The *Big Book* of **Car Culture**

The Armchair Guide to Automotive Americana

The *Big* Book *of* Car Culture

The Armchair Guide to Automotive Americana

Jim Hinckley and Jon G. Robinson

MOTORBOOKS

First published in 2005 by Motorbooks, an imprint of MBI Publishing Company, Galtier Plaza, Suite 200, 380 Jackson Street, St. Paul, MN 55101-3885 USA

Motorbooks titles are also available at discounts in bulk quantity for industrial or sales-promotional use. For details write to Special Sales Manager at MBI Publishing Company, Galtier Plaza, Suite 200, 380 Jackson Street, St. Paul, MN 55101-3885 USA.

ISBN-13 : 978-0-7603-1965-9
ISBN-10 : 0-7603-1965-0

Edited by Dennis Pernu and Heather Oakley
Designed by Christopher Fayers

Printed in China

Contents

3 The Ride 98

4 The Culture of the Road 200

5 Gasoline Alley 228

6 The Open Road 254

Introduction

From the perspective of the twenty-first century, it is hard to imagine an America without the automobile, let alone a time when it was such a wonder that it received top billing over the fat lady and the albino at the Barnum and Bailey Circus. Likewise, with a highway system that allows motorists to traverse the continent in a cocoon of climate-controlled comfort, it is difficult to imagine an era when a coast-to-coast drive was worthy of headlines throughout the world.

Initially even astute businessmen saw little future for the horseless carriage. Montgomery Ward is credited with saying the automobile was "something you should take the children to see before the fad passes." But this view was short-lived—less than a decade later, automotive pioneers were setting speed records approaching 150 miles per hour as well as establishing auto manufacturing and related industries at a meteoric rate.

In 1909, United States manufacturers produced 828,000 horse-drawn vehicles compared to fewer than 125,000 automobiles. By 1929, the horse-drawn vehicle and its supportive infrastructure had been almost entirely swept from the stage; in that year fewer than 4,000 horse-drawn vehicles were produced.

No fabric of our national identity was left unscathed. By 1920, it was more common for families to have an automobile than indoor plumbing. Farmers were set free from the constraints of rural isolation and prospered from expanded markets. Factory workers enjoyed a new phenomenon, the family vacation, and embarked on weeklong safaris into the countryside that sparked an explosion in tourism-related industries.

Sunday drives became a national obsession. In less than a generation, the nation's entire culture was turned upside down.

The American landscape, in many places largely unchanged for a century, was transformed in the blink of an eye. In 1919, the world's first tricolor traffic signals appeared on the streets of Detroit. In 1929, in Woodbridge, New Jersey, the first cloverleaf interchange opened. By the end of the following year, the federal government was averaging 10,000 miles of paved highway construction annually.

Billboards began to crowd the skyline, and vacant lots blossomed with filling stations and car lots. From coast to coast and border to border, a wonderful cornucopia of diners and roadside attractions vied for the attention of the increasing number of motorists. Some resembled wigwams and pagodas, while others were advertisements in themselves—built to resemble giant milk bottles or teapots. Even our lexicon was rewritten with words such as motel, Duesey, and road trip.

The words to jingles and slogans ("See the U.S.A. in Your Chevrolet," "Ask the Man Who Owns One," and others) became better known than the national anthem. The automobile soon became a quintessential symbol of America and it reflected the pulse of the nation.

The 1950s were a time of optimism with wild visions of the future that lay just over the horizon. The automobiles produced during this period, with their garish chrome trim and rakish fins, mirrored the mood. The 1960s can be encapsulated within the confines of a few select vehicles: the Volkswagen camper, the Pontiac GTO, the Olds Vista Cruiser wagon, and the Corvair. Likewise, the quirky little Gremlin, the pudgy Pacer, and powerful Trans Am sum up the 1970s, while the Plymouth Voyager represents the decade of the 1980s.

The automobile was the driving force behind one of the largest societal changes in history. Within one generation, the United States became a nation on wheels and a nation on the move. Within two generations, it became a car-culture nation and it never looked back.

This book is in essence a scrapbook containing a series of time capsules that chronicle the evolution of our national obsession with all things automotive. As such, it is also a trip down memory lane for a few and a peek into the past for those who are too young to remember.

1

Only Twenty Miles to . . .

In the era preceding the completion of the Interstate Highway System, it was possible to drive coast to coast and never leave the big top, for the roadsides of America were like a never-ending sideshow. In Oklahoma there was the opportunity to see albino buffalos and in the Ozarks there was a hillbilly village. In the deserts of California, and later Arizona, you could become part of the conspiratorial league that knew the mysteries of "The Thing" but would never tell. There were mummies and pecan logs, motels where the view included a drive-in theater, and roadside stands that offered everything from oranges to Navajo jewelry.

But somewhere between tailfins and unleaded fuel, the very nature of travel on the highways of America changed. Even for leisure travel, the destination became more important than the adventure of getting there and generic offerings replaced unique sights. The result was a cluster of cookie-cutter motels and eateries nestled around the off-ramp.

Yet, there were attractions, motels, and restaurants that had become larger than life; these wonders survived into the modern era to be rediscovered by a new generation. Others, now legends of the highway, live on only as fading memories or in yellowing black-and-white photos.

At the very heart of travel during these halcyon days was the lure, the signs that revived the weary soul with proclamations that it was only 20 miles to. . . .

Legends, Icons, and Mysteries

Americans' fascination with unsolved mysteries dates to at least the time of the lost colonists of Roanoke Island. Larger-than-life icons and legends are such an integral part of our national identity that it is impossible to imagine an America without the likes of Paul Bunyan, Pecos Bill, Daniel Boone, or Davy Crockett.

Enterprising individuals such as P. T. Barnum have often found ways to profit from this fascination. The advent of the automobile raised these endeavors to the level of an art form and made it possible for even the most remote community to capitalize on them.

Exemplifying such communities is tiny Rachel, Nevada. With a population of 100, it lies in close proximity to Area 51. First used as a training strip for flyers based at Nellis Air Force Base during World War II, this super-secretive military installation is a made-to-order mecca for those who love conspiracy theories and mystery. Over the years it has been known as Groom Lake, Dreamland, Nevada Test Site, Paradise Ranch, the Pig Farm, and

Billed as the "Mystery of the Mojave Desert" and the "Most Unique Show in America," The Thing on Highway 91 in California represents the quintessential roadside attraction of the 1950s.

Nellis Test Range. Add in the rumors that the government is using the remote base for the evaluation of recovered UFOs, and you have an instant tourist attraction—something the little of community of Rachel has done nothing to discourage.

The social center of town is the Little A'Le'Inn, a combination café, bar, and small motel. It also serves as a UFO information center complete with photograph-covered walls, a small library filled with related volumes, and a souvenir shop with everything from alien keychains to T-shirts emblazoned with smiling green alien faces.

Even the state of Nevada has jumped on the bandwagon. It recognized the potential for using this international fascination with things from another world to attract tourist dollars to a remote area. In 1996, with great fanfare, State Route 375 was officially designated the Extraterrestrial Highway.

In the world of roadside attractions, where at one time it seemed as though P. T. Barnum had established sideshows at every wide spot in the road, curiosity is the ultimate reason travelers decide to stop and have a look. One such attraction, which used a purposely vague advertising campaign as its lure, is "The Thing?" along Interstate 10 in southern Arizona (the original site was in the remote accesses of the Mojave Desert in California). For miles, billboards offer simple slogans like "The Thing?" "What is it?" and "Mystery of the Desert" to pique travelers' interest. And countless numbers of them can't resist, so they take a little detour and pay two dollars to discover what The Thing really is.

Just how many have stopped and paid is a carefully guarded secret. The exhibits on display, which have included a Rolls-Royce and a vintage matchlock rifle, hint that there have been enough visitors to make this a profitable venture.

Area 51 does not technically exist, and it is in the middle of nowhere, so what better souvenir than a post card that encapsulates the fancy, the mystery, and the empty desert?

Ducks, Elephants, and Shoes
Larger-than-life attractions

Legend has it that in 1931, Martin Maurer and his wife, Jeule, received a revelation for a novel way to promote their duck business while visiting a California coffee shop built in the shape of a giant coffee pot.

Upon their return to Long Island, New York, they set out to bring their dream to life. They sought assistance from George Reeve, a local carpenter, and two brothers, William and Samuel Collins, who were unemployed stage-show set designers. A live duck tied to the porch with a string served as the model. A cooked chicken served as the engineering diagram for the basic structure.

Upon completion of the wire-mesh frame, concrete and several coats of brilliant white paint were applied to the entire structure except for the bill. The end result was a big duck that measured 30 feet from beak to tail, 15 feet from folded wing to folded wing, and 20 feet from its base to the top of its head.

Originally designed to be a whimsical advertisement, the Big Duck has become a landmark on Long Island, an icon of the highway, and now a visitor's center that will soon be the centerpiece for a park celebrating the history of the American highway.

The paint had hardly dried before the Big Duck, originally on West Main Street in Riverhead, New York, began to receive worldwide attention. Its opening was featured in *Popular Mechanics*, and the Atlas Cement Company, which had supplied the cement for its construction, featured the duck in its annual company calendar.

In 1987, the property on which the Big Duck stood was sold, and for the third time it was moved to a new location, the Sears Bellows Pond County Park. Its purpose also changed. Today the Big Duck is listed on the National Register of Historic Places and serves as a gift shop that specializes in unique duck-styled merchandise as well as a tourist information center for the Long Island Convention and Visitors Center. Long-term plans for the Big Duck are to make it the centerpiece of an entire park dedicated to roadside art, such as neon signs and vintage gas pumps. That's quite an accomplishment for what began as a low-budget advertising gimmick and was until quite recently scorned by architects and those who preferred more conventional construction!

Eccentric roadside architecture, however, predates the automobile. In Margate, New Jersey, one of the most famous of these early attractions dates to 1881 when Lucy the Elephant was built as an attention-getting centerpiece for a beachfront real estate speculation venture.

Conceived by James Lafferty, the giant pachyderm standing on the seashore—ship's logs indicate that on clear days it can be seen up to 8 miles from shore—was a way to attract potential buyers from nearby Atlantic City. But there was a problem: even though it was theoretically possible by then-current engineering standards to build the proposed six-story elephant, it had never been done before.

Undaunted, Lafferty hired the services of an architect to design the building. Next, he retained a patent attorney to ensure that his creation would be one-of-a-kind. The U.S. Patent Office granted his request and gave him exclusive rights for 17 years to build and sell animal-shaped buildings.

The completed project was truly a wonder. More than a million pieces of wood were shaped into an intricate array of curves that functioned as load supports for the 90-ton structure. The entire outer surface was constructed of hammered tin. Even more amazingly, Lafferty built two more giant elephants. One of them, the Elephantine Colossus, was erected in the center of the Coney Island amusement park and stood 12 stories high, twice that of Lucy. Another, The Light of Asia, on the scale of Lucy, was designed for another real estate project. Today only Lucy survives.

Animals were not the only choice for those who chose to build larger than life models of everyday objects for their roadside establishments or as monuments to their success. In Hellam, Pennsylvania, millionaire shoe magnate Mahlon Haines built his dream house in the shape of a giant shoe in 1948.

The innovative residence is 48 feet long, 17 feet wide, and 25 feet high at the rear of the shoe. It has three bedrooms, two bathrooms, a kitchen, and a living room with everything laid out on five staggered levels. The garage in the instep is now an ice cream parlor, and the furnace and water pump are in the heel.

The shoe theme is evident throughout the house and property. The large stained-glass window in the front door features Haines holding a shoe in each hand with a sign that reads "Haines the Shoe Wizard." For the children, there is a shoe-shaped sandbox, and for the dog there is a smaller shoe house. The fence features shoe cutouts.

One of the most intriguing facts about the house is that Haines never lived in it. Instead, he offered it to elderly couples and employees for all-expenses-paid weekend getaways. After his death in 1962, the house became a combination private residence/ice cream stand/souvenir shop. In 2003, it was listed for sale with the stipulation that it would remain open to tourists.

A similar-looking home, in Webster, South Dakota, appropriately serves as a shoe museum. Inspired by the fairy tale about the old lady who lived in the shoe, another large shoe was constructed and serves as a residence in South Africa.

Along Highway 61 near Natchez, Mississippi, stands another unique example of unconventional roadside architecture. Mammy's Cupboard is a 30-foot-high concrete, stereotypical black mammy. For more than 60 years, she has stood as a local landmark with earrings made of horseshoes and a red-brick hoop skirt punctuated with arched windows.

Over the years, she has served local residents as well as passing motorists in numerous guises in between periods of abandonment. Originally, she was a gas station and restaurant. In recent years, her most common uses have been as a small restaurant and a secondhand shop.

Mammy's Cupboard is a unique time capsule from a time long past. In an era of political correctness run amok, her very appearance along the verdant roadside can be almost startling at first sight.

Mammy's Cupboard, the Big Duck, and Lucy are survivors of an era when America's roadsides were dotted with such monuments to individuality. For the adventuresome, many other memorable attractions are scattered throughout the country. These attractions are a reminder that quite often the most memorable structures are those built on a monumental scale. In the days before the introduction of the Interstate Highway System, the franchise, and the chain motel, this type of architecture was even more common. What better way was there to make your business stand out than to build it in the shape of a giant teapot or a sombrero or whatever?

Above: *Lucy the Elephant has been a landmark of the New Jersey shore for more than a century and is the only survivor of a trio of giant pachyderms, one of which was an important part of Coney Island's allure.*

Below: *The shoe house may seem unique but in actuality has proven to be a relatively popular form of mimetic architecture, appearing in various guises in countries throughout the world.*

Mammoth Orange
Mimetic citus

California State Highway 99 was once U.S. Highway 99. Much of it has been fenced into limited-access freeway, but there are substantial stretches of old expressway—unfenced, ground-level, at-grade intersections, with dimpled islands up the middle that scream of the original widening of U.S. highways after World War II.

Nostalgists can drive north on SR 99 past Fresno, California, cast their eyes to the right at Fairmead across the at-grade intersection with a county road, and see one of the last remaining mimetic, or imitation, roadside stands. The Mammoth Orange has been here since the 1950s, when motorists stopped for freezing-cold orange juice to cool their throats after a long un-air-conditioned ride. Some enthusiasts claim there were 50 such stands along SR 99 in this era, but now only one remains.

As such, eating at the Mammoth Orange is a bittersweet experience—sweet because one can avoid looking at the modern cars in the parking lot and imagine cars from the 1940s and 1950s to get feel of the past, but bitter because someday this orange will also become just another memory.

Will the Mammoth Orange make it very far into the twenty-first century? Let's hope so, because it seems to get plenty of business, and its separately created cousin in Redfield, Arkansas, has been serving nostalgia seekers and the curious since 1966.

The Mammoth Orange in Fairmead, California, is all that remains of the 50 of these hunger and thirst relievers that one time were located along Route 99. The fencing along the highway froze them out as the route was necessarily converted into freeway, stretch-by-stretch.

Cadillac Ranch
Waste in your face

The flatness of the short-grass plains east of the Rocky Mountains is a shock to people who've never seen it before. A perfectly horizontal horizon—green in the spring, brown in the summer, and frosty white in the winter—slams into the blue sky from below.

"There is a Hell, and you can see it from Amarillo," one young man once said of his hometown after returning from living in California. Yes, even a native was shocked by the landscape, a plain that others see as a perfect canvas.

It's a painful sight for anyone who loves old American cars—ten Cadillacs buried to their windshields, nose-first in a wheat field. Yet these weathered old beauties are like art to others. Even though they're in their final resting place, these automobiles, to car lovers, are not machines, but rather, living, breathing creatures. For true car fans, a visit to the Cadillac Ranch is like watching someone shoot a good horse.

The pain grows when the rest of the story comes to light. Each of the cars was bought for less than $1,000. The artists bought the 1959 Cadillac for $150. The seller of the 1949 Cadillac held out for $700, and after sealing the deal, the artists smashed the front of the car with sledgehammers in front of the seller, who reportedly felt every blow.

The ranch was established by Stanley Marsh 3, an eccentric oil-industry heir known for fully owning his reputation for pranks, and Ant Farm, a three-member group of architects that were known for viewing buildings and art through an innovative prism. Their partnership was based on this deal: Ant Farm would come up with the design, and Marsh 3 would put up the land and a $3,000 budget for the cars. The backhoe revved up on Monday, May 28, 1974, and the Cadillacs soon had back ends raised to the same angle as the Great Pyramid along Interstate 40 on the south edge of Amarillo.

The Cadillac Ranch has been described many times as documenting the rise and fall of the tailfin—starting out as more of a hump than a fin in 1948, reaching laughable heights in 1959, quietly lowering in 1960, and disappearing completely in 1964. Chrysler Corporation had sincerely tested its late-1950s tailfins for aerodynamics, but Cadillac had never made a secret of its fins simply being fashion statements, and like all fashion statements, they fell out of fashion. These Cadillacs, which had all been quiet, comfortable, high-quality, technologically advanced cars when they were made, were thrown away by the millions only because they were a little weathered, worn, and—worst of all—out of fashion. In the twenty-first century, the car lover's heart breaks to see the Cadillac Ranch, but Ant Farm's only sin was putting the waste out for all to see instead of hiding it behind the metal fences of junkyards. The Cadillacs were nearly worthless by 1974, and that is the real sin.

The Cadillac Ranch was made to be vandalized, and graffiti abatement is performed only sparingly. Oil heir Stanley Marsh 3 owns the open-access Cadillac Ranch outside Amarillo, Texas. Chip Lord, Doug Michels, and Hudson Marquez were collectively known as Ant Farm, an art/architecture firm that operated out of San Francisco through most of the 1970s. Marsh 3 put up the land and the budget, and Ant Farm came up with the design. Jeff Meyer photo. "Cadillac Ranch" copyright 1974, Ant Farm (Lord, Marquez, Michels)

Graceland
Elvis Presley's sentimentality

The rural South was poor well after the Great Depression and World War II, and the small city of Tupelo, Mississippi, shaped Elvis Presley's personality. When the 20-year-old man with huffing masculine voice, gyrating knees, and the sneer that was always on the verge of laughter hit the big-time, he gave.

Elvis Presley formed sentimental attachments to things he valued and kept them throughout of his short life. He lived in the same home in Memphis, Tennessee—Graceland—from 1957 until his death in 1977. One of his prized possessions was a pink 1955 Cadillac, which he couldn't bear to part with after his many adventures in it.

Out of the blue, in the mid-1950s, millions of American teenagers suddenly had a way to define their generation—rock music. To the irritation of their parents, they lurched for the car radio when the unmistakable bass thumps, guitar strums, and saxophone riffs beckoned. The kids of the 1950s learned to love rock and Elvis by listening to it on their parents' car radios. Now, as parents and grandparents themselves, they drive their own cars to Elvis' home to remember. But Graceland has become a destination for more than just the children of the 1950s. People born well after his death tour Graceland and wish they had been there when Elvis was the King.

Elvis Presley was born in 1935, and in the early 1950s he got his first car, an exhausted 1941 Lincoln. He never forgot his first car, and many years later, he was heard to laughingly reminisce that he had pushed the worn-out Lincoln more than he had driven it.

Elvis liked to drive. Even after success had smiled upon him, he wasn't eager to have a chauffeur. Yet in his early years, there wasn't much opportunity to be chauffeured. Elvis and his band dashed all over the South in the first years of his success, playing one-night gigs in ever-more-prestigious venues, but always returning to Shreveport, Louisiana, where he was under contract to the Louisiana Hay Ride radio show. Elvis and his band racked up a lot of miles together, riding in the same car much of the time. As Elvis became more and more successful, he wanted to feel successful and comfortable, so he bought his first Cadillac. The pink 1954 Cadillac had a short life. His band was following Elvis down the road quite a distance behind when they saw a fire up ahead. They soon spotted Elvis sitting on the side of the road, looking very upset as his Cadillac went up in flames from a mechanical failure.

Elvis replaced the charred car with a 1955 Cadillac. According to the paint codes on this car, it was blue when it came out of the factory. Elvis must have requested a repaint from the dealer or elsewhere because eventually it was pink with a black roof. This Cadillac was another comfortable car with custom upholstery and air conditioning to keep the humid southern summers at bay. It was also equipped with a removable roof rack for the band's instruments and luggage.

Elvis bought the car in July of 1955, and it was put into the same rough non-stop service the first Cadillac had seen. Two months later, on Friday, September 2, Elvis and the band were headed for Texarkana, presumably on U.S. 71, for a gig that also featured country music artists Johnny Cash and Charlene Arthur. Guitarist Scotty Moore was driving, and within 15 miles of Texarkana, an oncoming car passed a pickup truck at the wrong time and headed straight for Elvis and the boys. The accident was apparently not a head-on collision and the boys were not injured, but the Cadillac did take a beating and needed fairly extensive repairs.

*Opposite: **Elvis Presley bought this 1955 Cadillac new to replace a '54 Cadillac that burned in a fire. Elvis did a lot of hard traveling between gigs early in his fame, and this Cadillac was a working car. Guitarist Scotty Moore was driving when an oncoming car passed a truck unsafely, and the Cadillac was damaged in the accident. Elvis had the car repainted and reupholstered, and he gave the car to his mother as a gift. Millions of music fans discovered Elvis' music through their car radios, and it's worth the trip to Graceland to see the car that served Elvis through the early days.** Elvis Presley Enterprises/Graceland*

The Cadillac came out of the repairs nicely, with a white roof and a new upholstery job. Elvis presented the car to his mother, Gladys, in early 1956 (Graceland staff often correct the rumor that Elvis bought the car specifically for his mother). Gladys Presley never drove, but Elvis' father, Vernon, often drove her around Memphis in the pink Cadillac, and the car has always been known as Elvis' mother's car. Gladys died suddenly in 1958 in her 40s, and Elvis kept her car until his own passing 19 years later.

The Cadillac is on display at Graceland along with costuming from Elvis' movies, personal effects, and other cars, motorcycles, and vehicles used around Graceland. The 1955 Cadillac has something special to offer the car and music lover: a connection to Elvis' early fame that involved a lot of hard, unglamorous traveling between shows. It became a gift to a mother who loved her son, and it's worth the trip to Graceland just to see this one car that was never a toy.

South of the Border
Roadside attractions with an ethnic flair

Wanting to capitalize on the romanticized perception of an event or place has long been an impetus to promote it. Tombstone, Arizona, has survived and prospered solely on what took place in a few seconds at the OK Corral on October 26, 1881. In a similar manner an entire highway, Route 66, has become an internationally recognized symbol of America.

Yet, we have become a bit more thin-skinned than in the past, and as a result, attractions with an ethnic flair are not always viewed favorably. Because of that, Sambo's and many similar establishments have quietly faded into obscurity. One that has prospered, though, is Alan Schafer's South of the Border, located along I-95 just south of the North Carolina border in South Carolina.

As so many legends do, the story of South of the Border begins simply enough. In 1950, Schafer opened a small roadside beer and bait stand at this location. As increased business necessitated expansion, he ordered supplies that were delivered addressed to Schafer Project: South of the Border. With an uncanny ability to spot opportunity, Schafer decided to give his attraction a Mexican theme, importing all kinds of souvenirs.

Today Schafer's brainchild has morphed into a complete tourist complex that is a truly unique blend of cartoon-like stereotypical Mexican and old Dixie themes. A 97-foot Pedro, billed as the largest freestanding sign east of the Mississippi, serves as the entrance. Then, inside, there are 14 different gift shops; a miniature golf course, Golf of Mexico; Pedro's Rocket City, a huge fireworks shop; the Sombrero Room Restaurant; and Pedro's Southern Fried Chicken Restaurant.

The "Mexican speak" billboards that were once a trademark of the irreverent, one-of-a-kind South of the Border complex have succumbed to political correctness and have been replaced.

There is also a 300-room motel and an RV Park.

Pedro's Pleasure Dome features an indoor pool, steam room, Jacuzzi, bar, and wedding chapel. The site also has El Drug Store and the Dirty Old Man Shop (adults only), Pedroland Park, and a 200-foot-high tower topped by a colorful sombrero where visitors can stroll around the brim to view the heavily forested countryside.

There have been some concessions to the modern era. "Mexican Speak" billboards featuring Pedro once numbered more than 250 and could be found between New Jersey and Florida. But those legendary billboards now have been replaced with less offensive versions.

Left: *The entrance for the South of the Border motel provides shelter to 16 cars under the wide brim of the sombrero.*

Below, Left: *At night the towering Pedro is a becon that can be seen for miles.*

Left: *Fort Pedro's fireworks, motel, Pedro towering over the entrance, properly attired staff, and other Mexican kitsch set the atmosphere for this unique roadside stop.*

The Big Texan

4 1/2 pounds of beef take center stage

According to legend, everything is bigger in Texas. Even though Bob Lee didn't originally plan it that way, the Big Texan in Amarillo, Texas, has become an internationally recognized monument to that axiom. Best described as part John Wayne movie set and part Route 66 kitsch, this landmark eatery has become a must-see for Route 66 roadies.

Relocated to its present location along I-40 in 1970, the Big Texan has grown to include a 450-seat western-themed restaurant, a motel with a Texas-shaped swimming pool, a shooting gallery, and a gift shop. The biggest attraction, however, is the now-legendary free 72-ounce steak dinner contest.

The Big Texan and the steak dinner contest are all the result of founder Bob Lee's inability to find a big steak dinner in an authentic western setting. The weight for the steak dinner was, according to Lee, derived from how much a ravenous cowboy ate at his original restaurant.

The famous contest has but one rule: the $50 steak dinner that consists of a 72-ounce steak, baked potato, salad, shrimp cocktail, and roll must be eaten within one hour, without leaving the table. To make things even more interesting, the table is set on an elevated platform at the front of the restaurant, so that everyone can see those who were brave (or perhaps foolish) enough to make their dinner such a spectacle.

Since 1959, the year the contest was introduced, more than 27,000 have made the attempt and nearly 5,000 have succeeded. Frank Pastore, a pitcher for the Cincinnati Reds, holds the record for completing the meal in just nine and a half minutes. The oldest person to do so was a 69-year-old grandmother, and the youngest was an 11-year-old boy.

Today, the Big Texan is relatively unique. It offers not only a gastronomic challenge, but a time capsule back to when the adventure to be found along the road made getting there half the fun.

The Big Texan's towering cowboy is an icon for Route 66 roadies and an Amarillo landmark recognized by all who travel I-40.

McDonald's
As Familiar as McAnything

Wags call two-story tract homes that all look the same "McMansions." They are houses that appear to be large, crammed onto small lots. Ultimately there are only a few floor plans available for these houses, with no design input from the buyer. They are not well-crafted houses, but they are built well. They are not unique, but they are affordable. They are not creatively designed, but they are tasteful.

Yet, is that bad?

Nostalgic car enthusiasts miss the individually owned mom-and-pop diners, even though there are still plenty of them out there. The little eateries scattered along the original U.S. highways were individual, but they were also unpredictable and could actually be a little scary. Their signs touted good eats, but the salivating stranger driving down the road took a risk at every one of them—sometimes getting treated to a delicious local recipe, other times later having to pull over and lean out the window.

McDonald's was once just a local spot. The first one opened in 1940, on E Street in San Bernardino, California, and was owned by Mac and Dick McDonald. It used its company mascot Speedee to tout its "Custom Built Hamburgers" with a sign. At some point, Ray Kroc, a salesman from Oak Park, Illinois, became interested in franchising the restaurant. He knew about it because the McDonald brothers had bought a large number of Multi-Mixers from him so they could whip up milkshakes in a hurry. Kroc's first McDonald's opened in Des Plaines, Illinois, in April 1955, and by July he opened his second location in Fresno, California.

By 1960, the 200th McDonald's opened, and by 1961, it was clear that the neon 1950s were over. Speedee said goodbye, and the restaurants' new trademark became a modern-but-plain golden M sign. At the dawn of the next decade, McDonald's had grown to 1,500 restaurants, and by the year 2000, the franchise had more than 25,000 locations.

While the restaurants aren't very similar to the mom-and-pop eateries of the 1950s, they are often family-owned and are considered a part of many Americans' hometown hangouts. Mom can fill the station wagon with kids and go to the local McDonald's, and so can the lonely truck driver or salesman who wanders in tired and hungry, wanting the same favorite lunch he eats back home, possibly thousands of miles away.

Above: In the late-1950s, McDonald's established the Santa Wagon to deliver hot coffee and hamburgers to the Salvation Army's bell-ringing Santas in the Upper Midwest. In this case, the Santa Wagon was a Volkswagen. **McDonald's**

Below: In the twenty-first century, a plain, earth-toned, 1970s-era McDonald's in Lancaster, California, was torn down and replaced with a retro-1950s building that put Speedee back where he belongs.

23

Bob's Big Boy and Howard Johnson

The beginning of the generic age

For most of the mid-twentieth century, the bright orange roof of a Howard Johnson's was a welcome sight for travelers. With standardized architecture and menu, customers were made to feel welcome. Each restaurant felt as familiar and comfortable as the one in their hometown. Ironically, the conformity that reassured the motorist of the 1940s and 1950s is today viewed with disdain by the traveler in search of pre-interstate-highway America.

Howard Johnson began laying the foundation for his revolutionary concept in roadside dining with a $2,000 loan and the purchase of a small drugstore in 1925. It soon became apparent to Johnson that the soda fountain was the bread and butter of the business. Thus, armed with his mother's ice cream recipe, which had a butterfat content exceeding that of any other brand as a secret ingredient, he began to expand.

Soon Johnson had 28 flavors and, in addition to the soda fountain, a beachfront ice cream stand. Over the next few summers, he opened additional beachfront stands and expanded the menu to include hot dogs.

Flush with success and another loan, Johnson opened the first Howard Johnson's Restaurant in Quincy, Massachusetts. The menu was simple New England fare: fried clams, hot dogs, baked beans, chickpeas, and his now-famous 28 flavors of ice cream.

Enter a fortuitous set of circumstances. Boston's mayor led the fight to prohibit Eugene O'Neill's play Strange Interlude from running in the city, so the theater guild moved the production to nearby Quincy. Because the play was quite lengthy, it was shown in two segments, with an intermission long enough for dinner. Because Howard Johnson's was the nearest restaurant, business profited accordingly. An additional bonus was that many influential people from the Boston area discovered the restaurant. The rest, as they say, is history.

In late 1929, Johnson initiated plans to launch a franchise of his now-famous restaurant. However, the economic conditions of the time were not conducive to a great deal of expansion. Still, he persisted, and in 1935 was finally able to sell the first franchise to an acquaintance, and the second Howard Johnson's opened on Cape Cod.

In rapid succession more franchised locations opened, and by the end of the year there were 17. By 1937, the number jumped to 39. Then when the Pennsylvania, Ohio, and New Jersey turnpikes were built, Johnson bid and won exclusive rights for roadside service. So soon, the

The original Bob's Big Boy opened in Toluca Lake, California, in 1949 and still has carhop service on weekends.

Simple Simon and the Pie Man weathervane, a Howard Johnson trademark developed by Joseph Alcott, was found all along East Coast highways.

Meanwhile, on the West Coast in 1936, another icon of the American highway was founded. To raise capital for his new venture, Bob Wian sold his car for $350 and opened a small 10-seat eatery known as Bob's Pantry to modest success.

Legend has it that the legendary Big Boy sandwich came into being when some traveling musicians asked for something more than just a plain burger. Wian cut a regulation bun into three slices, added two beef patties, the traditional garnishments, and his new experimental sauce.

The trademark roly-poly Big Boy, with his checkered overalls, upraised arm with tray and burger, and curl of hair, came about because of a sketch on a napkin and a chubby youngster—so the story goes. Wian later recalled, "He was about six and rolls of fat protruded where his shirt and pants were designed to meet. I was so amused by the youngster—jolly, healthy-looking, and obviously a lover of good things to eat, I called him Big Boy."

Howard Johnson's clean colonial styling, brightly colored roof, and trademarked Simple Simon and the Pie Man were once a welcome sight for weary travelers in an era without standardization.

Bob's Big Boy, like Howard Johnson, expanded through franchise. In time the trademark Big Boy could be found in more than a half-dozen states. Even though it was never a real competitor of the orange-roofed Ho Jo's (they grew in different markets), their paths would converge in the decades that were to follow.

World War II and gas rationing did what the Great Depression had been unable to do—it brought the Howard Johnson franchise to near collapse. In 1941, there were 200 restaurants, but by the summer of 1944, only a dozen remained. The franchise grew after the war, though, and by late 1947, more than 200 new restaurants were being built. They were slightly smaller than the originals, but still offered standardized fare and Howard Johnson's legendary 28 flavors of ice cream.

By 1951, the company was the largest of its kind, with sales totaling $115 million. Three years later there were 400 Howard Johnson restaurants in 32 states, of which 10 percent were highly profitable company-owned turnpike restaurants. With the addition of motor lodges during this period, the company entered a new era.

In 1961, the year the company went public, there were 88 franchised Howard Johnson Motor Lodges in 33 states and 605 restaurants. As highway roadsides became more generic, Howard Johnson continued to expand.

The year 1973 would prove to be the company's peak, with more than 1,000 restaurants and 500 motor lodges operating in 42 states. Beginning with the gas embargos of the time, things began to change on the highways of America. A dramatic decrease in pleasure travel, coupled with an increasing number of competitors and the company's failure to adapt to the increasing popularity of fast-food restaurants during the 1960s, resulted in ever-diminishing profits. The next blow came with the Pennsylvania Turnpike's decision to take advantage of the scheduled contract renewal with Howard Johnson and instead added fast-food franchises to the roadway's service exits.

The resultant decline pushed Howard Johnson into the acceptance of an acquisition bid from Imperial Group PLC of Britain in September of 1979. This was almost immediately followed with a complete restructuring that included elimination of some properties, updated facades for many others, and a redesigned company logo.

The changes were just beginning. In 1985, the Imperial Group sold the majority of its assets to the Marriott Corporation. The new owners quickly sold the motor lodge division to Prime Motor Inns. The restaurants, particularly the toll-road operations, were rolled into Marriott Travel Plazas.

The remaining Howard Johnson restaurants were to be converted into Big Boy restaurants, another Marriott company. However, this plan met with resistance from franchisees who had built their businesses on Ho Jo and did not want to incur the expense of remodeling. Joining together as a new company, Franchise Associates, they acquired all rights to the Howard Johnson restaurant business from Marriott.

Franchise Associates' first endeavor was to reintroduce a new generation to an American classic. Simple Simon and the Pie Man, the trademark that had been retired in the 1970s, was returned. Menu covers and other promotional items featured images from the company's historic past. Yet, the competition was relentless and many stores were closed or transformed into a Denny's or other brand. The future for this roadside icon still remains on shaky ground.

Coney Island
Freak shows and
fresh ocean breezes

For more than a century, amusement parks have been a destination, an escape from the worries and troubles of the day. Initially they were located close to urban centers and connected by rail or streetcar for easy access. With the advent of the automobile, rural settings where size of the park was limited only by the imagination and the finances of its creator became the norm.

Long before Walt Disney ushered in the modern concept of the amusement park, Coney Island, in Brooklyn, New York, set the standard for all other parks. The foundation of the park as a destination for urban fun lovers can be traced all the way back to 1829, with the establishment of the Coney Island House and Shell Road.

With the addition of scheduled horse-drawn trolley service in the final quarter of the nineteenth century, and the Prospect Park & Coney Island Railroad later in the century, numerous hotels were established to serve the growing number of visitors who came to the beach for a weekend holiday. More than one million passengers in the railroad's first year of operation attested to the growing popularity. However, the popularity of the area soon attracted a rather unsavory element, and by 1880, Coney Island had become known as a haven for con men, prostitutes, and gamblers.

In 1895, a new chapter began at Coney Island when Captain Paul Boyton, an eccentric inventor made famous for swimming the English Channel in an inflatable rubber suit of his design, opened Sea Lion Park. This was the nation's first enclosed amusement park with an admission fee. The centerpiece was his highly successful aquatic circus with 40 trained sea lions as headliners.

Boyton's creative talents soon turned toward the creation of other diversions and amusements. On July 4, 1894, the Shoot-the-Chutes water ride opened. Its popularity encouraged him to open others, and soon the park included the Flip Flar, the Flip Flap, as well as the first commercial circular-looping coaster and the Cages of Wild Wolves.

The Steeplechase, Steeplechase Park, Coney Island, N. Y.

By 1910, Coney Island, with its breathtaking rides, fresh ocean breezes, freak shows, and shooting galleries, had become one of the most famous attractions in the United States.

The Tornado — Whirlwind Scenic Ride — Co...

16804

104

In 1903, Sea Lion Park was replaced by Luna Park. Steeplechase, which featured the latest mechanical-amusement attractions and a 25-cent entrance fee for unlimited fun, established a standard for future parks. In the decades that followed, Coney Island continued to set new standards for the industry. After numerous periods of decline and restoration, Coney Island is again entering a renaissance. After more than a century, Coney Island is still one of the most popular resort areas in the nation, and there are indications that its best days are yet to come.

Cabins, Courts, and Inns
Ports in the storm

Before 1925, early motorists had but two time-honored choices: sleeping under the stars (perhaps in the back seat) or at a local inn or hotel. Even into the 1930s, travelers often chose the open-air option, largely as the result of financial conditions. Countless small companies thrived by catering to this demand. Nash even went as far as making seats that folded into a bed as an option.

However, the foundation for change had been laid in 1925 when an enterprising Los Angeles architect, Arthur Heineman, introduced a new concept in lodging tailored to the unique needs of the automobilist. Roughly halfway between San Francisco and Los Angeles, in San Luis Obispo, he built a series of two-room bungalows that all faced into a central courtyard. Each unit featured a small kitchen and a private adjoining garage. Other services included a swimming pool and picnic tables for outdoor dining. The cost was just $1.25 per night.

The design was revolutionary, but the moniker bestowed upon it was even more so. The property was named Milestone and was promoted as a motor hotel, a term subsequently shortened by the owner to motel.

Yet even $1.25 could be an unjustifiable travel expense during the hard times of the Great Depression or when the hot nights of summer made it cooler to camp. After all, why spend the money for a room when in the summer it was most likely hotter inside than out? Still, the American entrepreneurial spirit found ways to triumph.

In Kingman, Arizona, a hard-rock miner and enterprising Russian immigrant by the name of Conrad Minka devised a novel scheme for ensuring year-round business. First, he quarried rock from a mountain to the west of town and then constructed an auto court from the pale stone along Route 66 in about 1930. He built a two-story box-like building from the same material that served as both office and residence.

Even though the entire complex was built on a foundation of solid rock, Minka dug utility tunnels under the motel and linked these with a tunnel to the office basement. These tunnels later lent credence to a persistent rumor that they also served another purpose: providing access for voyeuristic activity and the operation of a lucrative still.

The real crowning achievement was a tunnel that ran for several hundred yards up the mountain in the back of the motel and connected with an airshaft that ran to the surface. At the base of the airshaft was a large tank of water in which strips of burlap were hung, creating a primitive evaporative cooler. With floor vents in each room, the White Rock Motel was able to offer respite from the oppressive desert heat, and business boomed.

Individuality was the hallmark of motels and auto courts throughout the 1930s as well as in the immediate postwar years. Even in this cornucopia of diversity, a few businesses were able to stand out and rise to the status of roadside legend, such as John Carr's Coral Court on Route 66 near Saint Louis, Missouri.

Designed by architect Adolph Struebig in late 1940 and built in 1941, the Coral Court was a stunning complex. Each cabin contained two rooms that featured a private bath as well as a garage. The honey-beige ceramic brick exteriors, brown accents, wedge-shaped glass-brick windows, and rounded corners stood in stark contrast against the surrounding deep-green foliage landscape.

Even with the imposed gas-rationing limits, the Coral Court was well received when it opened for business in 1942. In 1948, the motel expanded by 23 units. For these, Mr. Carr utilized the talents of another local architect, Harold Tryer. These new cabins shared the same color scheme, but the glass bricks were changed to triangles and the entry bays were enlarged to create a sitting room with a foldout Murphy Bed. After the completion of the complex, the sign was changed to read, "Coral Court—Ultra Modern."

In 1953, Carr broke from the traditional design when he added three more buildings to the rear of the property. These additions were two-story structures with eight rooms each. For the final time, the sign was updated to a more modern chrome and neon that read, "Coral Court Motel—Moderate Rates." The final change came in 1961 when a pool was added to the complex.

There was, however, a seedy side to the Coral Court, and according to legend, it surfaced unintentionally. The Coral Court began offering special four-hour rates as a courtesy to truckers and to maximize profits. This rate, though, as well as the unique design features of the motel (such as garage doors and access to the rooms from the garage), made it ideal for the illicit rendezvous.

Then with the decline in business that resulted from the I-44 bypass, the once-stately Coral Court became the ultimate no-tell motel. By the late 1980s, the motel was in a state of disrepair and it even began to lose its illicit business. In 1987, the owner's widow was approached with an offer for the property.

A group of local citizens that recognized the motel as a historic asset formed the Coral Court Motel Preservation Society and intervened. This marked the beginning of the motel's final chapter.

The sale proposal was withdrawn, and as a result, demolition was averted. In 1989, the organization succeeded in adding the motel to the National Register of Historic Places. Meanwhile, souvenir hunters hastened the building's demise by snatching pieces inside and out.

In 1995, a developer purchased the property for construction of a new housing development. At the entrance was placed a sign that read, "It's checkout time at the Coral Court—No more one-night stands."

Though unable to save this interesting piece of roadside history, the preservation society did score one small victory. In conjunction with the Museum of Transportation in Saint Louis, the society moved one complete two-room bungalow from Coral Court with the intention to rebuild and restore it as part of an extensive display of roadside

Note: Sleeping Dutchman

WHITE ROCK COURT - ON HIWAY 66 - EAST END OF KINGMAN, ARIZ.

Above: *Now a private residence, the White Rock Court is one of the oldest auto courts to be found on Route 66 and is a monument in stone to the American entrepreneurial spirit.*

Below: *With the resurgence of interest in Route 66 during the 1980s, the Coral Court Motel was rediscovered. It became an icon of the movement and served as an example of the unique American roadside culture that has been lost.*

Above: *The origins of the Holiday Inn were based on simplicity and standardization that gave the traveler peace of mind. This post card from Memphis depicts one of the original Holiday Inn hotels.*

Below: *By the 1960s, the Holiday Inn sign with the proclamation "The World's Innkeeper" was a common sight along the highways of America and in countries throughout the world.*

America from the 1950s. Once funds for the project are secured, the display will also feature a vintage service station.

While individuality and innovation were often used to draw people to roadside accommodations, often those lodging options weren't very family friendly.

Kemmons Wilson, an entrepreneur from Memphis, found this to be the case in 1951 when he drove his family to Washington, D.C. He later wrote that he was appalled by the fleabags, greasy motels, low-rent tourist camps, and boarding houses filled with salesman that he encountered on the trip. F.B.I. Director J. Edgar Hoover had gone even further in his condemnation in a 1940 magazine interview in which he claimed that motor courts were little more than camps of crime.

Wilson was a businessman with vision. Rather than curse the darkness, he decided the time had come to change the face of roadside lodging. The idea was simple. He would do with motels what Howard Johnson had done with the standardization of restaurants and menus.

A series of identical motels would be built within a day's drive of each other. Each room would feature clean sheets, a Bible in the dresser drawer, and air conditioning. In addition there would be a pool and television. Legend has it that the name given the project, Holiday Inn, was the brainchild of a draftsman who had enjoyed the 1942 Bing Crosby film of the same name more and more after each viewing.

In 1952, the first Holiday Inn opened on Summer Avenue in Memphis. It featured a sign with the now-well-known emerald green background filled with bright white neon spelling "Holiday Inn" and a red pylon with an exploding yellow star. Three more Holiday Inns in the Memphis area soon followed.

The idea was long overdue. Coupled with Wilson's ability to raise capital, the result was a meteoric rise for the company. Soon Wilson was even exporting the idea. As a result, by 1970 a new Holiday Inn was opening somewhere in the world every two and a half days!

In a quarter century, roadside lodging had made quantum leaps. The transition was so rapid that few today can imagine a time when picking a motel for the night was akin to Russian roulette, or sleeping in the car might be seen as the most advantageous choice.

Movie Manor Inn
Room with a view

First, someone said, "Hey, let's show motion pictures in a theater for a profit."

Then, someone said, "Hey, let's show movies on a big outdoor screen so people can watch them from the comfort of their own cars."

Later, one man said, "Hey, let's build a motel in a drive-in theater outfield so people can watch the movies from the comfort of their own air-conditioned room," and it became a wonder that more of these didn't pop up all over the United States in the 1950s and 1960s.

George Kelloff grew up in the theater business. As a child, he watched the projectionist in his parents' Aguilar, Colorado, movie theater thread silent movies into the projector and helped the organist pump the pedals on the air-operated organ. Talkies took over, and by the time George was 12 years old, he was operating the big projectors himself.

When drive-in theaters really started booming in the 1950s, George and his wife, Edna, decided to open the Star Drive-In in Monte Vista, Colorado, a town that attracted tourists from Oklahoma and Texas to southern Colorado's fertile San Luis Valley. The Kelloffs' living quarters were right in the middle of the drive-in, and they enjoyed watching first-run movies right along with the paying audience. "We didn't have sound at first, so I had installed a speaker in our room. It gave me the idea," Kelloff recalls. "I told my wife about it, and she thought I was crazy, but I said, 'We'll see.' I saved up about eight years to start it, and I borrowed the rest. We started with 14 units, and we're up to 60 now."

The Movie Manor Motor Inn took shape in 1964, and grew from there. In the outfield, behind the audience parking, the motel is of very plain, functional architecture, but its gentle V-shape does have a certain graceful flying-wing air. Each room has a speaker and a sizable picture window facing the screen.

George selects his movies carefully and makes his theater a safe place for the whole family to take a vacation and watch a movie. He is adamant that the Movie Manor Motor Inn will continue to show only G-, PG-, and PG-13-rated movies, but he is frustrated by Hollywood's lack of G-rated entertainment. He also thinks many of the PG-13 movies should be rated R. He would like to show more classic movies from the wonderful era when movies were palatable for all audiences, but the prints are difficult to rent, and the audience for a classic movie must be a sure thing before it's a safe risk to take.

His Movie Manor Motor Inn is also popular with classic car buffs, who like to sit in their cars in the infield and get the feel of the 1950s or 1960s drive-ins that they may have missed because of their relative youth. Meanwhile, families can crawl under the covers with a bowl of popcorn in a motel room and wonder why this brilliant idea did not become one of those waves of the future.

The Movie Manor Motor Inn is shown from the sky above Monte Vista, Colorado. Every motel room faces the drive-in's big screen, and guests can watch the movie from their room in complete comfort.
George Kelloff

Dinner in the Car
Food with a twist

The basic fare may have been the same—hot dogs, hamburgers, malts, and fries—but in the age before the golden arches and Jack of the now legendary In-The-Box fame, that was often where the similarities ended. The local drive-in was just what the name implied: It was local and it was a drive-in.

Because of its location, travelers would often stumble upon it. If the drive-in was original in design, offered a local specialty, or was truly unique, it would be remembered. Then word of mouth would help it to become a regular stop for travelers.

During a stop in Muskogee, Oklahoma, Ed Waldmire Jr. discovered an intriguing "sandwich," a hot dog baked in a cornbread roll. The idea, as well as the taste, piqued his interest. The main problem with recreating the tasty treat was the length of time required for preparation, and various experiments in speeding up the process proved fruitless. In 1941 at Knox College, he mentioned the tasty dog and detailed his attempts to create his version to a fellow student, Don Strand, whose family was in the bakery business.

Fast-forward to late 1945: Waldmire is now stationed with the Army Air Corps in Amarillo, Texas. To his surprise, Strand had not forgotten their discussion and had been working on developing a batter that would stick to the dogs for fast frying. Using cocktail forks and the USO kitchen, Waldmire tried the new mix and was excited by the result, a tasty battered dog he christened the "crusty cur."

The dogs quickly became a hit at the USO as well as the PX. Strand supplied the mix and Waldmire did the cooking in his free time. By the spring of 1946, when Waldmire was discharged, thousands of dogs had been sold.

The popularity of the "crusty cur" encouraged Waldmire to open a small stand at Lake Springfield Beach House in Springfield, Illinois, that summer. Just as it had happened in Amarillo, the dogs became an over-whelming success. The little business then moved

The Snow Cap in Seligman, Arizona, is a rare survivor from the days when individuality was the norm that made travel an adventure. The empty highway in front of the drive-in is Route 66 and exemplifies the changes wrought in small communities when bypassed by the interstate highways.

to the corner of Ash and MacArthur in Springfield along Route 66. The product name was also changed, at his wife's prompting, to Cozy Dog, and a legend of the highway was born.

In 1953 in Seligman, Arizona, Juan Delgadillo chose another avenue for his little roadside diner—pure zaniness. Between then and now, much has changed along Route 66, including the bypassing of communities by Interstate 40 and the subsequent resurgence of interest in the "Mother Road." Through it all, Juan held on and developed his offbeat sense of humor into a true icon of the highway, the Snow Cap Drive-In.

The Snow Cap Drive-In has many distinct features, the first being its outhouse restroom with flush toilet. Another is the exterior of the building, which proclaims one of the drive-ins offerings as "dead chicken." Inside, a cut-down 1937 Chevy adorned with an inflated Santa and a Christmas tree greets visitors. Also, the food is served in original fashion, with a small Coke poured into tartar sauce cups and mustard bottles filled with yellow string.

The food is average at best, yet the establishment's originality has been its real draw. Today the little stand is recognized throughout the world. It has been featured on French calendars and German Christmas cards, in more than a hundred magazines, and in countless documentaries.

The Snow Cap Drive-In wasn't the only place to become a unique local hangout, though. In fact, one of the earliest establishments to attract a faithful customer base was the Pig Stand, which opened in Dallas, Texas, in 1921. It introduced Dallas, and later the whole country, to the concept of carhops, drive-through windows, onion rings, and drive-in dining, all of which made the stand popular enough to become a franchise.

It also fueled the construction of independent drive-ins, including Mel's Diner in San Francisco. Built in 1947 and owned by Mel Weiss and Harold Dobbs, it later became enshrined as the classic drive-in eatery in George Lucas' classic film American Graffiti.

In Seattle, Ralph Grossman and Ernie Hughes capitalized on the craze by building a large double igloo at one of the busiest intersections in town. Its large neon sign, depicting a smiling Eskimo above the diner's name with the enticing words "Good Food" soon became an icon of the city.

In the end, local drive-ins, as with so many businesses, were unable to compete with the franchise and chain stores. As a result, they have been for the most part relegated to memories, period post cards, and yellowed photographs.

Here and there, a few icons such as the Snow Cap and the Cozy Dog have survived into the twenty-first century. They serve as living time capsules from a time when the highway had only two lanes, the station wagon was king of the road, and Studebakers still rolled from the factory in South Bend, Indiana. Moreover, in the time-honored tradition of capitalizing on the traffic that rolls by, more than a few eateries have risen from the ashes like the mythical Phoenix as "recreated" time capsules, catering to the needs of those in search of adventure on the road.

Mr. D'z Route 66 Diner located in the old Kimo Café, in Kingman, Arizona, represents a new era on Main Street, America, as it strives to capitalize on the romanticized perception of what the highway once was.

Sonics and the Car Hop

Dolores in a top hat goes super-Sonic

It's always hard to trace who was first to do what, but there's one believable story that can explain the origin of the change-belted sometime-roller-skate-wearer who brought food right to people's cars in the 1950s and 1960s. The story goes like this: Vince Stevens opened the Dolores Restaurant in Oklahoma City, Oklahoma, in the 1930s. The Dolores was a white-tablecloth sit-down restaurant on one of the earlier Route 66 paths through the city, right near the state capitol. It was a popular place, and at some point someone thought it would be even more popular if people could be served food in their cars. It's a concept that still winning people over at the drive-in joints that have survived to see the dawn of the twenty-first century.

At the Dolores, the term "carhop" stemmed from the way the waitresses assigned to work outside handled the customer traffic. First, presumably, they would determine whether the car's occupants intended to dine-in or get food to go. If the patron wanted to eat in the car, the waitress would literally hop onto the car's running board and direct the driver to a parking space, take the customer's order, and bring the food.

In no time, the carhops were a hit, and in 1944, as the cruising culture swept America, the Dolores opened a second location in Los Angeles.

By the early 1950s, the drive-in restaurant business was flourishing. Many restaurants were adding drive-in eating as a way to expand their business. Troy Smith, whose first restaurant in rural Oklahoma was too small to be profitable, at first planned that his second restaurant would succeed by offering great steak. But it was the root beer stand in the parking lot—the Top Hat Drive-In—that really attracted customers.

Eventually, Smith wanted to make more room for cars in his parking lot, so he invited all his friends to bring their cars to the Top Hat and park them for maximum capacity while he went from car to car, marking parking spaces on the pavement with paint. Then he put the carhops to work. He had seen a drive-in restaurant in Louisiana that used drive-in movie theater speakers for communication between customers and staff, and so he adapted the idea for the Top Hat. With the Cold War silently raging, and the U.S. Air Force breaking the sound barrier, going supersonic, Smith made the Top Hat's motto "Service With the Speed of Sound." He also hired teens to work for him, giving them a dollar a week to buy records that he could play through the Top Hat's P.A. system, making his restaurant the one featuring all the latest music.

Charlie Pappe, a supermarket manager in Woodward, Oklahoma, liked the Top Hat Drive-In's style so much he asked Smith if he could open one in Woodward. The Smith/Pappe partnership eventually had four Oklahoma locations: Shawnee, Woodward, Enid, and Stillwater. The partners later wanted to offer franchises, but they found the Top Hat name was already taken. So with the supersonic theme already in place, the Top Hat became the Sonic, and it enjoyed great Midwestern success through the golden age of carhopping, from the Jet Age through American Graffiti. However, by the late 1960s, times were changing. America was suddenly more dangerous, teenagers were less prone to social gatherings, and Space Age neon glitz came to look junky and old-fashioned. Then in 1975, the McDonald's megafranchise opened its first drive-thru, replacing the smiling carhop with an anonymous arm.

Narramore

By the 1990s, Americans were missing the optimistic postwar car culture and began searching for the remnants of Route 66. This renewed interest restored many automotive attractions all over the country. It also rekindled interest in Sonic, which had weathered the storm—the end of the American Graffiti era, the anti-nostalgic counterculture, the gas crunch, and a period of automobiles that were too cruelly economical to enjoy. Soon the restaurants' carhops were staffing new locations designed to reflect the classic drive-in restaurant.

Another restaurant enjoying the drive-in resurgence is The Bob's Big Boy in Toluca Lake, California, which offers carhop service on weekends. And walk-up order survivors include Andre's in Bakersfield, California, and Zesto in Jefferson City, Missouri, both now authentically "retro." They never went out of business, and their brush-script signs and bright colors are original. You can't say the same when a new Sonic appears in town. But it is a continuation of something that never ended.

A smiling carhop serves young people in a new Oldsmobile in 1967 at the Greenville, Texas, Sonic. Sonic Corporation

Mount Rushmore
King of the hill

The guiding principle behind Mount Rushmore was a belief by its sculptor that "a monument's dimensions should be determined by the importance to civilization of the events commemorated." That was Gutzon Borglum's genius, and how he approached the granite face of the mountain as his easel. The result was a masterpiece of both art and engineering that has served as a roadside attraction of unparalleled proportions and symbolism.

The Black Hills were an important destination long before one mountain was selected to be a monument. For the Lakota Sioux, these mountains were sacred. The discovery of gold in the 1870s sparked a stampede that would result in full-scale war between those who had long held the hills in high esteem and those who came for riches. One of the more famous casualties of these skirmishes was George Armstrong Custer.

Shortly before the automobile became the favored mode of transport, the Black Hills had lured the adventuresome tourist with the promise of clean mountain air, unparalleled scenic wonder, and historic sites. By 1927, when initial construction of the Mount Rushmore National Memorial began in earnest, the western mountains of South Dakota had become a popular destination for a new breed of daring explorers who were known as automobilists.

Throughout the following decade, this engineering marvel encouraged travelers to visit this rugged land in numbers not seen since the gold rush of the 1870s. As a result, motels, service stations, gift shops, and other businesses that catered to tourists sprang up, giving new life to forgotten mining communities such as Deadwood, Keystone, and Custer.

Another boon for these communities was the presence of the hard-rock miners who worked on the project. They spent many months there, bringing the sculpture to fruition in record time.

By 1941, the year Mount Rushmore was actually completed, it was already listed as a top-10 destination for the vacationing traveler. Today, its popularity has not faded as tourists from around the world come to see the dream of Gutzon Borglum. They come to see a monument to the American spirit of liberty and the men who gave it life, represented in the towering 60-foot faces of George Washington, Thomas Jefferson, Theodore Roosevelt, and Abraham Lincoln.

Long before completion of the Mount Rushmore National Monument, the construction itself made the Black Hills a major tourist destination, as evidenced by this vintage post card.

Dairy Queen
The rise of royalty

It began with a series of experiments and a goal to create a unique, soft frozen dairy product. The result was test marketed on August 4, 1938, at Sherb Noble's ice cream parlor in Kankakee, Illinois, in the form of a 10-cent all-you-can-eat trial sale. To say the new dessert was an instant success would be a gross understatement; in just two hours, the store had sold 1,600 servings!

Food franchising was a relatively rare business practice during the late 1930s, but the new soft serve was a different sort of product. It seemed to be tailor-made for promotion. For most of 1939, the focus was on further development of the frozen confectionery, the formation of a company, and the initial sale of franchises.

In 1940, the first Dairy Queen opened its doors in Joliet, Illinois. Initially the franchise concept moved rather slowly for Dairy Queen. By the end of 1941, there were only 10 stores in operation. Rationing of essential war materials for the next four years brought efforts of expansion to a halt.

After the war, amid an atmosphere of hope and prosperity, Dairy Queen exploded onto the scene. In communities throughout America, it became the gathering place for local Little League teams as well as travelers in search of a respite from summer heat.

In 1949, Dairy Queen expanded its market penetration by adding milkshakes and malts to the menu. In 1951, the chain started offering banana splits. The big news for the company in 1953 was the opening of stores in Canada. As those stores succeeded, International Dairy Queen was born in 1962, leading to the chain's expansion into 20 foreign countries.

By the end of 1947, there were 100 stores in operation. The number had mushroomed to 1,446 by 1950 and to 2,600 in 1955. There has been little respite in the popularity of Dairy Queen, and with the company's acquisition in 1998 by Berkshire Hathaway, the growth has continued unabated.

By 1959, Dairy Queen was firmly established as an American institution, and its logo was a welcome sight for travelers hoping to beat the heat in the years before air conditioning. This 19th-anniversary flyer for Dairy Queen highlights the two cornerstones of the company's initial success, the family and ice cream sundaes.

A Night on the Rails

A link to the past

No one knows for sure who originally devised the idea to use old cabooses and other assorted railroad rolling stock for lodging, but the idea was a good one because it combined people's love of the open road with their love of trains.

In Chattanooga, Tennessee, the Chattanooga Choo Choo Holiday Inn complex (named after the famous Glen Miller song released in 1941) draws many railroad enthusiasts because an original 1909 depot serves as the hotel lobby. Beautiful flower gardens fill what used to be the terminal yard full of tracks.

Vintage rolling stock, dining cars, and private sleepers were permanently placed on the remaining rails and now serve as deluxe suites, a fine-dining restaurant, a laid-back pizza parlor, and a chocolate factory. A vintage New Orleans trolley car provides transportation to the actual hotel, which was built in the former switchyard. Upstairs in the depot, a mammoth incredibly detailed model-railroad layout provides entertainment for children of all ages, even those who remember the depot in its glory days.

The caboose, for most railroad enthusiasts, encapsulates the romance of the rail. With that in mind, it should come as no surprise that most motels choose the caboose for their railroad rolling stock. In Strasburg, Pennsylvania, this concept was taken to the extreme with some 35 cabooses and a vintage dining car.

That complex, which is now known as the Red Caboose Motel and Restaurant, started as a joke that soon became a mission, an adventure, a quest, and a nightmare for Mill-Bridge Craft Village Museum founder and president Donald Denlinger. In January 1970, at the height of a blizzard, Denlinger learned that his bid on some 19 cabooses, which he had submitted as a joke some six months before, was accepted. Not only that, but the cars had to be moved immediately, so Denlinger quickly got an education in railroad regulation and construction, red tape, the legal system, logistics, and in-depth planning.

The result is a unique complex; each unit is outfitted with attention to detail that makes ingenious use of space. The doors of a cast-iron potbelly stove open to reveal a television. The stovepipe curves to hide an overhead lamp. A Pennsylvania Dutch cabinetmaker created a space-saving combination desk/settee/chest and chair.

The Red Caboose is now world famous. Its story has been featured in National Geographic, Reader's Digest, Ripley's Believe It or Not!, Guinness World Records, and even Chinese Life magazine. The popularity has made it a destination for tourists from throughout the world as well as a landmark on the American road.

RED CABOOSE MOTEL
STRASBURG, PA. 17579

The Red Caboose Motel exemplifies the success to be found in catering to the needs of family, to children of all ages, and to those who have a love for the railroad. It is also an example of what once was, in the era before the franchise.

Stuckey's
An empire built on pecan logs

The devastating storm that became the Great Depression was just beginning to roll across the land when W. S. Stuckey, Sr., took to the back roads of rural Georgia to buy pecans, which he sold to a large warehouse and distributor in Eastman, Georgia. His enterprise had begun as a result of a failed job search, and he started his business with the help of his grandmother, who loaned him $35 for the venture.

In the first months of the endeavor, Stuckey often exhausted his cash quite early in the day. So he would wait until the banks closed and begin writing checks. He would sell the pecans that night and deposit money to cover the checks the next morning.

Within a few short months, the need for such risky business practices was a thing of the past. In 1933, the best credit the banks offered was a $200 loan. By 1936, the local bank backed Stuckey with $20,000!

Expansion came in 1936 in the form a roadside stand that sold pecans directly to tourists. To supplement their income from the sale of shelled and unshelled pecans, Stuckey's wife, Ethyl, started making and selling a variety of pecan candies.

In spite of the hard times, the Stuckey business continued to grow. When Stuckey opened the first retail store in Eastman, Georgia, the old roadside stand was no longer needed. It was purchased by a local farmer who quickly converted it into a henhouse. In short order, Stuckey opened two more stores in Georgia; those stores were followed with a store opening in Florida, the first outside of Georgia, in 1941.

Stuckey's pralines and pecan logs were the foundation for the building of a roadside icon that soon stretched far beyond its origins in the deep South.

With the rationing of gas and rubber during the war, Stuckey pulled back and kept only the store in Eastman open. By this time, the popularity of Ethyl's candies was such that sales reached far beyond the store in rural Georgia. Commissioned sales to military PXs as well as shipped sales carried the candies to every corner of the world.

The war's end brought prosperity and a wave of tourism. By 1948, the candy sales had far outstripped the company's production resources, so large-scale candy-making equipment was set up in the warehouse behind the store.

The ability for increased production and the increasing number of those traveling on southern highways sent the company's fortunes skyrocketing. By 1953, there were 23 stores. A decade later, the store count had risen to more than 100. In 1964, the company merged with Pet Foods, and the dynasty of the landmark teal roof entered into what appeared to be its final chapter.

Between 1970 and 1980, a number of circumstances affected Stuckey's growth. These included the retirement of Stuckey in 1970, the energy crisis and inflation, and Pet's acquisition by IC Industries. Stuckey's growth was at a standstill, and shortly thereafter a period of reversal followed. Some stores were simply closed, others were sold for their real estate value.

The end of the story has yet to be written. The company has been sold once again, but this time to Billy Stuckey, son of the company's founder. Slowly, with a return to what made the company famous, Stuckey's is once again returning to the highways and byways of America.

Totem Pole Parks
Big bands and family fun

Totem poles in name or actuality have long been a mainstay for roadside business promotion. Along Route 66 in Oklahoma, an artist built a towering totem pole monolith as a monument to the American Indian. In the Pacific Northwest and Alaska it was possible to find the real thing, but in most other instances the totem pole was merely suggestive or symbolic. On Woodward Avenue in Detroit, it was a local hangout. In the Northeast, the totem pole was synonymous with unforgettable evenings of fun and music during the glory days of big bands.

Opened in the summer of 1897, Norumbega Park in the Auburndale section of Newton, Massachusetts, was a contemporary of Coney Island. Built by the Commonwealth Avenue Street Railway as an effort to increase profits on the trolley line running between Boston and Auburndale, the park featured a small zoo, a penny arcade, a variety of rides, an outdoor theater, and fine dining at the Pavilion Restaurant. The popularity of canoeing on the Charles River, which bordered the park, provided an additional lure.

The totem pole has long been an important part of promoting roadside attractions. This unique souvenir card dates to the 1940s.

By 1905, to accommodate the tens of thousands customers who came to the park each season, extensive expansion and remodeling was initiated. Most notably, the theater was enclosed and programs were added that ranged from vaudeville and melodramas to moving pictures. The all-new Great Steel Theater was now the largest theater in New England.

For the next 25 years, expansions and improvements largely centered on rides and the zoo, and as a result, the latter became the largest in the Northeast. The big news for 1930 was the replacement of trolleys with buses and the conversion of the Great Steel Theater into the Totem Pole Ballroom.

By 1940, more than 100 ballrooms were advertised in the greater Boston area, but the Totem Pole outshone them all. Anton Myrer's The Last Convertible captured the fondness of a generation that remembered this legendary dance room.

The park and the ballroom supported each other rather well. A couple could enjoy the park, the rides, and the shooting galleries, and then dance the night away to the sounds of Benny Goodman and Artie Shaw. Young lovers could cuddle in the paddleboats and canoes, enjoy the lush gardens, and listen to the music that made memories, which lasted a lifetime and carried them through a world war.

The prosperity of the postwar years and the need to forget the friends who had been lost induced families to travel farther from home for entertainment. The younger set sought the sand and surf in the pursuit of creating memories for their generation. Norumbega and the Totem Pole Ballroom began a precipitous slide with the opening of new mega-parks such as Disneyland.

On Labor Day, 1963, Norumbega closed its gates forever. A few months later, on February 8, 1964, The Totem Pole closed too, and an era as well as an icon came to an end.

TALLEST TOTEM POLE
IN THE WORLD--120 FEET
HOTEL AND DANCE HALL
BUILT IN A REDWOOD STUMP
World Famous Drive Thru Stump
REDWOOD OCTOPUS STUMP
Redwood Pierced by a Rail
GIANT MAN-EATING CLAM
Museum of 1000 Wonders
TOTEM POLE PARK
and MUSEUM
CRESCENT CITY, CALIF.

Wall Drug
An empire built on kindness

The South Dakota Badlands in the early 1930s hadn't changed much since it became new frontier in the West. The roads were in large part nothing more than dusty, muddy, or snow-covered trails. In the summer, the sun often created shimmering mirages on the far horizons, while winter winds whipped up snow that brought visibility to zero.

Wall, South Dakota, a town with fewer than 350 souls, was but a speck in this vast prairie when Ted Hustead, a pharmacist, and his wife, Dorothy, bought the only drugstore in town in December 1931. At the time, many farmers had left the area because of a drought, and bitter winter winds didn't make life in Wall more hospitable to newcomers. Business reflected the poor weather conditions, but Ted decided to give himself five years to make the drugstore profitable.

By the summer of 1936, nearing their fifth anniversary in business in Wall, the family had a new member. And even though the Husteads weren't starving, the business continued to be stagnant. Then came a fortuitous afternoon where stifling heat and the noise of traffic on nearby Route 16A made it impossible for Dorothy to rest.

After numerous attempts to nap, Dorothy went to Ted with an idea. As she saw it, the travelers on the nearby highway wanted a break from the dust of the road and something cold to drink more than anything else. So why not put up some catchy signs, similar to those used by Burma-Shave, and offer free ice water?

Over the next few days, Ted made up a few signs, went out to the highway, and set them up. By the time he got back to the store, Dorothy was already serving many customers in search of the promised respite from the dust and heat.

The rest of that day sped by as they poured gallons of water, made and sold ice cream cones and such at the fountain, provided directions, and gave the cash register bell a real workout. Throughout the summer, business continued to grow. By the close of the following summer, it had become necessary to hire eight local girls to meet the needs of the business.

The signs, like the Rock City barn slogans, began to spread far and wide, including to the military theaters of operations throughout the world. Then Lady Bird Johnson's well-intentioned drive to clean up the roadsides of America began. The campaign was manifested in the America the Beautiful Initiative, and its cornerstone was the Highway Beautification Act, launched in January 1965. The plan brought the age of such signage to an abrupt end.

From its humble origins and an act of kindness, Wall Drug has grown to be a roadside stop recognized throughout the world.

However, the demise of the famous signs was not enough to eclipse the legendary status of Wall Drug. Today the expanded store, under the able guidance of the founder's son Bill, is still a welcome respite for the weary motorist crossing the prairie. The store often draws 20,000 visitors in a single day and is now the largest employer in the small town of Wall.

Wigwam Village
Politically incorrect lodging

Long before he patented the idea in 1936, Frank Redbird had dreamed of a motel that would be unique, something that would stand out from the auto courts that were springing up along the highways of America. The idea was to create a lodging experience that was out of the ordinary and would ensure a steady stream of customers with little more than word-of-mouth advertisement. This was not an easy goal in an era when roadside establishments were built in the shapes of teapots, whales, fish, elephants, milk jugs, airplanes, and ducks.

In time, fantasy became reality, and the Wigwam Villages were the result. Comprising a semicircle with 15 rooms built in the shape of teepees outfitted with western decor, each village featured a larger, centrally located teepee that served as the office and gift shop. Quite often, a gas station was also operated from the office, as with Wigwam Village Number 2 in Cave City, Kentucky. Two smaller teepees were built on both sides of the office as restrooms, with one for each sex.

Wigwam Village Number 1 was constructed at Horse Cave, Kentucky. The second, at Cave City, was built to serve guests visiting nearby Mammoth Cave. Later five more were added, with one each in Alabama, Arizona, California, Florida, and Louisiana.

Of the seven Wigwam Villages, two have been restored and modernized: the first at Cave City, and the second, now a Route 66 landmark, in Holbrook, Arizona, which originally opened in 1950. A third in California has also survived, but it has a very uncertain future due to its poor condition.

After almost 70 years, Wigwam Village No. 2 in Cave City, Kentucky, still does the job for which it was designed: provide travelers with a unique lodging experience.

See Rock City
Mountaintop time capsule

"**S**ee Rock City." There was a time not so long ago when this message could be found emblazoned on countless barns throughout the Southeast, as far west as Oklahoma, and as far north as Michigan. This, as well as slogans such as "See Seven States From Rock City" and the "World's 8th Wonder," were as much a part of a drive through the Land of Dixie as RC Cola, Moon Pies, and sweltering summer evenings thick with the scent of magnolia blossoms.

It was one of the most successful and simplistic advertising campaigns ever devised. Simply select a barn facing toward a heavily traveled road and offer the owner a monthly sum for the use of the wall, or roof, for the slogan plus the promise of repainting the entire barn on a regular basis. A similar idea had worked quite well for the Chattanooga Medicine Company in the late 1890s, and there was no reason to expect different in the modern era.

In time, the slogan "See Rock City" became better known than the attraction itself, and during World War II it appeared on everything from helmets and tanks to ammunition crates and jeeps. In Korea and Vietnam the tradition continued, and a PX near Saigon sported a sign that read, "Only 13,000 miles to Lookout Mountain and Rock City."

Today the barns have for the most part vanished from the roadside and only post cards and faded photographs remain to mark their passing. But Rock City itself, located high atop Lookout Mountain in extreme northern Georgia, is alive and well as a near-perfect time capsule from an era when cars made their way on small winding highways from coast to coast.

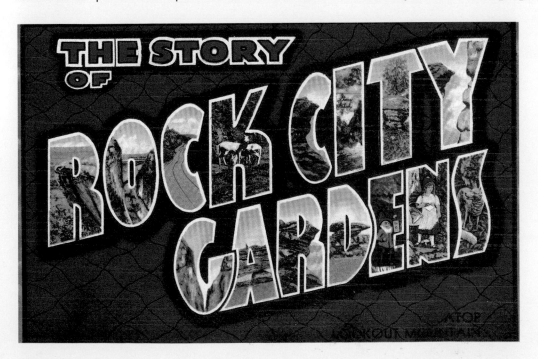

This souvenir brochure from 1938 accentuates the simplistic blend of natural beauty and whimsical fancy that has made Rock City Gardens a popular roadside attraction for more than 70 years.

However, the wonder-inspiring stone pinnacles sheltering shaded avenues and the breathtaking vistas were attracting visitors long before that time. In 1832, a Christian missionary to the Cherokee Indians, David Butrick, was fascinated by the mountain citadel where, "immense boulders were arranged in such a way as to afford streets and lanes."

During the American Civil War, the mountain summit was the scene of intense fighting. Both sides fought to control it because it overlooked the extensive network of river and railroad traffic that lay just below.

By the dawn of the twentieth century, Lookout Mountain had become a refuge for those seeking respite from the cloying summer heat of the Tennessee River Valley. As a result, fine homes soon dotted the lush mountainsides. In 1924, Garnet Carter, an entrepreneur whose family had moved onto the mountain when he was 11 years old, began construction of an exclusive residential subdivision next to the rock gardens near the mountain's summit to capitalize on its popularity.

His wife, Frieda, had a deep fascination for German fairy tales as well as European folklore. And since the stone gardens had long been associated with stories of goblins, it seemed natural to christen the project Fairyland. Names such as Peter Pan Lane were selected to fit the theme, and even the businesses received fanciful names such as Fairyland Gas Station.

While Carter focused all his attention on the project at hand, his wife turned hers toward transforming the "Rock City" into a storybook dream brought to life—the ultimate rock garden. With balls of twine, she began to lay out trails through the formations to the giant outcropping known as Lovers' Leap. She gathered and planted wildflowers as well as other native

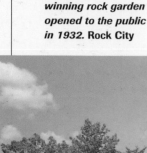

Rock City's award-winning rock garden opened to the public in 1932. **Rock City**

In 1832, a missionary to the Cherokees was fascinated by Lookout Mountain's immense boulders and natural lanes. **Rock City**

plants. Statues of gnomes and other figures from folklore were imported from Germany as well as other European countries and placed in carefully chosen locations.

The hard economic times of the Great Depression brought the Fairyland housing project to a near standstill. So Garnet Carter turned his attentions to the promotion and further development of his wife's award-winning mountaintop rock garden that had opened to the public on May 21, 1932.

Initially the paying customers who came to see the mountaintop wonderland were few in number. Then in 1935, the now-famous barn-painting advertisement campaign began. By the mid-1960s, more than 1,000 barns in 19 states were adorned with Rock City slogans, and the attraction was welcoming more than 10,000 visitors annually.

During the Cival War both sides fought to control lookout mountain for the views it afforded of the river and rail traffic. **Rock City**

Today, Rock City's scenic trails lead through beautiful gardens to awe-inspiring vistas, past thundering waterfalls, and among rock formations with whimsical names like Fat Man's Squeeze and Goblin's Underpass, as they have for more than half a century. The caverns filled with gnomes, goblins, elves, and other forest creatures still delight children of all ages, just as they have since the gardens opened in 1932.

In a recent interview, Bill Carter, a member of Rock City Gardens' founding family, summarized what has made it a popular attraction for more than 70 years: "We have a lot of people that were here as kids come back and bring their kids and grandkids," he said. "They remember it and tell us it was a big hit [on] both vacations."

Characters from German fairytails have long been a theme of Rock City. **Rock City.**

2

Safety, Comfort, and Style

The Evolution of Automotive Essentials

In the infancy of the automobile, what we today consider automotive essentials—air conditioning, heaters, doors, windshields, and so forth—were as distant in thought to the motorist as a road trip on Mars would be in our time. Simply having personal transportation without Dobbin leading the way was enough of a miraculous accomplishment.

But with each passing year, the luxurious options of the previous model became the standard features on the current one. Quite often, the features soon transcended luxury and became necessities.

The trend started in 1912, when Cadillac transformed the automotive industry with the introduction of the first practical electric starter. In an instant, electric and steam-powered vehicles became hopelessly obsolete. With the exception of Ford and a few small-volume companies, the industry had adopted the starter as standard equipment within two years.

Yet the evolution of the automobile has not always been linear, nor has it always been logical. When one considers that the Essex closed sedan made its debut in 1919, it seems only logical to think that creature comforts soon followed. Yet, it wasn't until 1947 that heaters were a factory-installed option in Chevrolet trucks.

Crashes and Survival
The Modern Era of Automotive Safety

The bumper hits the wall, but the rest of the car keeps going. The car finally stops, but the driver keeps going. The skull hits the windshield, but the brain keeps going. The brain hits the skull, and everything stops.

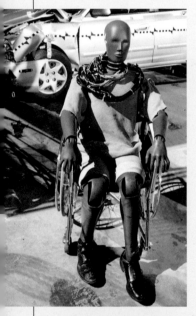

Meet GM Hybrid III, the world's smartest dummy. He was born in 1997, and he's taking car safety into the twenty-first century. He is a descendent of Sierra Sam, a crash-test dummy invented in the 1940s to test aircraft ejection seats. This example is the 168-pound, 5'-10" male, and this size and weight represents the most common driver on the American road. There are many other dummies representing big men, tiny women, children, and pregnant ladies.

This was the outcome of traffic accidents for decades. The accidents still happen, but the continued motions of body-to-car and brain-to-skull have been greatly eased with advice from a very wise, but very quiet family of crash-test dummies.

Sierra Sam was this family's first member. Sierra Engineering developed Sam in 1949 to test ejection seats for the U.S. Air Force, but he didn't see much action in the automotive world until the passage of the National Traffic and Motor Vehicle Safety Act of 1966. Before that, Nash offered optional seatbelts, until 1956 when Ford Motor Company stressed safety in its ad campaigns with the introduction of seatbelts, deep-dish steering wheels, and improved door latches. The public, however, didn't dig either effort. The Vehicle Safety Act leveled the playing field so that all the car companies were testing and perfecting the same safety devices without losing their competitive edge. Sources in the crash-test field stress that it was never the car companies' intent to build unsafe cars, but rather, they didn't know what specifically to do and were afraid to spend millions of dollars on the wrong things. They didn't want to raise the price of the cars without the desired safety results.

When Jerry Kratzke of Karco Engineering entered the crash-test field while working for another company in 1967, he and his colleagues crashed a dozen pre-1963 American cars to test camera and lighting equipment. Every one of the cars had catastrophic failures of gas tanks and steering columns. The gas tanks ruptured, some of them winding up in the back seat with the passengers, and the steering columns rammed backward toward the driver like a jouster's lance. As soon as the Vehicle Safety Act guidelines were implemented on 1968-model-year cars, steering column failures went to zero, and Kratzke has only seen three fuel tank failures in the following 36 years.

Sierra Sam's lineage evolved, culminating in the GM Hybrid III of 1997—a dummy with a lot of smart things to say. The most common dummy is the 5-foot, 10-inch tall, 168-pound male who represents the most common driver on American highways, and he's the one who hits the wall the most. The first step is seeing if seatbelts fit and stay on different sizes and weights of dummies—average men, average women, big men, short women, children, and pregnant women. Can people of radically different builds and weights get into the same car and be equally protected in a crash by the same safety devices? The technicians ask this question and the dummies answer.

The Head Injury Criteria—or HIC, pronounced "hick"—tell a story from sensors in the dummy's head. A complicated formula, involving deceleration rates and angles, arrives at the HIC number. A tolerable impact force has an HIC number under 1,000. Prior to the 1968 safety improvements, HIC numbers over 2,000 were common. By the 1970s, the crash-test dummies had helped reduced the HIC number to 700–800, and in the twenty-first century, the dummies are tap-dancing over HIC numbers under 300.

The crash-test dummies also measure chest "clip," a quick, hard impact of 60 Gs for 3 milliseconds, where the car should not exert more than 2,200 pounds to the dummy's thigh bones.

While it may cost up to $100,000 for such a high-tech dummy, their sensors tell a hell of a story—an intricate, terrifying drama contained in a split second.

Power Accessories
Luxuries that became necessities

Many power accessories started out in the flurry of bright ideas inventors had in the 1920s, before automobiles and the auto industry took their final forms. It was a time when any idea might make a million dollars.

At first these ideas manifested as aftermarket items, things drivers could add to their own cars after they bought them. Then car companies realized they could make money selling the accessories as add-ons to their product, letting cars leave the showroom already outfitted with every option an owner wanted.

The convenience accessories were powered by three main sources: electricity, hydraulics, and an engine vacuum. Many accessories started out powered by one source, only to be changed to another later.

Genuine necessities like fuel pumps and windshield wipers operated on engine vacuum in the early 1930s and 1950s, respectively, but others, like power door locks on Chryslers and Lincolns, were operated by engine vacuums well into the late 1950s. Later, power door locks were actuated by electric solenoids. Many modern heater/air-conditioning controls use vacuum pressure to operate the shutters and baffles that direct the air flow through different parts of the climate-control system.

Most power brakes have always been operated on engine vacuum. In the 1940s, master cylinders were under the driver's side floorboard on most cars. Thus, Chrysler's vacuum-operated power brake booster was under the floorboard, but its shape forced Chrysler to cut a large hole in the floor under the driver's seat and install a dome to accommodate the bellows of the brake booster. Chrysler used this under-floor brake booster to operate its innovative four-wheel disc brakes in the late 1940s. While most automobiles and light-duty trucks use engine vacuum as the power source for their power brakes, big trucks and motor homes have a hydro-

By the early 1950s, power accessories were fast becoming an important sales tool, and Chrysler was often an industry leader in their development.

boost that uses hydraulic pressure from the power steering pump as the power source for making braking safer and easier to apply.

Hudson is remembered for using engine vacuum to operate its automatic clutch in the 1930s. When the driver let off the accelerator to shift gears, the increased engine vacuum was used to operate an automatic clutch, and the driver shifted gears without pushing the clutch pedal. By the end of World War II, Hudson had added other vacuum-operated mechanisms to actually shift the manual transmission automatically. Hudson called it Drive Master.

Power steering has an identifiable inventor named Francis Davis, who had worked for Pierce-Arrow and was known for his contributions to the technology of heavy trucks. Big trucks were so hard to steer in the 1930s that truckers were known for having serious back trouble from operating the heavy clutches and hard steering. Davis set to the task of making trucks easier to steer. In 1938, he invented the power steering that most drivers are familiar with today—a hydraulic pump applying pressure to diaphragms that assist the driver. Power steering appeared on many American cars right around 1950 with varying results. The former owner of a 1950 Buick Roadmaster may recall the emblem that read "Experimental" right under the Roadmaster emblem on the front fender. The Buick's experimental element was power steering. The owner says the power steering was a dream to drive, but the gear ratio was too quick for the ease of the steering. The slightest movement of the steering wheel steered the car a lot further than the driver usually intended. Chrysler enthusiasts describe the opposite problem with Chrysler's power steering in the 1950s. Chrysler's Hydra-Guide and later Coaxial power steering units had ratios no faster than the ratios of mechanical steering. These ratios required just as much wheel-turning as mechanical steering, but the steering was so easy that it felt like the steering wheel wasn't connected to anything—it was as if the steering wheel were a bicycle wheel mounted on a broom handle.

Most automotive power steering pumps were mounted on the back of the car's generator in the 1950s and ran off the generator's shaft. Power steering is needed most when maneuvering a car through tight parking areas, meaning that the power steering is needed most at low speed. The power steering pump needed to be turning fast enough to do its job, so the car had a giant pulley on the water pump and a small pulley on the power steering pump. The resulting ratio made the generator and the power steering pump run at nearly three times the engine's speed. That's great while idling around a parking lot, but it also made for frequent replacement of generator brushes.

Truck drivers who drove semis in the 1960s will remember that some power steering units on big trucks operated on compressed air. When driving slowly, the air-powered steering was dangerous. The truckers learned quickly to keep their hands on the outside of the steering wheel when driving slowly because uneven ground or an accidental bump into a curb caused the steering to kick backward with great force. If the trucker's fingers were in the way of the steering wheel spokes, there were grave consequences.

Most modern drivers think of power windows as electric, but many may be surprised to learn than many power windows were hydraulic in the late 1940s and early 1950s. They were fast and silent, but they may have been too powerful to be safe when a person's fingers accidentally got caught in the way.

The big, long touring cars in the 1920s took a lot of muscle, precise geometry, and cussing to extend the 8-foot-long convertible top. Some companies proudly advertised their spring-loaded "one-man" tops that could be raised or lowered by a single person standing outside the car. In 1939, Plymouth got the credit for offering a power convertible top. Plymouth's power top ran on vacuum, but the auto industry quickly developed tops that ran on the other two forms of power, electricity and hydraulics.

Turn signals are thought of as essential legally mandated equipment, but they started out as conveniences. Many modern drivers have forgotten the venerable hand signals, but in the 1920s and 1930s, they were all a driver had available. Aftermarket companies eventually took a cue from the trucking industry, which had been using a form of the mechanical turn signal, and made these signals for cars. The early truck signals consisted of an arm with reflectors on it hung outside the trucker's cab. When the trucker needed to make a turn, he reached for a lever or a set of strings and swung the arm out into the appropriate position for the turn he was making. The mechanical arm mimicked the same hand signals other drivers made with their own arms. Some of the mechanical signal arms even had lights on them.

The 1939 Buick gets the credit for introducing the modern flashing turn signal. In the middle of the trunk, a large, stylized Buick emblem housed rounded arrows on each end, and when the driver hit the signal switch, the appropriate arrow started flashing. Buick's signal switch was on the right side of the steering column and in front of the gearshift. Buick kept it there out of tradition until 1950, long after the rest of the industry, and even the rest of General Motors, had settled on the left side of the steering column.

It's amazing how long it took for cars to have adjustable seats. In the 1920s and early 1930s, most car seats were not adjustable at all. One of the Chrysler Airflow's showy innovations was its adjustable front seat. Not only did it have a big chrome acorn nut on the side of the seat for adjusting the seat up and down, but there was a precise gauge next to it with a needle passing over numbers. Each person could adjust the seat to what he had determined to be his optimum seat adjustment number. Sources differ tremendously regarding which company actually installed power seats first. It's quite likely they were invented by an aftermarket company much earlier than anyone would imagine, but power seats started showing up on the options lists for expensive cars in the 1950s. First, they moved forward and back. Then, they moved up and down. Then, they even tilted forward and back, making the six-way adjustable seat everyone dreamed of in the 1960s. By the 1990s, even truck-based SUVs had seats with power-adjusted lumbar supports.

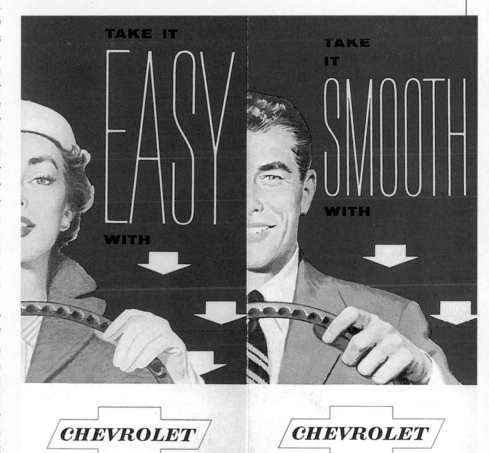

Power accessories are very addictive. Once the public gets a taste of them, they don't want to go back to driving a car without them. Even people on small incomes expect cars to have all the power accessories that only a decade before were expensive luxury options. It's a foolish trend because anyone who restores old cars knows that it was often the power accessories that sent 1950s and 1960s cars to the junkyard. Cars were deemed junk when the power windows would not roll down on a hot day, the power seat got stuck in the forward position so its 6-foot-tall owner couldn't get in, the power steering started leaking, the vacuum-operated heater/air-conditioning control sprung a vacuum leak, or the battery went dead preventing the driver from unlocking the doors. Who knows how many hundreds of thousands of cars with perfectly good drivetrains and major components went to the scrap heap because the power accessories stopped working?

This will be the death of millions more twenty-first-century cars, which include even more power accessories and are sold to buyers at even lower prices. The ultimate demise of so many cars will rise sharply, not because of the cars themselves, but because of extras that have been installed in them that are supposed to make them easier to drive.

"Relax in traffic! Traffic holds no terrors for even the frailest lady. . . ." Other advantages of Chevrolet power steering noted in this period brochure include increased resale value, parking with ease, and enjoying long trips.

Heater
Comfort first, then came safety

First, the car companies had to make cars go down the road reliably, and they competed to see which company could offer the most reliable car at the best price. It didn't take long before the cars were reliable enough to compete in other areas, so comfort and style became big selling points.

Cars were still motorized stagecoaches through much of the decade after 1910, and motorized transportation didn't make a Minnesota winter any warmer. With time, cars with fully enclosed bodies became more affordable. By the early teens, expensive, technologically advanced cars from McFarland even had heated steering wheels, but better answers were still to come.

One of car culture's best trivia questions is this: What actually powers cars? Most people will say gasoline, but that's only half the answer. All fuel-burning cars actually run on heat. Heat is the form of energy that pushes a car down the road. The heat also helps warm the inside of the car. From the 1920s and into the twenty-first century, most heaters have worked by pumping hot water from the engine's cooling system through a mini-radiator in the passenger compartment, and a fan simply blows air through it, warming the passengers. Some makers of expensive cars developed thermostatic temperature controls in the 1940s, and long-standing GM car dealerships miss the under-seat heater their cars offered the public in the 1940s and 1950s. In the 1930s and 1940s, Southwind heaters mounted under the dash had a small line to the car's fuel system and burned gasoline. Because of that feature, it's more accurate to call the Southwind a furnace instead of a heater.

Many car enthusiasts are unaware that, for some time, heaters have had a specific set of legal requirements. Crash-test facilities and proving grounds test new-car heating systems for proper glass defrosting and defogging. Federal Motor Vehicle Safety Standard Number 103 divides a car's windshield glass into two areas. Area A is the entire windshield, and Area C is the critical area that must be clear so the driver can see to drive. The test facilities put cars in refrigeration units over night and freeze them to a pre-determined temperature. Then, from a cold start, the car's defroster must defog and defrost Area C in a certain amount of minutes and Area A within so many minutes. Something that was once simply a comfort device to give the buyer more car for the money has become a serious safety device, similar to seatbelts and air bags.

Right: *This 1950 DeSoto shows off a thermostatically controlled heater made before cars were said to have climate-control systems.*

Opposite: *With the introduction of closed cars, making the vehicle comfortable in all seasons became even easier, especially when equipped by Tropic Aire Motor Vehicle Heaters.*

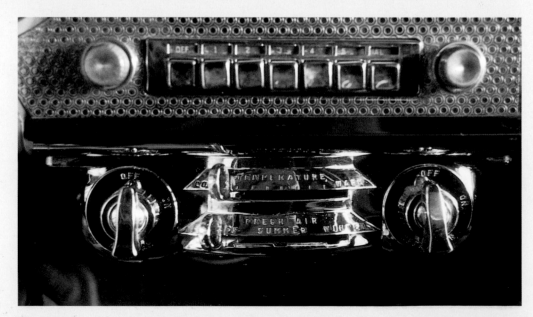

The New Modernized

THE ORIGINAL FAN EQUIPPED
TROPIC-AIRE
HOT WATER
MOTOR VEHICLE HEATER

Eye Appeal plus Purse Appeal

Ask Your Jobber's Salesman for Details !

Your biggest money-making car heater opportunity for 1935-36 season is in this new TROPIC-AIRE line. Get the complete story before you place any heater orders.

Here are heaters designed in appearance, in size and in price to meet the needs and desires of every automobile owner. Styled in the latest, smartest mode . . . to satisfy those who want things that are finer.

Developed by the Originators and Pioneers . . . heaters tha attain still higher standards of mechanical perfection, that exce in quality and performance, that introduce important new ad vancements . . . revolving Tri-plane deflectors, rubber-cushioned rust-proof radiators, advanced flat-type motors, modernized switches, new universal rigid bracket mounting . . . and others

A complete line . . . *DeLuxe, Senior, Tri-Flo* (Downdraft) and *Universal* . . . a model for every purse and each model easily installed in any car!

TROPIC-AIRE, Inc.
71 Eleventh Ave. N.E., Minneapolis, Minnesota
Patent Numbers 1684900—1746985—1830691—1834141
1879152—1892506, others pending.

Air Conditioning
There's no such thing as cold

It's easy to picture a dry sponge soaking up water from the kitchen counter and being squeezed out in the sink. It's a little harder to imagine a gas soaking up a form of energy and squeezing it out somewhere else, but that's how air conditioning works.

There's no such thing as "cold." There is only the absence of heat, just as dark is the absence of light. Refrigeration does not create cold. Refrigeration soaks up heat, moves it someplace else, and releases it.

Compressed-gas refrigeration was one of the many automotive innovations to spring from Charles Kettering's fertile brain, along with electric starters, generators, magneto-less ignition systems, and leaded gasoline. In his several decades with General Motors, Kettering also made ingenious refinements to diesel engines, and his successful and unsuccessful experiments with air-cooled engines eventually led directly to the Chevrolet Corvair. Kettering was still teaching at the General Motors technical schools in the late 1950s, and many GM dealers have fond memories of taking classes from the gentleman genius.

Kettering gets most of the credit for perfecting compressed-gas refrigeration. While ammonia and, worse yet, sulfur dioxide are efficient refrigeration gasses, they are too dangerous and even deadly to use safely. So Kettering developed Freon, a safe, odorless gas that Floridians secretly worship every summer.

The air-conditioning compressor compresses the Freon, and the Freon gets very hot—the equivalent of squeezing the water out of the sponge. Then the hot, compressed gas is run through a set of coils in front of the car's radiator, where the heat is released from the gas, condensing into a cool liquid. Then, it's allowed to suddenly expand back into a gas, which gets really cold. This cold gas is run through a mini-radiator in the car's passenger compartment, and it sucks the heat right out of the air blown through it—the equivalent of soaking up water with a sponge.

Through the 1930s, '40s, and into the '50s, the Thermador Car-Cooler was an extremely popular aftermarket accessory. It looked like a tube-type vacuum cleaner, and it was actually an evaporative cooler—something Californians and Southwesterners have on the roofs of their houses and often call "swamp coolers" or "swampies." The body of the Car-Cooler was half-filled with about a gallon-and-a-half of water, and lining the inside of the cooler was a screened tube filled with balsa-wood shavings. The cooler had a string hanging down in the passenger compartment, and the driver or passenger pulled the string as needed, which rotated the pad of balsa shavings in the water. The air rushing into the front of the cooler from the car's forward motion would blow through the water-soaked pad, and blow through a vent into the passenger compartment. The Car-Coolers didn't cool like A/C, but they worked better than most people would expect.

Packard is credited as the first car company to offer factory-installed air conditioning, and it was quickly followed by Cadillac, Chrysler, and DeSoto. The A/C compressors ran off the engine, but the output units were in the trunks with the cool air blowing into the passenger compartments from the package tray behind the back seat. Chrysler and DeSoto vehicles had

The Thermador Car-Cooler is an evaporative cooler like southwesterners have on their houses. The unit holds a gallon and-a-half of water, and inside the unit's tub-shaped outer skin is another tube-shaped pad of balsa shavings encased in screen. The passenger pulls a string inside the car's passenger compartment, and the inner tube rotates into the water where the balsa shavings absorb the water. The air entering the front of the unit blows through the water-soaked balsa shavings and into the passenger compartment, making it blissfully cool. It doesn't work as well as refrigerated air conditioning, but it works generally better than people first imagined.

an additional oddity in that the only way to turn off the compressor was to open the hood and take the belt off. The only controls in the car for the air conditioner were those that worked the blowers. With time, electric compressor clutches came along and relieved drivers of this chore.

By the 1950s, Chrysler products and GM cars had stand-up air intakes next to their rear windows. GM cars had clear plastic tubes that took the cold air from the output in the package tray up into the headliner, and the cool air blew into the passenger compartment through vents in the headliner. Owners of Chrysler products report that the cold air blowing out of the package tray followed the inside roofline of the car and came down right on the driver's knees, making for bone-aching travel.

Aftermarket air conditioning was available for all cars by the late 1950s, and by the 1960s, air conditioning output units were under the dashboards. Coincidentally, many cars had fewer and fewer vents as alternatives to air conditioning, almost forcing buyers to have that option on their cars.

As the U.S. highway system expanded to four-lane expressways throughout the country, drivers were able to sustain 65- and 70-mile-per-hour speeds on their long drives. Yet driving into headwinds made the noise inside the car almost too much to bear, so car companies had to insulate and soundproof cars for higher-speed driving, and air conditioning played a role in that advancement.

By the 1990s, most consumers couldn't buy a car that didn't have air conditioning. Its price dropped considerably, and drivers just couldn't live without it. In fact, used-car dealers found that even customers with very limited budgets would insist on getting an air-conditioned car. It was common for these buyers to walk right past older used cars with few miles on them to purchase worn-out, beat-up, high-mileage cars with air conditioning.

Automatic Transmission

By the late 1930s, all American cars ran down the road pretty well. Even the economy makes had achieved respectable reliability. Competition no longer centered around which brand of car ran the best but, rather, which one offered the driver more comfort and convenience.

There are two kinds of gearboxes found in most automobiles. Most manual transmissions have a sliding gearbox in which two shafts lie next to each other—the main shaft and the countershaft—and gears with different numbers of teeth slide along the shafts and mesh with each other during gear changes. In high gear, the main shaft locks into one piece, the power goes straight through it, and the transmission's output shaft turns at the same speed as the input shaft. The planetary gearbox may have three or four sets of gears. Each set has a sun gear in the middle, surrounded by three planet gears, and still farther out is a ring gear that holds them all together. The power will be running straight through the sun gear, with the planet and ring gear coasting along, until a hydraulic mechanism suddenly clamps a band around the ring gear. This motion stops it and causes the planet gears to walk around inside the ring gear, which is driven by the sun gear. The power will then be taken at a different ratio from the planet gears. When it's time to change gears, one band will let go and allow one gear set to coast, and another band will clamp down to engage another gear set with a different ratio. Ford's famous Model T had a planetary gearbox, and the driver's foot operated the bands instead of a hydraulic mechanism. To come to a stop, most automatic transmissions use a fluid coupling within the flywheel that looks like a spinning doughnut-shaped tank of liquid. When the driver steps on the gas, the engine spins the tank faster, and the centrifugal force

The big news for 1940 at Chrysler was the option of fluid drive, a forerunner of the modern automatic transmission.

Why Shift Gears?

DRIVE IN "HIGH" ALL THE TIME WITH CHRYSLER FLUID DRIVE

throws the liquid to the outside of the tank, where it grabs blades attached to the output shaft. This simple fluid coupling was refined further into a true torque converter by adding other sets of blades that captured the violent currents created in the liquid and redirected these currents into productive forces.

By the early 1930s, several American car companies had experimented and marketed forms of automatic and semi-automatic transmissions, but some became more popular and influential than others.

Bendix made all sorts of automobile equipment—braking systems, starters, generators—and Bendix was responsible for some of the earliest popular automatic-like shifting systems. The Electric Hand was a stylish chrome arm off the right side of the steering column with a pod on the end that had slots in the familiar H-pattern. The driver moved a tiny gearshift through these slots to the next gear he wanted to car to be in, lifted his foot from the gas, and waited for the transmission to click into that gear. It was called a pre-select transmission, and it appeared on Cords, Packards, and Hudsons in the late 1930s.

Hudson introduced a vacuum-operated automatic clutch in the late 1930s. With the addition of a vacuum operated pre-select self-shifting mechanism, Hudson called it Drive-Master.

The real stroke of marketing genius came from General Motors in 1937, with the introduction of Oldsmobile's Safety Automatic. This was simply a fluid-coupling clutch with a planetary gearbox that did not shift on its own. This transmission was crude, but it set the stage for great things. Oldsmobile brought out the truly automatic Hydra-matic in 1939, and it quickly appeared on Cadillacs.

That same year, Chrysler installed a fluid coupling between the engine and a manual gearbox under the name Fluid Drive. These Chryslers and DeSotos gained a great reputation for controllable traction in ice and snow, as well as long-lasting universal joints, differentials, and rear engine main bearings because of Fluid Drive's cushioning effect. Chrysler installed various automatically shifting

Free wheeling in the early 1930s was heralded as an advancement in fuel economy, but it proved to be a very dangerous option in light of the quality of brakes featured during the period.

The gear selector on this 1956 Oldsmobile is attached to GM's wildly successful four-speed Hydra-matic.

gearboxes behind the Fluid Drive unit up through 1954, and with a lift of the foot from the accelerator, they shifted with a soft click and were some of the most reliable automatic transmissions ever produced.

GM's Hydra-matic took the world by storm, setting the trend for all automatic transmissions to follow. But, because of restrictions on the manufacture of civilian automotive components during World War II, Hydra-matics were not maintained during the war years, and they were known to become jerky and harsh while shifting. It's possible that GM hung the Buick division with soft suspension and the ultra-smooth, non-shifting Dynaflow in 1948 to counter customer complaints that GM's cars were too jerky. The Dynaflow was hard on gas, and a six-cylinder Fluid Drive Chrysler could easily outrun a Dynaflow Buick with a big straight-eight. Through the 1950s, the Dynaflow steadily improved, and by 1960 a Dynaflow Buick could peel rubber with the best of them.

The four-speed Hydra-matic was convenient when coupled with a flathead Cadillac V-8, but the Hydra-matic became exciting when installed behind new overhead-valve Cadillac and Oldsmobile V-8s in 1949. The rest of the industry ran to catch up. Hydra-matics appeared in Nashes and Hudsons under an arrangement with GM, making Hudson Commodores and Hornets as well as Nash Ambassadors some of the automobile world's most underrated cars.

Chrysler shot off into the distance with the hemi V-8 in 1951, and while they still had the semi-automatic gearbox behind them, Chrysler had caught up to GM by installing a true torque converter in between. Ford Motor Company got into the act in 1951, and retired employees of the Ford Arizona Proving Ground discovered and corrected many heat-related torque converter problems while testing the transmissions in the Mojave Desert. The Ford-O-Matic was a pleasant two-speed unit that really came to life on the 1953–1955 Lincolns with their advanced V-8s and road race–inspired designs. Ford brought out the Cruise-O-Matic in 1958, and this basic design served the company for many years.

Chrysler went fully automatic in 1953 with the two-speed Powerflite. Chrysler may not have been the first with a fully automatic transmission, but when it finally came out, its design was simpler, with fewer moving parts and a lot less to go wrong. While Chrysler's first three-speed Torqueflite automatics were troublesome in 1957 and 1958, these transmissions were quickly refined into something bulletproof. They took the punishment of truck use under the name Loadflite and took the beatings meted out by the muscle-car era. Chrysler's and Edsel's push-button transmission controls are charming artifacts of the Jet Age.

By the late 1950s, the automatic transmission world had settled into norms that lasted into the twenty-first century. No one was wowed by them anymore, but thinking back, it's fun for car enthusiasts to drive a Hydra-matic from the 1950s or a Fluid Drive Chrysler from the 1940s and imagine the excitement their grandfathers felt about the coming technological age.

Windshield Wipers
Where the rubber meets the glass

In the early automotive world, when gasoline was bought in gallon jugs at drug stores, there were no roads to speak of and really no fixed roofs. Who was driving in the rain?

Times changed quickly, and driving when the world said you were supposed to, no matter what the weather, became more common. By 1920, even many expensive cars still had manual windshield wipers, and the driver would reach up and flip the little lever back and forth to clean his straight-ahead field of vision only. If the rain got bad enough, he pulled over and sat out the storm.

By the end of the 1920s, even inexpensive cars had vacuum-operated wipers, but they were quirky and almost as much work as manual wipers. The engine built up vacuum pressure in the intake manifold, and a rubber hose ran up to the wiper motor. The motor was a curved, semicircular chamber with a pivoting diaphragm inside. Outside the motor, levers connected the diaphragm to the wiper arms. When the valve on the dash was opened, vacuum pressure pulled on one side of the diaphragm, and it swept across the inside of the chamber. When it reached the end of its travel, it automatically closed a little internal valve and opened a valve on the other side of the diaphragm, which was then pulled in the other direction. It repeatedly pulled the diaphragm back and forth, and the windshield wipers cleared water from the glass.

There were problems, though. When the car accelerates, the manifold vacuum drops, and the wipers stop. They started moving again when the gas pedal was let up a little for steady speed, but when the driver decelerated and let off the gas completely, the manifold vacuum would jump, and the wipers would go crazy, slapping back and forth like a flag in a windstorm. On a road with lots of gentle rises and falls, the driver constantly adjusted the speed of the wipers.

It's amazing that it took so long, but Chrysler finally brought out electric wipers in 1940, and they operated at constant speed no matter what the car was doing. They simply had an electric motor with a rotating crank that swept the wipers back and forth smoothly, with none of the sudden, nervous reversals in direction that characterized vacuum wipers.

It took the rest of the industry into the late 1950s to catch up, but there were some innovations in vacuum wipers that made them work a little better. Around World War II, several car companies installed vacuum pumps on top of the fuel pumps. The wipers still operated off manifold vacuum, but the vacuum pump smoothed out the variations and kept the speeds steadier under different accelerator conditions.

From the late 1930s and into the early 1950s, cars all had split windshields, and each side had its own wiper, but there was no way for them to overlap and clean the whole field of vision, especially in snow. The design of the windshield makes this forgivable, but less forgivable are the wiper designs on American cars from the mid-1950s with the big, beautiful wraparound windshields that car collectors love. The wipers swept from each end and met tip-to-tip in the middle, still leaving a big V-shaped area in the middle of the windshield uncleared.

By 1960, most American cars' wipers swept together in the same direction and overlapped, leaving only the outer edges of the windshield uncleared. By the 1990s, even rear window wipers were common, and some European cars even had wipers on the headlights. There's a lot of talk about where the rubber meets the road, but where the rubber meets the glass isn't talked about enough.

This 1949 Hudson carries its vacuum-operated windshield-wiper motor high in the middle of the firewall and has an ingenious, though some would say silly, system of little cables and pulleys connecting the motor to the wiper arms.

Radio
Theme songs for the road

The AM radio in this 1942 DeSoto sits in the dash like a piece of fine furniture and delivers a warm, rich sound that was quickly forgotten in the higher-tech but weaker-toned transistorized era. This DeSoto lives in the Chuck Zimmerman collection.

"**B**oss radio! Ninety-three, K . . . H . . . J . . . ! in Boss Angeles, and I'm the Reeeaaal Don Steeeeel! Don't touch me, 'cause I'm red hot, baby!"

Was it ever a good idea? Even in the early 1930s, automobiles traveled at 60 miles per hour on country highways and edged their way through tight old-fashioned streets of big cities. Should there have even been radios to distract drivers, and how many fender benders have drivers fiddling with radios caused?

It was never a good idea, but car radios are a reality, and they hum, crackle, and play the soundtrack to childhood memories for millions of Americans. The big tube-driven Philco, Motorola, and Silvertone AM car radios of the 1940s and 1950s delivered a warm, clear sound that was quickly forgotten in the higher-tech transistorized-radio era of the following decades, when AM radios became poor imitations of the fine equipment that came before.

A guy gets in his car, turns on the radio, and hears a live broadcast of Martian spaceships landing in New Jersey and the agonized screams of those shot with death rays. Those who

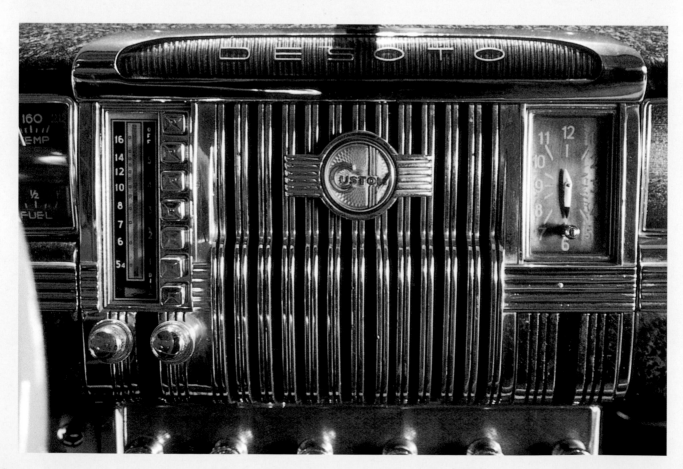

laugh at the people who believed Orson Welles' War of the Worlds broadcast on Halloween night of 1938 have never heard the recording—a terrifying, convincing masterpiece of broadcast history. How many people tuned in too late to know it was fiction and sat in their cars not knowing where to run?

A girl rides in her father's car looking at the back of a ration sticker, crying as she wonders if her boyfriend will come back from Europe alive. The Andrew Sisters sing "Apple Blossom Time."

Dad drives his first V-8-powered car on a family vacation to the Grand Canyon with mom singing along with "Tennessee Waltz."

A man approaching middle age crosses the Bay Bridge into San Francisco in his gleaming, finned DeSoto with dual antennas, mentally dissecting complicated rhythms he's never heard before, vowing that he will soon own this new Dave Brubeck LP.

A policeman and a trucker pass each other on a quiet, pitch-black Nebraska highway. Patsy Cline sings "Crazy" through the occasional crackles of distant lightning, and they both wish they were home.

A long-haired young man guides his multi-colored Volkswagen bus through the California hills and wonders if he can ever again be the child he once was, when "I Want to Hold Your Hand" comes on the air, evoking pre-counterculture memories. Was his father really that bad?

Booming Hip-Hop thumps from CDs, and live sports are beamed down from satellites into overly insulated SUV interiors. Car stereos are often more sophisticated than some home stereos, but none of them will ever have the romance and sentiment of the simple sincerity that hummed from the speakers of mid-twentieth-century AM radio.

This twenty-first century satellite radio brings in broadcasts from around the world on hundreds of specialized channels, but its very individuality takes it out of the collective mind. Decades from now, people won't share common sentimental memories about the music and shows they listened to on the radio.

Automobile Insurance
Another game of chance

In essence, insurance is a gamble. The insured pays, hoping he never needs it, but derives peace of mind knowing that in the event of loss or damage he will not suffer the resultant financial burden alone. The insurer accepts the payments and the premiums, hoping the customer never has a loss or suffers damage to that item of value.

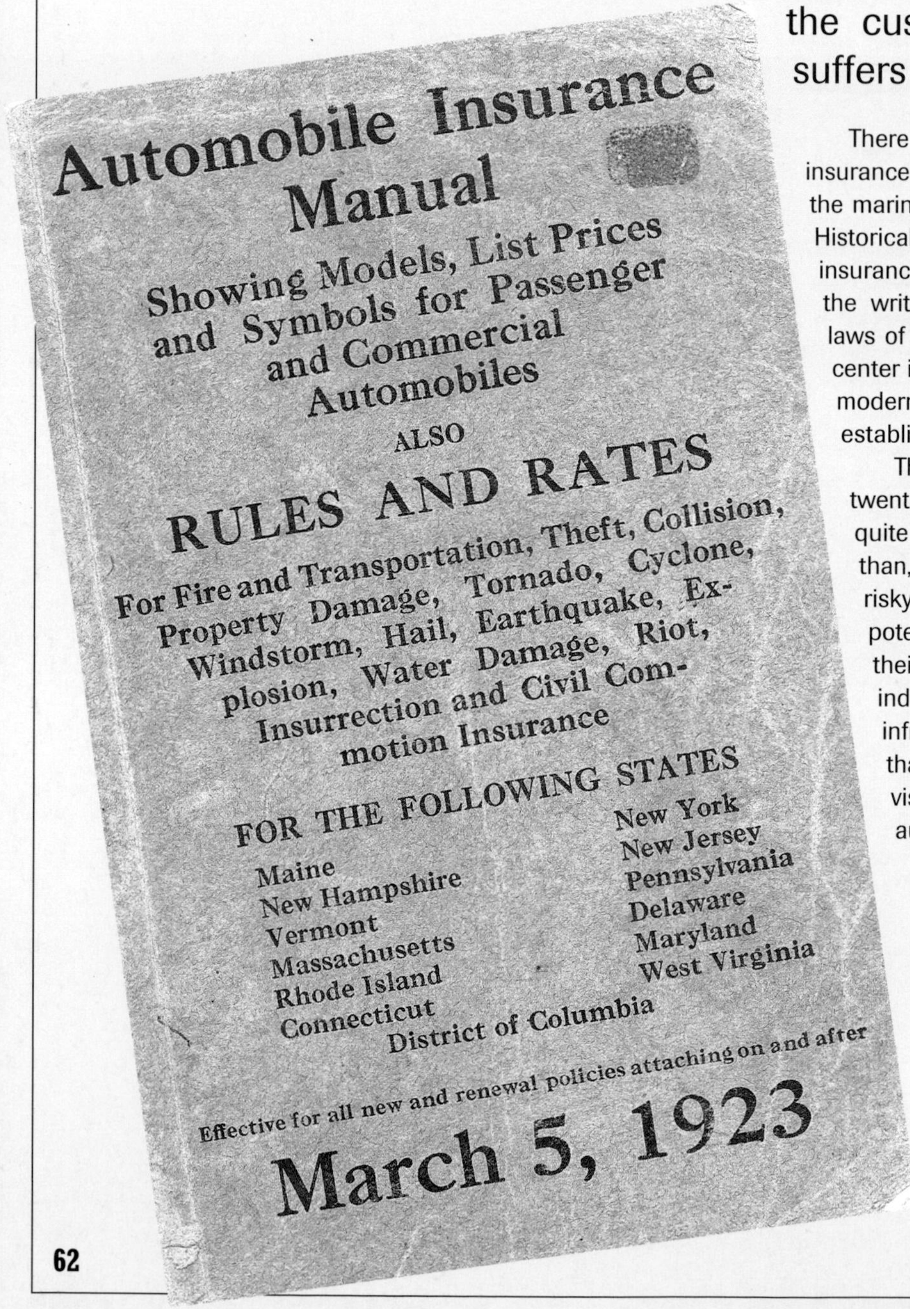

There are some indications that the concept of insurance was used in China as a form of loss control in the marine trade several thousand years before Christ. Historical evidence documenting the evolution of insurance can be found in the Babylonian legal system; the writings of Justinian, the Roman emperor; and laws of Venice during its pinnacle years as a trading center in the twelfth century. It could be said that the modern beginning of insurance dates to the establishment of Lloyd's of London in 1769.

The automobile during the first decades of the twentieth-century represented a costly investment; quite often they carried a price close to, or greater than, that of a house. The investment was also risky. A few companies were quick to see the potential profit in providing insurance, much as their predecessors had for the high-risk shipping industry. As with many aspects of the automotive infrastructure, the development of companies that offered insurance usually began with visionaries who saw the unique needs of automobile owners.

Automobile Insurance Manual

Showing Models, List Prices and Symbols for Passenger and Commercial Automobiles

ALSO

RULES AND RATES

For Fire and Transportation, Theft, Collision, Property Damage, Tornado, Cyclone, Windstorm, Hail, Earthquake, Explosion, Water Damage, Riot, Insurrection and Civil Commotion Insurance

FOR THE FOLLOWING STATES

Maine
New Hampshire
Vermont
Massachusetts
Rhode Island
Connecticut

New York
New Jersey
Pennsylvania
Delaware
Maryland
West Virginia

District of Columbia

Effective for all new and renewal policies attaching on and after

March 5, 1923

By 1923, the automotive insurance industry had become a complicated one, as indicated by the thickness of this rare insurance manual.

George Mercherle had spent a great deal of his life farming before accepting a job selling insurance for a small company. While he proved to be quite adept at sales, the rates as well as business practices bothered his conscience. When he brought these matters to the attention of the owner and proposed solutions, the response was derision and the blunt suggestion that if he was so smart he should start his own company.

So with the foundational premise that farmers should pay less for insurance because they drove less and had fewer losses as a result, Mercherle started a company he called State Farm in 1922. Another revolutionary aspect was that it was a mutual automobile insurance company owned by its policyholders.

The company grew at an amazing pace and, as a result, the board voted to decentralize in 1928. Employees from the original Bloomington, Illinois, office as well as new employees hired for their knowledge of the local community became the core for the new office in Berkeley, California. As with the Bloomington office, this one provided support for regional agents who in turn provided faster and more personalized service to the customer.

Today the concept behind the formation of the Berkeley office has given rise to 25 operation centers in 13 zones. Moreover, the company founded with the needs of the farmer in mind has expanded to 71.6 million policyholders in the United States and Canada.

Catering to the unique needs of the automobile owner served as the catalyst for the formation of numerous insurance companies. Now, with the weight of regulation, insurance has become a necessity rather than a luxury as well as a multi-billion-dollar business.

The cost of the premium and the value of the vehicle may be quite different from comparative costs today, but the overall policy is surprisingly similar.

AUTOMOBILE POLICY

Expires   November 10th, 1926

Property   Ford

Amount   - - - $ 200.00

Premium   - - -
A. B. Moody   - $ 3.50

No.   377

National Liberty Insurance Company of America

STOCK COMPANY

INCORPORATED 1859

CASH CAPITAL $1,500,000.00

HEAD OFFICE: 709-717 SIXTH AVE., NEW YORK

FRANCIS H. SLATER
INSURANCE SPECIALIST
THE TIP-TOP TOWN OF THE ADIRONDACKS
TUPPER LAKE, N.Y.

NOTIFY US OF VACANCY
REPAIRS REMOVAL ASSIGNMENTS
AND CHANGE OF OCCUPANCY

Edition 1923

30M 6-25

Whose Idea Was That?
Unsung heroes of the automobile culture

In ancient Greece, warriors and athletes were the heroes of the day, with their deeds becoming more legendary with every telling. With the passing of the years it became increasingly difficult to separate fact from fiction, and soon many had achieved a dubious form of immortality; their names were spoken in nearly every household, but the men behind them were forgotten.

In America during the first years of the twentieth century, it was the industrialist and the inventor who were elevated to the status of legend. Just as with the heroes of old, a few, such as Louis Chevrolet, Henry Ford, Walter Chrysler, and David Buick, obtained a shadowy immortality, with the men themselves forgotten but their names known throughout the world. More than a few, including many who made the success of their more famous contemporaries possible, have been denied even this brush with fame.

Ralph Teetor had an inquisitive nature and a sharp mind, a near perfect combination at the dawn of the automotive age. He liked working with his hands, which in part led to him losing his sight in a shop accident at the age of five. He didn't let his blindness stop him, though. In 1902, at the age of 12, he and a cousin rebuilt a discarded engine, machining each part by hand. They immediately tried to use it in a car of their own design.

Ten years later he graduated from the University of Pennsylvania with a bachelor of science degree. Almost immediately after, he devised a revolutionary technique for balancing steam turbine rotors used in torpedo boat destroyers. He then became a mechanical engineer for the Light Inspection Car Company, a firm that had been founded by his family. Later, the company was reorganized as the Perfect Circle Corporation, which manufactured piston rings. Eventually, he became president of that company.

In the years to follow, Teetor developed numerous innovative solutions to mechanical and manufacturing problems. His most memorable creation was patented in 1945, and it became known by a variety of names: Controlmatic, Touchomatic, Speedostat, and Cruise Control. Because of his legendary invention, as well as several other innovations, he was inducted into the Automotive Hall of Fame in Dearborn, Michigan.

Robert Stempel developed a fascination with all things automotive before he was old enough to walk. This fascination turned profitable when he worked in a local garage to earn money for college and repaired students' cars to have money while he was in school.

His driving ambition was to be employed by General Motors, a goal that he met rather quickly. Among his many contributions to the company and to the automotive world were the development of the intricate front suspension on the 1966 Oldsmobile Toronado and playing an instrumental role in the development of the catalytic converter, as well as the positive crankcase valve.

In recent years, he oversaw the project that built General Motors' first solar-powered car and the first modern electric vehicle. After leaving GM, he continued to spearhead technological development, including the production of nickel metal hydride batteries for electric vehicles and, most recently, preliminary work on fuel cell technology.

To many, Charles Kettering was the Thomas Edison of the automobile. In 1909, after developing an electric motor for National Cash Register, he and a colleague from that project founded their own research firm, Dayton Engineering Laboratories Company (DELCO). Within three years they had developed an electric starter, an improved electric ignition system, and electric lights, all for automotive application. These innovations made their debut on production vehicles with the 1912 Cadillac.

From today's perspective, his creations may seem rather dubious: Freon, Duco paints, and leaded gasoline, to name but a few. Developing leaded gasoline was the result of his work to develop an air-cooled engine for General Motors in 1921. (An interesting historical footnote is that the air-cooled engines installed in Chevrolets resulted in one of the first automotive recalls).

Shortly before the advent of World War II, General Motors published an informative booklet that profiled the history of the diesel engine, its advantages, and why diesel would be the fuel of the future.

Rudolf Diesel was fascinated with engine design. In 1893, he published a scientific paper on a proposed internal combustion engine. The following year he applied for a patent on his device, listed as the diesel engine; the patent was granted in 1898.

The first practical commercial application of this technology was a 60-horsepower 2-cylinder unit built in Saint Louis, Missouri, as a stationary powerplant. From those humble beginnings, the diesel engine has become the engine of the modern age—our trucks, our trains, our heavy equipment, the very lifeblood of modern commerce and transport, all have at their heart the creation of Rudolf Diesel.

Where would our car-crazed culture be today if it weren't for the contributions made by these men? How would we roll merrily along in our Oldsmobile if not for the pneumatic tire made practical by John Dunlop or the contributions of André Michelin or Charles Goodyear?

CB
Reach out and touch someone

Today, with cell phones in almost every driver's hand, it can be difficult to believe that fewer than 50 years ago the ability to communicate with the office while on the road was reserved for the wealthiest customers or companies. During this period, even police departments were often operating with equipment that had changed little since the early 1930s.

The earliest use of mobile telephone technology was for law enforcement. In the summer of 1931, California Highway Patrol Chief Raymond Cato approved experiments to evaluate the feasibility of dispatching patrols by radio. In spite of the favorable results, the formal adoption of radio equipment would not come for another four years. At this time, the radios were just that—modified car radios that operated as simple receivers.

However, the economic conditions of the 1930s made it difficult for police departments to fund the new equipment. As a result, many early transmitters were either hand-built by the men themselves or were funded through raffles. In late 1941, as a response to the perceived threats that resulted from the United States' entry into World War II, the development of two-way capability became a priority.

Personal use of mobile phones dates to this period as well. However, technological limitations, regulation, and resultant disinterest prohibited further development at this time.

By the mid-1970s the CB radio craze was nearing its peak, and companies such as Radio Shack profited greatly from offering all manner of related equipment and material, such as this informative booklet.

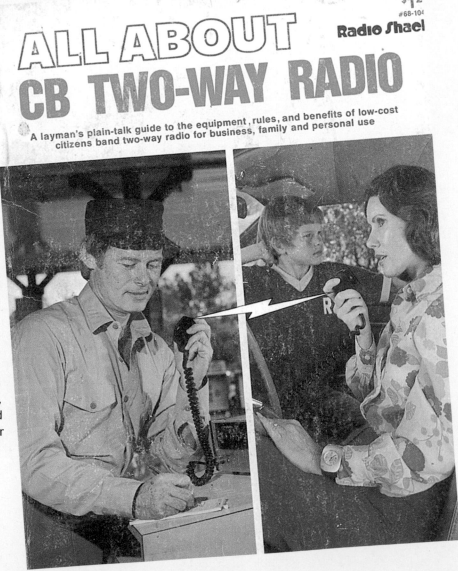

$12
#68-104
Radio Shack

ALL ABOUT
CB TWO-WAY RADIO

A layman's plain-talk guide to the equipment, rules, and benefits of low-cost citizens band two-way radio for business, family and personal use

On June 17, 1946, in Saint Louis, Missouri, a joint effort between AT&T and Southwestern Bell resulted in the establishment of the first commercial mobile radio/telephone service in the United States. The cornerstone of this new service was the issuance of radio/telephone licenses by the Federal Communications Commission. However, the cost of nece-ssary equipment as well as the limitations of service prohibited its use for many.

The initial revolution in making personal communication from the automobile a possibility for the common man began in 1962 when Midland CB Radios introduced into the noncom-mercial market the citizens band radio, which had initially made its debut in 1943. An interesting historical side note has to do with the man accredited for its invention, Al Gross. Additional inventions and gadgets invented or developed by Gross would include the walkie-talkie, made famous during World War II, and the digital stopwatch.

In essence, the CB radio is a private two-way, short-distance voice communications device. Between its introduction and the founding of the Citizens Band Corporation, it would be 15 years before the FCC in 1958 introduced the first 23 channels of the citizens band.

In retrospect, it seems that in the blink of an eye the CB went from being the mainstay of the long-haul trucker to a cultural phenomenon, with popularity fueled by the film and music of the time. Leading the charge in this revolution of personal communication were songs such as "Convoy" by C. W. McCall (aka Bill Fries), a ballad filled with truckers' slang released in 1976. McCall's popularity from this song alone resulted in his becoming the spokesman for Midland Radios. Movies like Convoy and Smokey and the Bandit also fueled the meteoric rise of the CB.

The CB Line *REALISTIC*® That Says it All

The national popularity of the truck-driving ballads reached its peak in January of 1976, and the CB craze peaked shortly after when "Convoy," from McCall's second album, Black Bear Road reached the number-one position on both the pop and country charts of Billboard.

Even though it is still an important part of life on the road, today the CB radio has largely been replaced by the cell phone, except for those who make their living on the road, such as long-haul truckers. But for a brief time, almost no one could imagine cruising the four-lane without his ears on.

The Dashboard
The scenery that never changes

Dashboards predate automobiles. On a horse-drawn wagon, a dashboard was a vertical piece of wood in front of the driver's feet that kept mud, rocks, and manure from being kicked onto his shoes by the horse.

The earliest automobile dashboards were no more sophisticated than those found on wagons. Oldsmobile made one of the first strides into aesthetic dash design with its gracefully curved dash in 1901, and Chevrolet advertised that its 1912 Classic Six had a dash that was lit with electric lights. Still, most automobile dashboards looked as though they belonged behind a horse until the 1920s, when cars became enclosed and provided a more protected environment for delicate, decorative materials and designs. The stage was set for the greatest period of dashboard design.

Art Deco sliced into automobile design in the early 1930s, and cars quickly left behind their stagecoach roots to embrace Buck Rogers-era sweeping lines, symmetry, and V-shapes. Not only were dashboards wood-grained, but many of them had the look of inlaid designs, as if finely crafted wood pieces had been laminated together to negotiate curves and create the beautiful Vs of the time. Symmetry was everything in the late 1930s, a speedometer dial on the left side of the dash was usually echoed by a clock or instrument cluster on the right side. Sometimes there would even be a glove box on each end of the dash.

New and super-powerful airplanes came to public attention during World War II, and three-spoke steering wheels that mimicked airplane propellers became common in cars. By 1950, wood-grained Art Deco was disappearing quickly and being replaced by asymmetric designs of Streamline Modern, which featured a pod of instruments in front of the driver, with plain panels sweeping over to the passenger's side. Chrysler and Nash set the instrument pods on top of the steering columns to further play on aeronautical themes.

In the mid-1950s, Chevrolet and Plymouth had a brief, nostalgic flirtation with Art Deco symmetry that was echoed on each end of the dash. Ford had a radio dial in 1955 that put the tuning knob in the middle of a round face that looked like a washing machine control and echoed some of the round radio dials from the 1930s.

By the late 1950s, the Jet Age became the Space Age, and Chrysler's push buttons and GM's acres of laboratory-style chrome and glass heralded the Sputnik era. Speedometers were backlit, buttons were pushed, and radios were self-tuning.

Chevrolet was an expensive brand in 1918, and this high-tech V-8-powered Chevrolet Model D in the Tom Meleo collection has a very functional dash with electric lights and well-crafted wood trim.

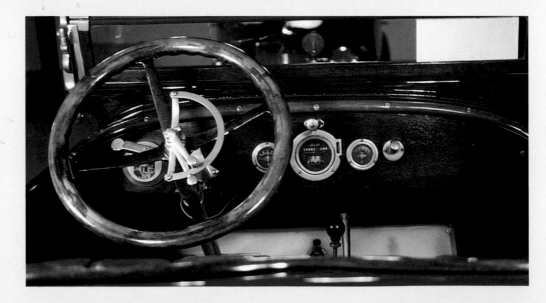

Left: *This 1942 DeSoto in the Chuck Zimmerman collection has one of the most beautifully designed dashes ever to grace an American automobile. With copper-colored instruments and plentiful-but-tasteful ornamentation, this dash fits the rest of the car and its era perfectly. Its Art Deco roots show, but it also predicted the Jet Age.*

Below: *The twenty-first-century dash in a Chrysler 300.*

The rebellion came quickly, though. In the early 1960s, the public suddenly revolted against gaudiness. Dashboards became plain and functional, with an almost aggressive prohibition on any kind of beauty. By the 1970s and 1980s, a plain look was matched by poor quality. In the 1990s, quality improved, but twenty-first-century dashboards are as plain as they were in the mid-1960s.

Many people who are attracted to old cars will look at the dash and exclaim over its beauty. Mechanics have always hated looking under them for problems, but there was a time when people loved their dashboards as much as their side-mounted spares or their two-tone paint.

The Gas Gauge
Between E and F

It's a relatively simple concept: a float connected to an electrical sending unit is tied to a gauge, which most often has an E at one end, an F at the other and, perhaps, some numbers such as 1/2 in the middle. On the Volkswagen Type 1, an R near the E indicates a small reserve. Even in the modern era of electronics, the overall concept remains the same.

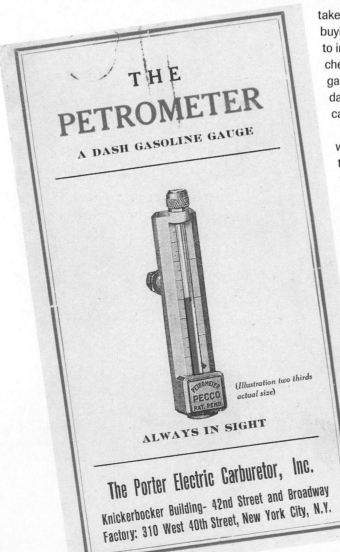

THE PETROMETER

A DASH GASOLINE GAUGE

(Illustration two thirds actual size)

ALWAYS IN SIGHT

The Porter Electric Carburetor, Inc.
Knickerbocker Building- 42nd Street and Broadway
Factory: 310 West 40th Street, New York City, N.Y.

The gas gauge is another one of those little goodies that is taken for granted to such a degree that it is impossible to imagine buying a new car without one. As a result, it might even be harder to imagine buying a new car that came with a measured stick for checking fuel levels or not laughing at the concept of a gas gauge that was mounted directly on the tank instead of in the dash. But this was the rule, and not the exception, for most new car buyers in the years before 1930.

Since one of the redeeming factors for the Model T Ford was its low price, the car continued to be a no-frills model in the extreme sense of the word until its demise in 1927. The tradeoff was inconvenience at best and endangerment at worse. In the matter of checking fuel levels, there was a degree of inconvenience: one had to lift the seat cushion and insert a measuring stick.

Even cars that carried a rather hefty sales price were not immune. As late as 1928, Franklin, a manufacturer that led in the technological development of aluminum usage in automobiles as well as air-cooling for engines, utilized an external gauge mounted on the tank behind the trunk. It was only natural that numerous companies rose to the occasion and offered supplemental instruments.

Modern motorists give little or no thought to the gas gauge unless they are on a lonely road at night and the needle is hovering near E. For the modern automobile owner, the gas gauge is just another miracle of technology that is simply accepted.

The absence of a gas gauge, or a tank-mounted gauge, provided many opportunities for aftermarket companies to fill the void.

ROCHESTER
DASHGAS GAGE
No More Empty Gas Tanks

RULE:—To adjust, face the Dial and turn the knurled Adjusting Sleeve in the same direction you wish Pointer to move

FOR CHEVROLET
(SUPERIOR MODELS)

EASY TO INSTALL
POSITIVE - ACCURATE

UNAFFECTED BY WEATHER OR ATMOSPHERIC CONDITIONS
RUGGED - ACCURATE - RELIABLE
NO GUESSING ——— NO WORRY ——— NO OVERFLOW

ELIMINATES WASTE
HELPS CHECK YOUR MILEAGE
NO DANGER OR ANNOYANCE
NO WASTED ELECTRICITY
NO PUSH BUTTONS
NO AIR PRESSURE
NO PUMP

POSITIVE
MECHANICAL
OPERATION

The regular filler cap is used

NOTE.
Adjusting sleeve on back of Dash Gage is provided, to bring pointer to agreement with Tank gage

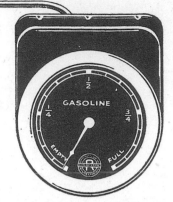

Gear Guard protects from injury by hose nozzles

Two lugs hook under filler opening to fasten gage securely in place

Specially treated floats Always Alive

...riven by the surge ...line makes positive ...f cam shaft

The I... ...TOR clamps on the Instrument Board and ins... ...t night and day.

The ... work a... unscre... **preve... gaso... getti...**

Satis... Ord...

DASHGAS EXPLANATION

The Impeller Vane in the tank unit operates as a wave or tidal motor deriving its power from the motion of the gasoline and thus driving the entire mechanism. The Float, not being required to do this work, is free to maintain its position on the surface of the gasoline and by so doing also governs the movement of the vane, and secures the extremely steady movement of the dial indicator.

The power developed in the tank by the surge of the gasoline against the "Impeller Vane" is transmitted through a small cam at the top of the shaft. This in turn moves a roller on a slide connected to a piano wire cable in the lubricated tube linking up the tank and dash units.

The longitudinal movement of the connecting wire is only 5/16 of an inch from one extreme to the other, slowly being drawn towards the Dash unit as gas is put into the tank, and back again as the gas is used up. There is no incessant see-sawing of the wire in the tube to rapidly wear out the parts at the curves.

In the "Dash unit" is a spirally grooved stem, not unlike that in the "Yankee" screw driver, which causes the dash indicator to turn, as this stem is pulled in and out. It is not *pushed* in either direction. The spring used in the dash instrument practically balances the float arm, and as the float rises this spring constantly takes up all slack and keeps the roller in contact with the cam. Gravity of course holds the float to the level of the gasoline as it is used, and any tendency to stick is overcome by the urge of the Impeller Vane geared to the float arm.

New England Representatives
PRUDENTIAL SALES SERVICE CO.
126 Massachusetts Avenue
BOSTON, MASS.

10 MILES
Eureka GAS STATIO...

Adverstisements and Jingles
Selling the sizzle, not the steak

Perhaps one of the most overlooked chapters in the evolution of the automobile is how it went from being a circus sideshow attraction to multi-million-dollar businesses within a decade. More incredibly, within 20 years, it went from being a luxurious toy to a necessity in the United States. The automobile almost completely replaced our primary mode of transportation for the previous two thousand years: the horse.

Technological advancements in the automobile and its related infrastructure played a key role in this rise to dominance. Yet, it can be argued that it was the silver-tongued wordsmith who truly sold us on the automobile.

Initially, automotive advertising portrayed the general confusion of just what an automobile was and what its purpose was. Another hallmark of early automotive advertisement was wordy Victorian-era prose.

An advertisement dated 1900 for the Porter Stanhope featured a small

This commemorative post card from Springfield, Massachusetts, features a Barnum and Bailey Circus poster from 1896, when the Duryea motor wagon was truly a sensation.

The Pierce Arrow

48 Horse Power, 7-Passenger, Suburban Limousine, 6 Cylinders, 130″ Wheel Base, Price $6100. Besides the Suburban Limousine, the other new types on this chassis include Roadster, Tourabout, Touring Car and Landau

LOUIS FANCHER 08

In a car for city use not only comfort but also elegance is needed. PIERCE ARROW Broughams and Landaulettes have all the smartness of a well-appointed carriage, and the perfect service that comes from the PIERCE engine and the freedom from repairs and other annoyances which is characteristic of all PIERCE Cars.

THE GEORGE N. PIERCE COMPANY, BUFFALO, NEW YORK

Members Association Licensed Automobile Manufacturers

lithograph-type picture of the car and a heading in bold print that read, "The Only Perfect Automobile!" Following were several hundred words of descriptive prose: "A handsome, stylish vehicle which can be started instantly and without previous laborious or lengthy preparation, can be stopped promptly, can be run at any speed up to 25 miles per hour, can be perfectly controlled by any person without special training, can travel over rough streets and roads, can climb stiff grades, can, in short, do anything and everything that a horse or span of horses attached to a vehicle can do, and do it more satisfactory, do it at a fraction of the expense and at the same time. . . ." And this was but the introduction! More than a hundred words followed, with the company's name and address at the bottom.

The sheer novelty of the automobile and seemingly endless stories of advancement made some question whether advertising was even necessary. With this in mind, Edward Goff, editor of Motorcycle, wrote in the May, 1897, issue, "The manufacturer of a motorcycle is in a position to take advantage of more free advertisement than any other industry."

Illustrations for early print advertisements were pen-and-ink sketches, retouched photographs, or airbrush work, and they were almost always black and white. Enter Ernest Elmo Calkins, who in 1903, began applying a degree of artistic standards to his work. Less than a decade later, his endeavors had grown into the formidable Calkins and Holden advertising agency, one of the first to work almost exclusively on automotive accounts.

The company's primary client was the stuffy, prestigious automaker from Buffalo, New York: Pierce-Arrow. To say the work Calkins and Holden produced for that company raised the bar would be a gross understatement. Calkins and Holden spared no expense in hiring the finest illustrators and artists of the day, including Edward Borein, a renowned artist who was world-famous for his Frederic Remington style of work; Joseph Leyendecker, renowned for his breathtaking Saturday Evening Post covers; and Newell Convers Wyeth, the illustrator of choice for writers such as Robert Louis Stevenson.

Many of the pieces produced for Pierce-Arrow transcended mere promotional advertisements and were often seen as works of art, quite befitting a company that promoted its cars as vehicles for a discriminating few. On many occasions the only mention of the company was the name across the top, at the bottom, or hidden in a corner. The vehicles themselves were often placed into a scene that seemed to wrap around them, highlighting their fine lines.

Cadwallader Washburn Kelsey, who for obvious reasons went by C. W. or Carl, is another forgotten pioneer in the development of automotive advertising. His initial work for Maxwell-Briscoe in late 1905 would have made P. T. Barnum smile. For the sake of promotion, Kelsey organized a wide variety of stunts including a journey up and down Broad Street with banners flying that eventually totaled a thousand miles.

Contracting with Lubin Film Studios, a pioneering cinematography company that supplied many of the nickelodeons in the northeast, Kelsey was to able promote Maxwell-Briscoe products to a larger audience in a more action-packed manner by having many of these stunts captured on film. The result was the first filmed automobile commercial and an explosion in sales that soon outpaced production capabilities.

Another important contribution Kelsey made was recognizing that a large sector of the market was being overlooked: the female motorist. To counteract this oversight and further promote Maxwell-Briscoe products, he contracted Alice Ramsey in 1909 to drive across the continent alone. As he expected, a few well-placed rumors were all that was needed for her to be closely followed by a covey of journalists. The result was international publicity in the form of attention-grabbing headlines.

Slogans and jingles—"See the U.S.A. in Your Chevrolet," "Ask the Man Who Owns One," "The Aluminum Six with Magnetic Gear Shift," "Ride in a Glide Then Decide," "A Car Worthy of Its Name,"—and some memorable advertising promotions have become forever entwined in the American love affair with the automobile. Nevertheless, unlike the dubious immortality granted to men like Louis Chevrolet, David Buick, and Walter Chrysler, the names of those behind their success and the names of the brilliant individuals who could sell the sizzle from a steak or the squeal from a pig have been in large part forgotten.

Pierce-Arrow

A car that looks equally good from the curbstone, from the driver's seat or from the tonneau.

The Pierce-Arrow Motor Car Company Buffalo, N.Y.

Hood Ornaments
Icons, mascots, and flights of fancy

The hood ornament is one of those little trinkets that has adorned automobiles almost since their inception. But unlike so many shiny baubles that have adorned automobiles over the years, the hood ornament speaks volumes about the owner as well as the manufacturer. Quite often during the 1920s and 1930s, they were chromed sculptures that represented a company's vision of the automobile.

Packard became famous for its flying lady. Duesenberg chose sharp, stylized Art Deco for the figurehead at its prow. The Franklin Airman featured a beautifully detailed radial engine monoplane (with spinning propeller) and cabin lights that came on with the headlights. In the postwar years, Pontiac, DeSoto, and a few others also featured lit ornaments.

Many of the earliest variations are highly sought-after collectibles today. However, in the beginning, the hood ornament often served as more than just a three-dimensional promotion of the manufacturer or a way for the owner to individualize his vehicle. There was a more practical purpose: an indicator of the engine's operating temperature.

The largest manufacturer, by a very large margin, of the latter type units was the Boyce Motometer Company, which utilizes the Boyce patents and its own design studios. The company began its rise to dominance in 1912 when the president of the company, George Townsend, obtained exclusive rights to patents for a thermometer coupled with a radiator cap.

The concept was quite simple. A sensor tip extended into the radiator to a point just above the water level, thus recording the temperature of the water vapor rather than the water itself. This was then reflected in a thermometer, which was visible to the driver. Townsend and Boyce Motometer transformed the concept into an art form with a graphics studio that allowed for the customization of the housing to an individual or manufacturer's unique needs or specifications.

Soon dozens of manufacturers were having custom units designed depicting their corporate mascots or logos. Individual dealers quite often had special additions made that incorporated their name into the corporate one as well. Associations such as AAA, the Lincoln Highway Association, the Masons, and countless others also placed special orders.

The optional hood ornament for the 1951 Chevrolet was stylish in a futuristic sort of way that accentuated the body curves and overall style of the vehicle.

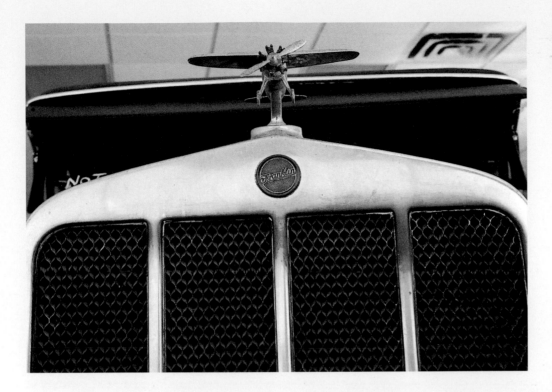

On occasion, a member of the country club set had a personalized version made to adorn the prow of his land yacht.

By 1927, Boyce Motometer's dominance of the market was so complete that the company employed more than 1,800 people in six countries and boldly advertised that "today over 10,000,000 Boyce Motometers stand guard over motors throughout the civilized world." But by then the handwriting was on the wall. More and more automobiles were beginning to feature in-dash temperature gauges. Within a few short years, the predominant placing of the radiator within the engine compartment made the radiator cap inaccessible without opening the hood. These updated designs brought the era of the Boyce Motometer to a close. However, the company management was farsighted. In 1926, it had purchased the National Gauge and Equipment Company, which was the largest manufacturer of dashboard-mounted instruments.

The Boyce Motometer would have faded into obscurity had it not been for the eclectic collector. The hood ornament continued into the modern era. Its popularity has suffered ebbs and flows, but it still serves as an indicator of manufacturer and on occasion as a symbol of status, just as it did in the past.

DENNEY TAGS W   STER, PA.

How to read the motometer

during the cold weather season

The motometer that is placed on the radiator filler neck cap registers the temperature of the AIR over the water in the radiator upper tank and does not register the temperature of the water in the radiator as is commonly supposed. The motometer is therefore affected very appreciably by atmospheric temperatures.

The summer driving range as shown on the motometer (see Fig. 1) should not be used during the winter months as the point on the motometer at which to open hand-operated radiator shutters.

These illustrations indicate the proper motometer readings at which to open your radiator shutters.

If the hand-operated shutter is not opened when it should be, not only will the motor probably knock and operate unsatisfactorily but the liquid in the cooling system will boil out through the radiator overflow pipe.

Fig. 1 Summer Average Reading.

Fig. 2. Height of Motometer liquid when water in cooling system reaches 160°—180° F. in weather between 32°—40° F.

Fig. 3. Height of Motometer liquid when water in cooling system reaches 160°—180° F. in zero weather.

Safety Glass
A vision of safety

The incongruity of automobile development during the closing decades of the nineteenth century and the first decades of the twentieth century is best displayed in the development (or lack thereof) of supportive infrastructure and safety features. Even items as fundamental as brakes were not always given priority, as evidenced by the Model T, which still utilized mechanical brakes (Ford would continue to do so until 1939), but only on the rear wheels!

Automotive glass progressed in a similar manner. The earliest windshields date to 1904 and were simple folding affairs. The majority of the shield was like a giant monocle attached to the steering column. The windshields were impractical at best and a threat to safety. Most were made of regular or even plate glass, which made goggles the more practical option.

Then two scientists working independently resolved the issue of glass safety. One, a Frenchman by the name of Edouard Benedictus, had accidentally discovered that an adhesive film of nitrocellulose applied to glass kept it from shattering.

British inventor John Wood had also arrived at a similar solution, but he took it a step further by pressing the adhesive film between two sheets of glass. Though it was developed in 1905 and produced under the name Triplex, it was not made available in the United States until 1926.

The dramatic rise of enclosed cars from roughly 1 in 10 in 1919 to 9 in 10 in 1929 prompted some manufacturers to address the issue of glass safety in novel ways. Promoted as the "Safety Stutz," the Model AA featured the company's own version of safety glass in 1926: hair-thin wires molded into the glass. Even the glass visors that crowned the upper exterior of each window frame were treated accordingly.

The next major step in the evolution of automotive glass came in 1924 with the development of a procedure to manufacture plate glass as a continuous ribbon instead of the more costly batch method. In 1928, Pittsburgh Plate Glass Company (PPG) led the industry with the introduction of Duplate laminated safety glass, which was an advancement over the earlier application that utilized a film between two sheets of glass to prevent shattering.

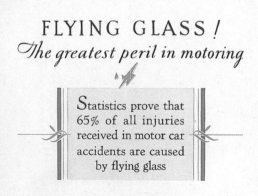

FLYING GLASS !

The greatest peril in motoring

Statistics prove that 65% of all injuries received in motor car accidents are caused by flying glass

You are protected against this danger when you ride in

Graham Sixes and Eights

First introduced in the 1934 Chrysler Imperial Airflow, curved windshields as well as the curvature of side windows and rear glass were an almost universal industry norm by the mid-1950s. The developments in glass production during this period included improved laminates that allowed for the maintenance of integrity with an impact velocity nearly three times that of glass just a decade before. This glass also allowed for more freedom in styling.

This increased use of glass did result in another problem: a dramatic rise in passive solar heat. Once again, PPG was the technological leader with the development of Solex glass. Introduced in 1952, the glass absorbed a percentage of the infrared solar spectrum. Green absorbent glass similar to Solex soon became an industry standard.

Today, PPG continues to lead in the development of automotive glass. The company recently introduced Sungate, a heat-reflecting laminate between two sheets of glass that effectively blocks 60 percent of ultraviolet radiation, thus keeping the car cooler as well as protecting interior materials from damage and deterioration.

Protected
from flying glass

In regards to promotion of safety glass in the late 1920s, it may come as a surprise to many that the technology had been available for more than 20 years.

Every Graham
is completely equipped with
SHATTER-PROOF
Safety Plate Glass

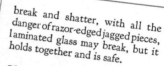

THE fact that all Graham cars are completely equipped with shatter-proof laminated plate glass, in all windows and doors as well as windshields, is the response to a public demand which grows every day in volume and intensity.

The shatter-proof plate glass used as standard and complete equipment in all Graham cars, at the lowest additional cost ever placed on such equipment, offers a protection never before available except in cars of the highest price ranges; and in some of them only at almost prohibitive extra cost.

Why Shatter-Proof Glass Is Safe: It is proof against shattering under impact, and though it may be broken by shock or the force of a flying missile, it will not shoot dangerous sharp particles and pointed slivers through the interior of the car.

Because it is laminated, it behaves in an entirely different manner from ordinary glass under the same circumstances of blow or strain.

Where non-laminated glass will break and shatter, with all the danger of razor-edged jagged pieces, laminated glass may break, but it holds together and is safe.

How Shatter-Proof Glass Is Made: Between the two sheets of finest plate glass is a tough, non-brittle bonding sheet. The three sheets are so firmly bonded together under pressure that the finished product is one of the most perfect examples of permanent lamination known in the glass industry today.

The center bonding sheet is invisible. Vision is clear and free from distortion and eye-strain—as clear as though you were looking through a single sheet of highest quality plate glass.

And that, in effect, is what you do in any one of the new Graham cars; for the two sheets of plate glass and the bonding sheet are a unit, to all practical purposes.

Learn the deadly difference in the two types of glass from any Graham dealer. Observe how fully the new Graham cars with complete protection of Shatter-Proof Glass, live up to the Graham assurance that—"Quality is the Best Policy."

Seat Covers
By the seat of your pants

Automobile seats covered with materials woven from natural fibers, as most vehicles featured between 1920 and 1950, did not wear well and quite often began to show signs of use relatively rapidly. Leather seats were much more durable, but they have always had several drawbacks, as do those covered with vinyl. As an example, try sitting on a leather seat in a convertible on a hot summer day, after the top has been left down, while wearing shorts. Even with leather, when a car became a second- or third-hand vehicle, the seats were quite often well-worn.

Enter the seat cover. Initially this was little more than a blanket. Even today, for those on a budget the blanket most often suffices. Classier options include having the seats reupholstered. This also provides an opportunity to add a personal touch, but replacing vinyl or cloth can be costly. Any restorer will also tell you that replacing leather is downright expensive.

In the postwar years, when it was easy to believe the miracles of modern science would solve all problems, synthetic fibers such as nylon ushered in a new era. Those obsessed with keeping their seats clean and in like-new condition turned to using clear plastic with raised squares or other geometric shapes in the late 1950s. While a boon to seat protection, these were a nightmare for those who had to sit on the material for long periods on a humid summer day.

Today the seat cover has come full circle, with one of the more popular types being a stylized western motif made with a heavy blend of long-wearing natural and man-made fibers. These durable covers often feature pockets and greatly resemble the saddle blankets of old. If you want to customize your vehicle on a budget, perhaps the first place to begin is with seat covers; they are now available in almost every imaginable pattern (such as spotted cow, leopard spots, or zebra stripes) as well as some that are best not imagined.

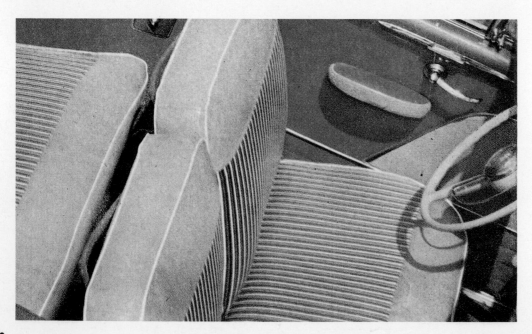

In the immediate postwar years, a multitude of new technologies, such as synthetic fabrics, was transforming the American auto industry. This was most noticeable in car interiors.

treat them rough...
show them off!

ALL PATTERNS AVAILABLE IN TRAVELON FABRICS BY HAFNER

....smart year'round seat covers are woven of

Firestone *Velon**

*TRADE MARK

Other uses of Woven Velon

© 1949, FIRESTONE PLASTICS CO.
POTTSTOWN, PA.

Guaranteed by
Good Housekeeping

Winter, summer, spring and fall, seat covers woven of Firestone *Velon* enhance the beauty and value of your car. They keep your car new-looking, because *Velon* resists practically everything under the sun (including the sun). There are seat covers woven of *Velon* by Hafner *still perfect after 10 years of wear.*

Year 'round smartness: More colors than the rainbow to choose from—to blend with the color of your car. Marvelous weaves in stripes, plaids, checks, solids to express your personal taste.

Years and years of wear: So cool in summer, so easy to slide over. Children, dogs, luggage, shoes, won't scratch or scuff them. Damp cloth removes dirt and grease. Don't let mud or snow ruin car upholstery. Ask for seat covers woven of Firestone *Velon* now, at auto dealers, auto accessory stores, Firestone dealers and stores, department stores, or write Hafner Associates, Empire State Build-

Other forms of Velon

FILM   YARN

This tag is your
Assurance of
first quality material

It's Made of
Firestone
*Velon**

Earl Scheib
"I'll paint any car any color for only $29.95! No ups, no extras!"

The austere Ford Model T was many common people's first new car, and Earl Scheib was the man who provided many common people's first new paint job. When classic cars are discovered, pulled out of barns, and found to have poor paint work, spectators usually leap to conclusions and say, "Well, it's got an Earl Scheib paint job." But, many are unaware of the fascinating story behind the name and the bright side to "getting what you pay for."

Earl Scheib was a native of San Francisco, California, but his fame started humbly when he opened his own gas station in Los Angeles at the corner of Whitworth and Fairfax in the mid-1930s. Scheib started painting cars as a sideline and realized there was a lucrative void for him to fill. He opened his first paint and body shop in 1937 at the corner of Pico and LaBrea when he was not quite 30 years old.

In keeping with Henry Ford's common-people's car, Scheib took an assembly line approach to painting cars. Scheib and his 10-man crew sanded, prepped, masked, and painted 30 cars per day, seven days a week. He charged $29.95 for sedans and $24.95 for coupes, and crowds of customers jammed the intersection waiting for their turn.

Was the quality high? Probably not, but that wasn't the point. There was finally a paint shop the working man could afford. His car may have been 10 years old, but it could shine like new and would be protected from the elements. Even at the tail end of the Great Depression, a regular guy didn't have to be ashamed of his car. With more work than he could handle, Scheib opened more locations, and an icon was in the making.

After World War II, America blossomed into the blissful and nostalgically remembered rhythms of postwar prosperity. Grown men were buying new cars left and right, and young men were buying used cars or accepting old hand-me-downs from their parents. None of the old cars had to look bad if there was an Earl Scheib in town, and Scheib hit the television airwaves with his unforgettable delivery: "I'll paint any car any color for only $29.95! No ups, no extras!"

"No ups, no extras" was an agreement between Scheib and

An especially decorative Earl Scheib location in the early 1960s. Earl Scheib, Inc.

Earl **Scheib**™
PAINT & BODY

the customer. The paint job cost a fraction of what a high-quality paint job cost, and the customer knew what that meant, but that constitutes a kind of honesty.

Prices rose incrementally through the decades, and classic-car enthusiasts are often heard comparing television memories as they see who can remember the lowest Earl Scheib price. Earl Scheib passed away in 1992 on his 84th birthday, but his company entered the twenty-first century still repainting cars for a base price of $159.95, and Earl's unique delivery found a new generation of fans on cable television networks that show his decades-old commercials along with classic TV shows.

Tail Fins
Monument to an era of dreams

It began simply enough as a styling statement on the 1948 Cadillacs: two small humps that formed little "fins" on the top of the rear fender, emulating the aircraft designs of the times. In the decade that followed, each manufacturer sought to introduce its version of this styling feature that came to symbolize the American auto industry of the 1950s. Common sense and good taste were subverted to competition. As a result, the fin grew to grotesque proportions in various guises.

The perception by some manufacturers was that the consumer would associate fins, like those on Cadillacs, with class. So what better way to hint at a car's prestige than to emulate? Sales of the Henry J and Sears Allstate, produced by Kaiser-Frazer in 1951 and 1952, made it painfully clear that the public was not fooled.

By 1955, the Cadillac hump on the El Dorado series had grown to be a real fin. By 1959, it had become the dominating feature on all models, standing more than two feet above the rear deck and accentuated with incredible bullet-style tail lamps.

The fins utilized by Buick stylists during this period were a bit more sedate. By 1958, the fins were hardly noticeable, as the rear fenders became a veritable sea of chrome. That year, Oldsmobile went even further in its use of glittering trim and adornment. Then for 1959, the fins were given a sweep to the side instead of rising vertically.

Chrysler was not immune to this styling trend, and by 1960 it had surpassed GM. That year the Dodge Polara two-door hardtop had a fin that swept back from the door opening higher than that found on the 1959 Cadillac. Even vehicles in that corporation's truck division, Dodge, were given the treatment.

Dodge truck sales had dropped steadily since 1949, and the popularity of GM's stylish Chevrolet Cameo as well as the GMC Suburban, introduced in 1955, made it clear that things were about to get even worse. Nevertheless, Dodge was not to be outdone, and the resultant competitor model introduced in 1957 was both unique and bizarre.

Utilizing the rear fenders and the rear bumper from the 1957 Dodge two-door Suburban station wagons, the company was able to give its dealers a modern-looking truck: the D100 Sweptside, a pickup truck with tail fins! Of even more importance to the cash-strapped division, this was accomplished with little modification or additional outlay.

All Sweptside trucks were assembled in the special equipment shop, not on the assembly line, due to their small production numbers. Their small numbers, as well as their discontinuation in 1959, have made the Sweptside one of the rarest of the finned vehicles.

Love them or hate them, the finned vehicles of the 1950s and first years of the 1960s feature truly unique styling. As a result, over the years some of the more unusual models, such as the 1959 Pontiac Catalina Safari station wagon, have developed a certain cult status, with a kitsch value that puts them in a league of their own. What fan of the nifty 1950s, Route 66, and the poodle skirt doesn't see them all in the 1959 Cadillac?

The towering fins on the 1959 Cadillac have come to epitomize the era of the poodle skirt, cruising under the neon, and Route 66.

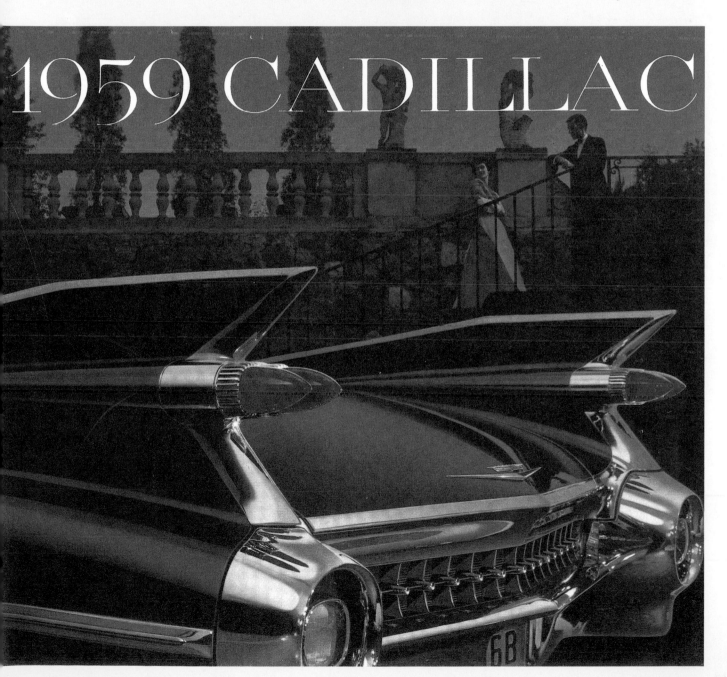

1959 CADILLAC

Only from the great traditions of Cadillac could there come a motor car as surpassingly fine as that portrayed below —the 1959 Eldorado Biarritz. Luxurious beyond description, it offers spectacular performance and handling ease. Every known motoring advancement makes each journey memorable. Standard equipment includes a custom engineered 345-horsepower engine, air suspension, electrically powered front seat adjustment, electric door locks and window regulators, power steering and braking, radio and heater. Interiors are offered in deep-grained Cardiff and Florentine leathers in tones of bronze metallic ... blue metallic ... gray metallic ... slate green metallic ... black ... white ... and red.

THE NEW STANDARD OF THE WORLD IN SPLENDOR!

ELDORADO BIARRITZ

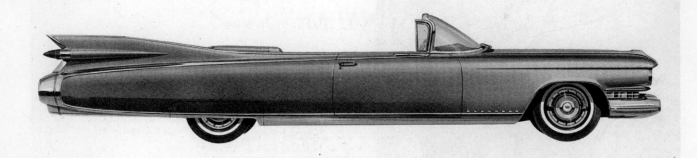

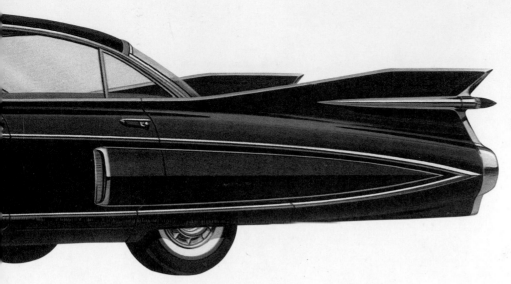

The size and lines of the 1959 Cadillac made it impossible to confuse it with anything else on the road.

THE NEW STANDARD OF THE WORLD IN DISTINCTION!

Sedan de Ville (Six Window)

Splendor is the constant companion of the owner of this supremely gracious version of the Sedan de Ville. Its advanced features of engineering and construction provide the most satisfying performance and superb comfort ever achieved in Cadillac's fifty-seven years of fine car leadership. And here, too, are all the elegant luxuries that have won for the Cadillac de Ville models the admiration of motorists everywhere. Interior selections are, of course, the same in all three distinguished de Ville creations.

The Club
Don't steal a winner's Cadillac

Stolen cars account for half the dollar value of all stolen property in the United States, so when a brand-new Cadillac was stolen from Sharon, Pennsylvania, in 1985, it wasn't unusual. But unfortunately for car thieves everywhere, this theft had worldwide consequences.

Jim Winner didn't like thieves from the beginning. In the Korean War, he wrapped chains around his army Jeep's steering wheel to keep scoundrels from driving off with it. For many years afterward, he sold theft-prevention devices used in department stores. The Sensormatic electronic article surveillance system is familiar to shoppers everywhere—a plastic tag attached to clothing, CDs, and even meats in grocery stores that sets off the alarm bells if a shoplifter tries to leave the store without paying for the item.

So when he bought his new Cadillac, Winner had the latest electronic alarm system installed on it. But the car was stolen anyway. Imagine Winner's disgust when his Cadillac disappeared right from under his nose one night. He stewed about the theft for days. Somewhere in the back of his mind, a memory stirred—chaining his Jeep's steering wheel during the Korean War—and he had an idea.

Some maggot stole a Cadillac from the wrong person in 1985, and the victim got mad. Jim Winner was the victim, and he created one of the most popular and effective theft deterrents in the world: the Club. Winner International

He consulted with engineers and patented The Club. In conjunction with police and former car thieves, Winner International tested The Club on Porsches in Los Angeles—the city where a Porsche was most likely to disappear, according to crime statistics. During the test period, none of the Porsches were stolen.

The Club hit the market in late 1986, and by 1987 Winner International got its first big contract when Sears saw the value of the ingenious device. It was not sophisticated, but rather simple and easy so people would use it. It was also inexpensive, making it even more attractive to buyers. Winner also designed The Club to be visible, so a thief would see it from the outside before breaking a window or jimmying a door. Winner called it The Club because that's what it looked like.

Winner International does not claim The Club will completely prevent theft. It is just a matter of reducing the likelihood by turning the car into a "hard target" by increasing the difficulty of theft enough that a thief will choose an easier target. Now, nearly 20 years after its introduction, The Club has been used in the tens of millions of cars, all because one guy decided to steal the wrong Cadillac.

Tires
A bias toward radials

Even in the early 1900s, race cars like the steam-powered Stanley could reach up to 127.6 miles per hour. But the tires used on these race cars were really nothing more than oversized bicycle wheels, with rubber compounds not much more advanced than the compounds used in rubber bands or pencil erasers. It would be another 60 years before tires really caught up to the technology of the rest of an ordinary automobile.

Tires had come a long way by the 1920s, but they still presented certain dangers. The wheel and the rim were two separate pieces. The tire and innertube were mounted on the spring-loaded rim, and the rim was mounted onto the wheel with a series of locks. Many large cars carried 70 pounds of air pressure in their tires. Between the high air pressure and the spring-loaded split rim, severed limbs and death were tragically common for mechanics mounting tires in garages. Motorists changing tires on the side of the road were also in danger when the tires and rims exploded off the wheels. Many big trucks still use split-rims on their front tires to withstand the side forces of heavy cornering. As pneumatic lifts were perfected in the 1930s to lift cars off the ground, mechanics would lay the split rim wheel on the floor and set the lift down on it before filling the tire with air. By the late twentieth century, garages working on split rims were required to lock the wheel in a safety cage for filling.

As the 1930s progressed, car companies announced low-pressure tires as comfort items that rode more softly than previous types and were a lot easier to change when necessary. Even with quickly improving roads and tires, it was still common for people to have to change several tires on a long trip.

Between 1910 and 1920, whitewall tires came along as decorative items. Through the 1920s, when the front-end designs of automobiles made both sides of the front tires visible, some expensive cars sported double whitewalls that gave off Jazz Age glitz in every corner. Whitewall tires were popular clear through the 1950s, but they disappeared during World War II and the Korean War, due to material conservation. Some car companies offered wheel covers with a small chrome hubcap in the middle and a white dish covering the rim that imitated whitewalls, and popular white Port-A-Walls could be glued to the sides of tires as add-on whitewalls.

The bad news about the whitewall era is that tires, especially affordable tires, were barely more sophisticated than the first low-

The whitewall radial tires on this DeSoto give the proper, historically correct appearance while delivering modern performance. The radials roll much more easily, and they do not jerk the car all over the road as bias-ply tires did for many years, thus preserving this classic's steering and suspension components.

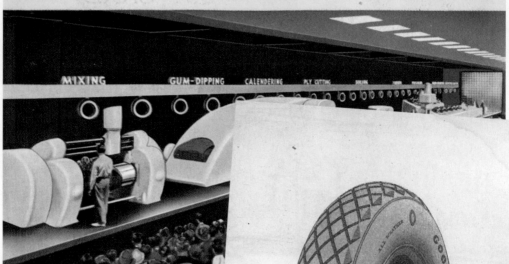

FIRESTONE BUILDS TODAY, THE TIRE OF TOMORROW — PRODUCTION LINE, FIRESTONE FACTORY AND EXHIBITION BUILDING, NEW YORK WORLD'S FAIR

The Facts about Balloon Tires

CITY MOTOR SUPPLY CO.
Eighth & Sibley
ST. PAUL.

GOODYEAR

pressure tires from the early 1930s. Tires get their strength from steel or nylon belts within, and for decades, bias-ply tires were the norm. The part of the tire that rides on the rim is called the bead. The bias-ply belts ran diagonally from bead to bead—starting at one bead, running up the sidewall at an angle, crossing diagonally under the tread, and ending up on the other side of the tire, having gone across the tire and around its rolling surface. They were interwoven in opposite directions and framed the tire like two hands interlocking fingers.

In the 1960s, radial tires were quickly perfected and were the preferred tires to have by the mid-1970s. The radial belts simply start at one bead and run straight across the tread area to the other bead, with a set of belts running straight around the tire's circumference to tie all the radial belts together. A radial leaves a bigger, fatter footprint on the ground and grips the corners a lot better than a bias-ply tire ever did. Bias-ply tires would "walk the road" by following all the pavement's imperfections, and if there was a crack running down the length of the road, the bias-ply tires would find it and ride it like a railroad track. It could steer the car right out of the driver's hands. It's very common for those restoring old cars to find even a low-mileage specimen to have terribly worn-out steering components from bias-ply tires jerking the car all over the road.

Radials don't even notice pavement irregularities, and they roll much more easily. When radial tires are applied to old cars that were built tough enough to withstand the poor road conditions and bias-ply tires of decades ago, the old car's steering and suspension become indestructible, because they were built tough enough for a hard life but now live an easier one. Tire companies that specialize in making tires for classic cars make radials with wide whitewalls to give the car the accurate look of the old days with the safety of modern times. With the decreased rolling resistance of radial tires, people are sometimes surprised at the fuel economy their classics suddenly deliver. With proper-looking radial tires on a classic car, times are approaching near-perfection.

The Care of Pneumatic Tires

The RUBBER ASSOCIATION
OF AMERICA *Inc.*
TIRE MANUFACTURERS DIVISION
250 West 57th Street, New York City

*Many tire
manufacturers
produced brochures
similar to these to
promote the advantages
of balloon tires.*

Inflation

To give maximum service a tire must contain the proper air pressure at all times, since it is the air cushion within the tire which supports the weight of the car.

When under-inflated the sidewalls bend or flex sharply with each turn of the wheel (Fig. 1).

When properly inflated the tire stands full and round (Fig. 2).

Fig. 1
Under-Inflated Tire

Fig. 2
Properly Inflated Tire

The bending and flexing produces heat which softens the rubber between the layers of fabric or cords. Finally the layers separate and begin to chafe and rub against each other. Separation of this sort is shown in Figure 3.

Sooner or later the layer next to the tube breaks. This break pinches or chafes the tube and results in a slow leak or blowout. Figure 4 shows a casing ruined in this way.

Clincher casings, when under-inflated, may also develop another condition commonly known as "rim cutting". When

2

Fig. 3
Separation of fabric due to under-inflation

the tire does not contain enough air to keep it properly rounded out, the side-walls chafe against the edge of the rim. The result is illustrated in Figure 5.

Fig. 4
Fabric injury inside casing due to under-inflation or overloading

3

Side-Wall Wear

The side of a casing is provided with sufficient rubber to withstand ordinary wear, but it is not nearly so thick as the tread rubber and is more easily injured.

Running and spinning a tire in ruts, scraping it against curbs, driving over

Curbstone Wear

Rut Wear

The Result

Fig. 13

rough frozen roads, and occasionally an accident, will tear and gouge off the sidewall rubber and expose the carcass of the casing.

When once exposed, the fabric may be badly damaged in a short time by water,

12

sand, dirt or foreign substances of any kind (Fig. 13).

Such side-wall injuries can easily be repaired if taken promptly to an experienced vulcanizer.

Rims

The average automobile owner pays very little attention to the steel rims on which his tires are mounted, yet this neglect often causes the loss of many miles of tire service.

Care should be used to see that the rims are true so that the tires fit perfectly. A bent rim or any variation in the rim contour (Fig. 14) will not allow the tire to fit properly at that point and sooner or later will cause tire trouble.

Running on a flat tire or on a rim from which the tire has been removed, or strik-

Fig. 14
Damaged Rims

13

The V-8
Song of the American Road

In a time not so long ago it was possible to identify the make, and sometimes even the model of a car, by the sound of its starter and the engine. The deep, throaty rumble of the Ford V-8 was distinctly different from the rattle of a Chevy six. There is no confusing the sound of a Model A Ford with that of a V-8-powered Lincoln of similar vintage. Likewise, a Dodge Challenger with a 440 and a six-pack with the throttle wide open is not likely to be mistaken for a Corvair.

Engines with a V formation of cylinders, such as the V-16 Cadillac, were almost exclusively the realm of high-end luxury cars until the introduction of the Ford V-8 in 1932.

If there were but one engine configuration that symbolizes the American auto industry and our love for the open road, if there were just one engine that could be selected to stand for all the power and self-assurance that is the United States, it would have to be the V-8. No other engine has powered so many of our favorite vehicles or served as the foundation for building our dream cars.

It might surprise many to learn that the V-8 engine is not an American invention. The first such engine is credited to Clement Adler, who built a vehicle to compete in the 1903 Paris-to-Madrid race. In 1910, the French manufacturer De Dion was the first to offer the V-8 in a production model. However, as with so many automobile-related technologies, American manufacturers took the ball and ran with it.

One of the more memorable and earliest milestones in the long and colorful history of the American V-8 engine dates to 1906, when Glenn H. Curtiss, aviation pioneer and early builder of motorcycles, built a V-8-powered cycle. In January 1907, he used the motorcycle to shatter the land-speed record at Ormond Beach (now Daytona), reaching an incredible 137 miles per hour.

The lightweight air-cooled engine was one of many, including single-cylinder, V-twin, and inline four-cylinder configurations he designed and built. The record-setting V-8 had been fitted to the motorcycle to test its reliability and power for aeronautical application.

The next evolutionary step came in September of 1914 with the introduction of the Cadillac V-8. Inspired by the De Dion V-8, Cadillac engineers led by Henry Leland refined the concept and further advanced Cadillac's slogan of "Standard of the World."

During World War I, Leland departed from Cadillac to found Lincoln, initially to construct aircraft engines. As an automobile manufacturer, the company under his direction was instrumental in the next stage of development when the Lincoln made its debut with a V-8 engine in 1917 (with actual production beginning in 1920). The engine represented innovative technology, pushed the envelope of precision engineering, and ensured 70-mile-per-hour performance.

The expense incurred in engineering and production of the V-8 engine during this period relegated the configuration to the realm of luxury cars such as Cadillacs and Lincolns. But it wouldn't be long before Ford, the company that had brought automobiles to the masses, made the V-8 engine affordable.

In late 1925, Ford began initial development of a replacement for the dated Model T. After the introduction of the Model A, this experimentation continued in two parallel directions: the development of an improved four-cylinder engine and a V-8 to compete against Chevrolet's six that was introduced in 1929.

In all fairness, it should be noted that General Motors had a brief flirtation with the V-8 engine besides that offered in the Cadillac. Oldsmobile produced a V-8 from 1916 to 1918 and again from 1919 to 1921. In 1929 and 1930, a V-8 was made available in the Viking series. The Model D Chevrolet of 1917 and 1918 also featured a V-8.

SIXTEEN CYLINDERS

Performance such as the world has
never witnessed . . . The most highly
individualized of all motor cars

CADILLAC MOTOR CAR COMPANY   DIVISION OF GENERAL MOTORS

For 1932, Ford unveiled two new models. The Model B had an improved four-cylinder engine that retained the dimensions of that offered in the Model A, but with a 25-percent increase in horsepower. The Model 18 had a 221-cid 65-horsepower V-8 at an astounding $460 in roadster configuration. Even with an extreme failure rate in the initial production run, the cars were a resounding success. The Ford flathead V-8 would be the mainstay of Ford products for the next 21 years.

The next chapter in the V-8 story debuted in 1949 as the Oldsmobile Rocket 88, a vehicle that some credit with presaging the era of the muscle car, and the "Futuramic" 98. The V-8 engine that powered these cars represented a complete departure from traditional concepts, most notably: higher compression, deemed impractical and not feasible just a few years previous; overhead valves; hydraulic lifters; forged crank with counterweights; aluminum pistons; and a dual-plane intake manifold.

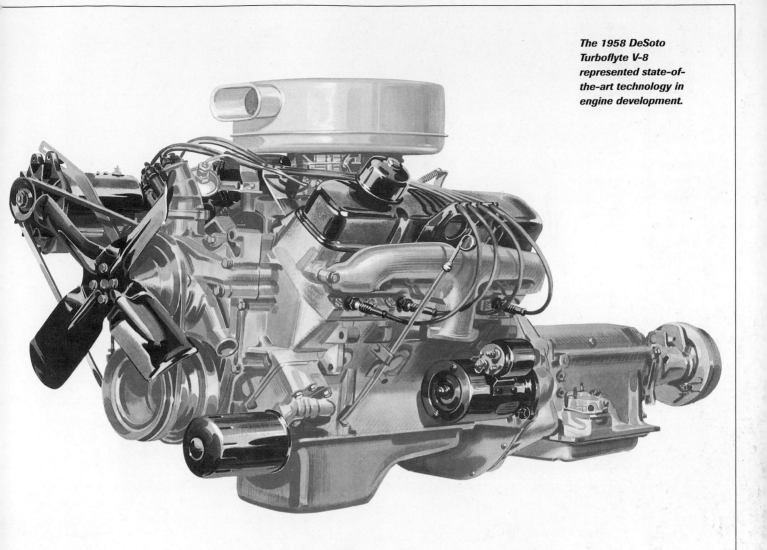

Initially the 98-series Olds garnered a great deal of attention upon its debut, but the real news came some six months into the model year with the introduction of the lighter-bodied 88. The performance of the new Olds made it a favorite on the NASCAR circuit, and by the end of 1949, the new Rocket 88 had won six of the nine sanctioned stock car races. More publicity was garnered in 1949, when an 88 convertible was selected as the Indianapolis 500 pace car. Then in 1950 the California Highway Patrol updated their fleet with the powerful cars.

The developments were now coming in rapid succession. For 1951, Chrysler introduced its Fire Power hemi-head V-8 in the Imperial series. The concept of a hemispherical combustion chamber for higher compression and improved performance was not new. Jules Goux in a hemi-powered 1913 Peugeot won the 1913 Indianapolis 500. Chrysler never took credit for the idea, it just developed it and perfected it on production-built automobiles.

Then came the era of the small block, with the introduction of the 265-cid V-8 made available on 1955 Chevrolet models. Improvements to the engine made another milestone in 1957 possible: an incredible one horsepower for each cubic inch.

For most of the following two decades, the V-8 was the powerplant of choice. Even today, these now legendary engines—the wedge, the 440, the 429, and the Cobra Jet, to name but a few—are spoken of with reverence and even awe among some automotive enthusiasts. Although it has faded from dominance in the American automotive industry, the V-8 engine carries a mystique and historical association that translates into sales. The popularity is evident based on the Cadillac Northstar system and, more recently, the reintroduction of hemi-powered Chryslers. An engine design that just a few short years ago seemed destined to become an historical curiosity in a dusty museum has entered a new era.

Odometer
The automotive calculi

Then: "My car is 10 years old and only has 62,000 miles on it!" One look at the worn pedals, crushed upholstery, bare armrest, and wobbly steering makes it clear the car has a lot more miles than that. Now: "My car is five years old, and it has 427,000 miles on it!"

One look at the new-looking pedals, comfortable seats, and tight steering makes it clear the car probably has many fewer miles on it. Even the six-figure indicator on the dash seems like it's lying when the rest of the car is examined.

People used to exaggerate how few miles a car had, and now, they brag about how many it has. There's lots of room for doubt in both camps. The death knell for many cars was 100,000 miles, and it was hard to sell anyone on the idea of buying a car so close to the end of its life. With twenty-first-century oil, coolant, component machining, tires, and roads, cars easily pass 200,000 miles—more from the products and circumstances than from qualities of the cars themselves.

It's relative, too. An economy car with 100,000 miles has a lot of mileage. A big-rig with 100,000 miles is brand new.

The number of miles represents a car's condition, use history, and memories. Car enthusiasts can often remember where they were when their car turned over 100,000 miles, and they enjoy recounting miles from a long pleasure trip added to the odometer. The little numbered wheels in a car's dash go unnoticed much of the time, but when they're looked at, it's usually important.

The Mormon pioneers counted the miles of their famous nineteenth-century migration from Iowa to Utah with this hand-carved odometer. Courtesy of the Church Archives, The Church of Jesus Christ of Latter-day Saints

The Roman legions had their own reasons for wanting to know the number of miles they traveled. They were conquering and measuring the known world. Their odometer was a big wooden-wheeled device that looked a lot like one of their famous chariots. The wheels had pegs in them that hit levers, and every 400 hits, a little trap door opened and dropped a marble into a box. Individually, a marble was called a calculus, and together, they were the calculi. Each calculus in the box at the end of the trip represented a Roman mile.

In the nineteenth century, early members of The Church of Jesus Christ of Latter-day Saints members settled in Nauvoo, Illinois, on the banks of the Mississippi River. But when they were attacked by vicious mobs, several thousand Mormons fled Nauvoo in 1846 to head west. They kept track of the 1,300 miles they traveled on their way to the Great Salt Lake by using a device with hand-carved gears and numbered teeth that rode on a wagon's axle. This rough-looking but accurate little machine may have been the first mechanical odometer used to measure distance across America. The Mormons' path included the Platte River wagon road, which later set the path of U.S. Highway 30 across Nebraska. This is also known as the famous Lincoln Highway, which nostalgic Americans are rediscovering just as they have rediscovered Route 66.

Mechanical automotive odometers haven't changed much since the 1920s. The car rolls forward, a transmission gear spins a flexible cable, the cable spins a magnet, and the magnet pulls a spring-loaded needle around a dial. The cable also turns a set of tiny gears in the odometer housing, and these gears turn the little numbered wheels seen through the odometer face. Thus, the miles are counted today.

Every time a proud car owner tells how many miles long a trip was and what happened along the way, he's having a conversation that links him directly to the Roman legions of the ancient world and to the Mormon pioneers who crossed a continent and tamed a desert. They all measured their lives and accomplishments by the calculi of travel.

Air Bags
The Debatable Bombs

It's like taking the cork out of a champagne bottle. The car hits something solid, a decelerometer feels the impact, ignites a sodium azide cap, and a high-pressure charge of nitrogen gas inflates a neoprene-coated nylon bag in $\frac{1}{20}$th of a second. By about $\frac{1}{3}$rd of a second, the bag has deflated and brought the car's passenger to a more gentle, skull-saving stop.

Air bag development took a while, but the debate took a lot longer. The technology was 90 percent ready for the marketplace by the late-1960s, but without proper seat belt laws, the air bag made a minor accident more dangerous, because, unless the driver is also restrained by seat belts and shoulder straps, the backward blast from the air bag could be more lethal than a 20 mile-per-hour accident. Television commercials in the 1980s showed the air bag inflating into a fluffy pillow in super-slow-motion, but the reality is that the air bag is a bomb that explodes into shape under thousands of pounds of pressure, which then immediately deflates, acting more like a parachute than a cushion.

In the early-1970s, General Motors spent $80 million to implement an air bag program and set up the factories and bought the supplies to produce 300,000 of them. The air bag system was optional, and the public only bought 10,000 of them when they were offered between 1974 and 1976 on Oldsmobiles, Buicks, and Cadillacs. Consequently, it cost GM $8,000 per car sold to install the air bags, which is what a new Cadillac cost at the time. The retail price of an Oldsmobile was half the cost of the air bag it carried. The auto industry was not trying to kill its customers by avoiding air bags. The industry just could not operate with numbers like these no matter how good the intentions.

Lee Iacocca, former Ford Motor Company executive and Chrysler Corporation savior, wrote in his 1984 autobiography that air bags were not feasible until the solidly enforced seat belt laws of the 1980s. Yucca told the story that a British newspaper had reported on an idea to use air bags as a form of humane capital punishment. Iacocca thought the article was a joke until he read further and found quotes from a Michigan engineer who was dead serious that air bags broke unrestrained human necks better than a hangman's noose. Air bags were deadly unless used in combination with seat belts.

Drivers of radically different physical weights and builds need to be equally protected in a crash. Crash test facilities test air bags by painting the test dummy's face with grease paint and seeing where the dummy's face lands on the bag during the crash, leaving an eerie ghostly image at the location of impact

Fortunately, effective public service announcements and changing public attitudes made seat belts cool by the mid-1980s, and the time was right for air bags to take their place in the American dashboard.

By the early 1990s, the proof was in that the air bag's explosive blast had killed a significant number of people, mostly children, and car company engineers and crash-test facilities took to the task of improving the air bag. Drivers were then able to turn off passenger-side air bags when small children were seated, and inflation and deflation rates were re-examined. One solution was a lighter inflation force and volume combined with a smaller outlet hole in the air bag. The bag inflates with less force, but the escape route is smaller and restricts deflation—less blast with the same cushioning effect.

Air bags are not perfect, but the bang of the bag is a lot better than the bang of hitting the steering wheel.

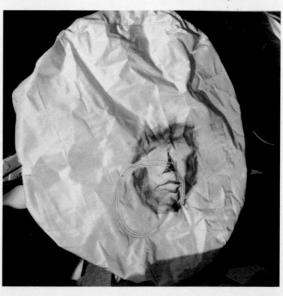

3

The Ride

How the automobile has affected the birth rates and mating rituals of the American citizen is a subject best left to the imagination. However, the average American's love/hate relationship with the automobile begins almost at birth.

A few of us have entered the world in an automobile. For the rest of us, as newborns coming home from the hospital, we experienced life in the car before life at home.

Soon after that first ride comes the interest in toy cars, then comes the need to craft detailed die-cast models. Somewhere along the way comes your first drive in a pedal car, your first bicycle ride. Then after reaching your teens, you reach the ultimate rite of passage: earning your driver's license and driving solo in the old man's sedan or wagon.

After that, it's the first car—most often a prize in our eyes and a relief for the seller who is tired of being stranded or pouring money into what seems to be a bottomless pit. With marriage and family, practical replaces fun. In the past, this time of life often meant the acquisition of a station wagon, but today it's the minivan and supersize SUV.

By the time the kids are grown, fond memories of one's glory days prompt two courses of action. We can relive that time as we wished it had been with fast sports cars, or we can remember it by buying the car we thought was so cool, but just couldn't afford then.

Finally, there's the golden years, and it's time to see the U.S.A. with all the comforts of home in a land yacht that makes a mockery of roughing it. Finally, there is the last ride; quite appropriate for a car culture such as ours, this is often the most stylish ride of all.

The Advance-Design Chevrolet

The pickup truck comes of age

There was a time not so long ago when the pickup truck, like the draft horse it had replaced, was seldom seen anywhere but on the job. As a result, truck manufacturers focused on durability, ease of repair, and economical operation. Styling and amenities were seldom given much thought when it came to truck design.

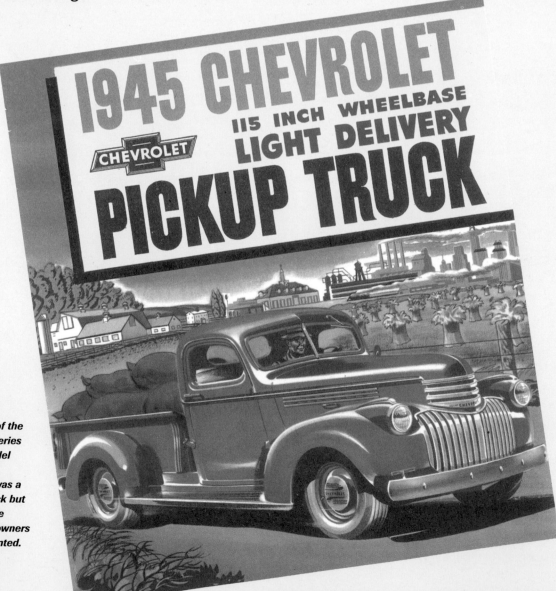

The predecessor of the Advance Design series was the 1941 model pickup, which ran through 1946. It was a stylish pickup truck but lacked many of the comfort features owners indicated they wanted.

CHEVROLET

ALL-AROUND UTILITY OVER-ALL ECONOMY

115-INCH-WHEELBASE
CHEVROLET LIGHT DELIVERY PICK-UP TRUCK

Popularly known as the all-round utility truck, the Chevrolet light delivery pick-up possesses all of Chevrolet's outstanding qualities—performance, dependability, long life and durability. In every part, it has been designed and engineered to do the job efficiently and economically. The large load space—78 inches long, 48½ inches wide, 16¼ inches high—is without obstruction of any sort and assures ample capacity for scores of uses by haulers of light payloads.

1945 CHEVROLET

...GNED BODY FOR DURABILITY

STRONG TUBULAR STEEL FLARE-BOARDS

STAKE POCKETS

ANTI-WARP MOISTURE-PROOF WOOD FLOOR

ANTI-RATTLE STEEL END GATE

The Chevrolet unit-designed pick-up body is precision-engineered to give maximum durability with maximum load space. The floor is rigidly built, of highest-grade suitable wood, reinforced with heavy cross-sills to withstand severe use. Flush-type skid strips hold the floorboards in place, leaving a smooth, even surface. The steel side panels are single-piece units with rigid side braces to hold them in alignment. The end gate, which lines up evenly with the floor when lowered, facilitating loading and unloading, will support extremely heavy loads.

THE UNSUPPORTED CORNER OF THE END GATE WILL HOLD A 200-POUND MAN WITHOUT BEING BENT OUT OF SHAPE

However, in the months immediately following the end of World War II, astute observers of trends and markets at the Chevrolet truck division felt that the time was ripe for change. An extensive in-depth survey of registered truck owners, the first of its kind, proved them right.

The "modern" truck buyer wanted a stylish vehicle for advertising appeal and prestige, but did not want to sacrifice durability or economy in operation and maintenance. It was also noted that a large percentage of those surveyed wanted roomier cabs as well as options for comfort and better visibility. The result was the Advanced Design series of Chevrolet trucks.

Introduced in 1947, these rugged workhorses fulfilled almost every dream, want, and desire that truck owners had called for in the survey. The styling was new, clean, and modern. Visibility had been increased by 174 square inches over the previous year's model, and the cabs were roomier, since they were widened by 8 inches. Doors were also wider, allowing for easier access. A lengthy options list included bright stainless-steel body moldings, radio, heater, corner windows, and a variety of colors.

Even in its fifth year, with little in the way of exterior changes, sales continued to climb from 259,533 units in 1947 to 370,982 by the end of the 1952 model year. In comparison, Ford's sales for the same period fell from 301,901 units, a market share of 22.6 percent in 1948, to 236,753 units, a market share of 19.2 percent in 1952.

ADVANCE-DESIGN

CHEVROLET TRUCKS

FINER APPEARANCE that creates prestige for you and the things you sell . . .

PANEL TRUCKS — protection for your loads

new

The Advance Design series Chevrolet trucks introduced in June 1947 were the culmination of the most extensive research and marketing survey of truck owners ever undertaken to that time.

Finer-looking, more spacious Chevrolet panel trucks are designed for bigger loads—for greater durability, comfort, convenience. Merchandise is protected from weather and theft. (De Luxe equipment at extra cost, is shown.)

INTERIORS—Panel bodies are wider, more spacious, with over 13 per cent more cubic-foot capacity! Seat riser at the right of the driver is flush with the floor, increasing load space by 20⅛ inches!

new

SEAT CONSTRUCTION—

MODEL	A	B	B'	C	D	E	F	G	H	J	GROSS VEH. WT
3105	116"	78"	120"	61¾"	51⅛"	196⅝"	77¾"	42¼"	49½"	48¼"	4600 LB.
3805	137"	109"	151"	62½"	51⅝"	227¼"	83"	42¼"	49½"	48¼"	6700 LB.
1508	116"	66¾"		56¼"	41¾"	196½"	66⅞"	34⅜"	34⅝"	48"	4100 LB.

FOR MOUNTING ON CHEVROLET

The *Utility...Dependable, Versatile*

The styling of the Advance Design series carried over to other product lines, including route delivery vans and large tractors.

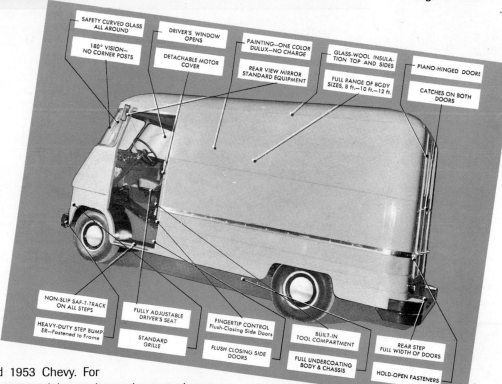

SAFETY CURVED GLASS ALL AROUND

180° VISION— NO CORNER POSTS

DRIVER'S WINDOW OPENS

DETACHABLE MOTOR COVER

PAINTING—ONE COLOR DULUX—NO CHARGE

REAR VIEW MIRROR STANDARD EQUIPMENT

GLASS-WOOL INSULA-TION TOP AND SIDES

FULL RANGE OF BODY SIZES, 8 ft.—10 ft.—12 ft.

PIANO-HINGED DOORS

CATCHES ON BOTH DOORS

NON-SLIP SAF-T-TRACK ON ALL STEPS

HEAVY-DUTY STEP BUMP-ER—Fastened to Frame

FULLY ADJUSTABLE DRIVER'S SEAT

STANDARD GRILLE

FINGERTIP CONTROL Flush-Closing Side Doors

FLUSH CLOSING SIDE DOORS

BUILT-IN TOOL COMPARTMENT

FULL UNDERCOATING BODY & CHASSIS

REAR STEP FULL WIDTH OF DOORS

HOLD-OPEN FASTENERS

There were relatively minor changes for 1952 and 1953 Chevy. For 1954 and the first part of the 1955 model year, the trucks were given a facelift of sorts: a new grill and a one-piece windshield, to list the most obvious. But the series had run its course, and the updates were not received well; sales slid to 292,202 units.

The sales dominance of the Advance Design series through 1952 and the industry standards that were pioneered with these trucks are the foundation for the success and social acceptance of the pickup truck today. As to the Advance Design series trucks, they may be even more popular today than when they were new. Among collectors they are rapidly becoming some of the most sought-after vehicles of the immediate postwar era.

Airflow

The end of stagecoaches

The surfaces were smooth and round with no sharp edges to hook the wind. The interiors were wider and more comfortable than any production car up to its time. More advanced geometry moved the rear-seat passengers off the rear axle and put the engine on top of the front axle where its weight smoothed out the miles. They go like rockets and stop on a dime—pleasantly quiet and completely comfortable.

None of it could save the Chrysler Airflow's reputation. For the rest of the twentieth century, even people who recognize and admire its advances ridiculed the Airflow as an ugly failure. The same people who ridiculed the Airflow's looks sat impatiently on waiting lists after World War II to buy the rounded fastback styling that characterized all those ultra-graceful 1940s cars—styling that evolved right out of the Airflow.

Some suggest it was ahead of its time, but it wasn't, really. Even in the midst of the Great Depression, miles and miles of gravel highways were paved, and treacherous grades and switchback curves were bypassed by new and, in some cases, multi-lane highways. The Airflow was right on time. The year 1934 was the perfect time to anticipate freeways and 70-mile-per-hour driving where the Airflow would be in its element, gliding along smoothly with its engine loafing along in overdrive and air flowing from bumper to bumper at great speed.

One dedicated Airflow enthusiast grew up in McCook, Nebraska, where he worked in a Chrysler dealership as a young man. He remembered the public being fascinated by the Airflow's styling and never heard the cars called ugly at the time. With Depression-era money tight, he says people were more afraid to try something new that might not stand up.

An eight-cylinder Airflow flies up a modern freeway on-ramp in second gear with the overdrive engaged, "Second-overdrive" as people used to say. When pulled into third-overdrive, the big straight-eight settles in at 70 miles per hour in a low-effort groan with lots left over. The Airflow feels nearly 20 years newer than it is, driving more like an early 1950s Chrysler than a car older than Gone With the Wind. Even the six-cylinder DeSoto Airflow makes the same grade. The interiors cradle the passengers far away from either axle on seats upholstered like Victorian-era davenports that are the height of a comfy office chair. More than any car manufactured up to its time or many cars made today, the Airflow was a car made for people to sit in. The interiors were tastefully ornate with elements that would make Frank Lloyd Wright and Buck Rogers envious, and the dash was high-tech. The speedometer not only told the car's forward speed, but also the engine's rpm in third gear and overdrive.

Chrysler hedged its bets by making a separate line of Chryslers and DeSotos with ordinary 1930s styling and lower-tech mechanicals, and these cramped cars bounced hard down the road in typical 1930s fashion. Although they went under the name Airstream, their time was over ultimately.

Even though the Airflow's era was confined to 1934 to 1937, its elements lived on in the form of aerodynamic car styling until the 1990s. This was when the clumsy, bumbling SUV came along and erased the Airflow. In the twenty-first century, Americans by the millions ride around in SUVs with sharp, flat fronts and backs that push and suck enough air to drag a freight train to a stop, and put the rear seat passengers right over the rear axle. They pay tens of thousands of dollars for the privilege of driving a vehicle less aerodynamically advanced than the Chrysler of 1934.

Above: *This is the Chrysler Airflow in its debut year, 1934, captured in one of its most famous poses.* DaimlerChrysler Corporation

Left: *The Airflow was in its last year in 1937, and this photo shows that the Airflow's nose had begun to resemble its more conventional Chrysler cousins with each passing year of its four-year life span.* DaimlerChrysler Corporation

Airstream
Roughing it in style

If one takes the time to give it some thought, it is really quite ironic. We take to the back- country to get away from it all, to get back to nature. For the "true outdoorsman" of the modern age this is often done in a climate-controlled 4x4, while the more refined prefer roughing it in an RV park.

This is not a recent phenomenon—it has been the case for most of a century now. By 1920, the modest price of cars such as the Model T even enabled the average person to be a tourist, escape the rigors and noise of city life, and take to the mountains or forests.

To take advantage of this growing trend, numerous companies began offering a variety of campers and trailers. Interestingly enough, many of them simply took concepts from horse-drawn trailers that featured little more than fold-down beds covered by a tent when raised, and modified them to fit on truck or car chassis. Variations on these themes and the addition of specialty modifications such as kitchen facilities and a lavatory remained the industry norm until the mid-1930s and the introduction of an American classic: the Airstream trailer.

The company's founder, Wallace Byam, was well acquainted with travelers and their needs. His childhood years often included time spent with his grandfather, who ran a mule train in Baker, Oregon. As a teenager, he earned money as a shepherd and called a two-wheeled donkey cart his home.

His interests and ambitions were broad, but travel was never far away from his thoughts. After leaving the merchant marine and studies of law at Stanford University, he founded an advertising agency and then became publisher of a do-it-yourself magazine. It was in that capacity that his future and the future of American camping were forever changed.

When readers began to complain that the plans for a travel trailer included in a feature article were flawed, Byam decided to try them out himself. As it turned out, the readers were correct, so he began to build his own model. This included the unique concept of dropping the floor between the wheels. Byam then wrote a detailed article on how to build the trailer for under $100.

The response was such that Byam began selling plans for five dollars each. He followed this with the sale of complete kits and finished trailers that were constructed in the backyard of his Los Angeles home. By the late 1920s, his career in law, publishing, and advertising was a thing of the past. In the first years of the following decade, he expanded and further developed his trailer concept.

His experiments in incorporating aircraft construction and design methods, such as a using a monocoque aluminum body, to provide better durability and wind resistance as well as improvements to the weight-to-strength ratio came together on January 17, 1936, in the Airstream Clipper. The $1,200 price was hefty during the hard times of the Great Depression. Yet, the trailer's many innovations—a tubular-steel-framed dinette that could convert to a bed, a self-contained water supply, electric lights, insulation, and even, as an option, a dry-ice air conditioner—resulted in the company's overwhelming number of orders.

By 1940, of the more than 300 trailer manufacturers that had been operating in 1936, only Airstream remained as a result of the crippling economic conditions of the Great Depression and the dominance of Airstream. World War II and the subsequent shortage of materials accomplished what the Depression could not; the Airstream Trailer Company closed its doors.

By 1970, Airstream trailers had become widely recognized for quality, and as a result often were used to enhance the perception of another product, as indicated by this brochure for the International Travelall.

FUN-LOVING WAGONS FROM INTERNATIONAL®
TRAVELALL®

In the interim, Byam had decided that the best contribution he could make to the war effort was to offer the experience he had gained in trailer construction to the aircraft industry. For the duration he worked with the two leading military aircraft manufacturers, Curtiss-Wright and Lockheed.

The postwar boom proved to be the catalyst for the rebirth of the Airstream trailer. By 1948, the products produced by the company were as widely recognized as Jeep, Chevrolet, and Coca-Cola. By 1950, the Los Angeles production facilities were proving to be inadequate for meeting the rapidly growing demand. So in July 1952, a lease was signed for a new facility in Jackson Center, Illinois. In August, California production was relocated to Santa Fe Springs.

In the early 1970s, Airstream expanded its product line by introducing the company's first motorhome promoted as the classic. In the 1980s, this was followed by the introduction of the Argosy fifth-wheel trailer. The innovation continues, as today the company has more products under development than at any time in its history.

Some of the most significant honors Airstream has received include being selected by John F. Kennedy to build his mobile presidential office and by NASA to be a part of its space shuttle program. Both the Smithsonian Institution and the Henry Ford Museum feature Airstream trailer displays. However, the greatest testimonial to Airstream's impact on America is that, according to a company press release, more than 60 percent of all Airstreams ever built, including some built from the original five-dollar plan, are still on the road.

AIRSTREAM LAND YACHTING—THE BETTER WAY TO TRAVEL

Post cards distributed by dealers in the 1950s often featured Airstream trailers in exotic locales and promoted the company-sponsored caravans that proved to be quite popular with owners.

Facing page photo courtesy Michael Karl Witzel

JUST ARRIVED...BIG TRAILER LUXURY IN A SMALL PACKAGE!

Winnebago, Independents, and Eccentrics
Pioneers of the recreational vehicle

While Lloyd Rounds never achieved the financial success or recognition awarded the founder of Airstream, his visionary efforts and talents exemplify the optimism of the postwar era as well as the entrepreneurial spirit that has made America great. Motorized campers had been built in numerous configurations since at least World War I. Rounds' idea, initiated in 1946, was to expand on this concept and to build a vehicle that was more home than transportation. As he saw it, the vehicle was to provide a practical solution for the postwar housing shortage or for construction workers whose trade required a move to new locations on a regular basis.

The culmination of these ideas was the Nomad III, completed in 1949. Built largely of war surplus, including aircraft aluminum framing as well as sheeting, and utilizing aircraft construction techniques, this revolutionary experiment on wheels had many features unknown even in most conventional homes of the time: full air conditioning, radiant heating in the floors, a water heater, cork insulation panels, and Lucite thermal windows.

However, this was but a small display of the innovative genius that was made manifest in the Nomad III. When parked, the driver's compartment converted to a study, with intricately hinged panels and a steering column that collapsed to be stowed under the dash. Power steering and front-wheel drive made it somewhat easier to operate a vehicle that weighed 15,650 pounds and was 40 feet in length!

An extremely overworked Ford flathead V-8 proved to be the Nomad III's Achilles heel. Additional mechanical shortcomings were found on the vehicle's maiden voyage from California to North Dakota. A return trip to California and short run to Arizona were the Nomad III's final voyages.

Dave Peterson was an avid outdoorsman whose idea for a motorized home was birthed as a solution for his frustration of being forced to decide whether to pull his boat or his Airstream trailer. Unlike the Nomad III, his Ultra Van actually made it into production.

A truly unique concept in recreational vehicles, the Ultra Van featured extensive use of aluminum and was built with the principles of monocoque construction. It featured more than six feet of headroom, was wide enough to seat four comfortably, and was fully self-contained as well as heavily insulated. The most revolutionary aspect was the choice of rear-engine configuration to ensure a lower stance, as well as elimination of the floor hump. What kind of drive train in 1959 would be adaptable for such an application? The all-new Chevrolet Corvair!

Initial testing of the prototype exceeded expectations, and simply through discussions with friends as well as fellow outdoor enthusiasts, Peterson found himself in the unique position of receiving orders for a vehicle that technically did not exist. From this juncture, things began to move rather quickly.

Prestolite Corporation began limited production of the vehicles under the Travalon name. Then in 1965 publishing magnate John Tillotson received rights to mass-produce the Class A motorhome and relocated the entire operation to Hutchinson, Kansas. By the end of 1966, eight units per month, with a selling price of $8,995, were rolling from the factory.

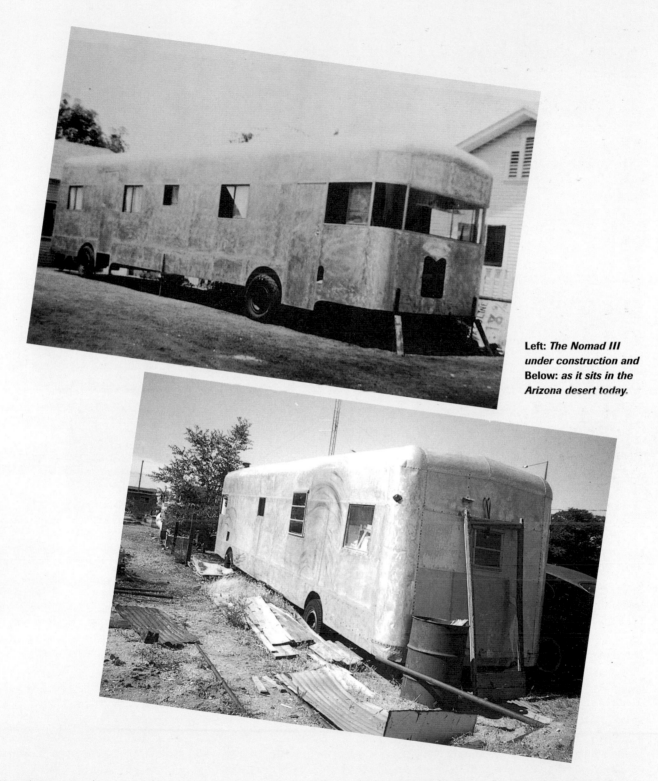

Left: *The Nomad III under construction and* Below: *as it sits in the Arizona desert today.*

Also, there was a $250 "bird dog" rebate for those who used their vehicle to attract business. By 1969, the year the Corvair engine was phased out, 305 units had been built. Remaining units on hand were adapted to the Oldsmobile Toronado configuration. Next was the series 500 with a reverse-facing, Chevrolet-built 307-cid V-8 engine. However, the cost of these transitions pushed the sales price with options to $14,000 when a Winnebago could be had for $11,000. In June 1970, production ceased and the Ultra Van became just another forgotten chapter in American automotive history.

John K. Hanson had a long list of successful business accomplishments—manager of a farm implement, furniture, and appliance store, and funeral home director, to name but a few—to his credit when he joined several other investors to launch Winnebago Industries in 1958. The company's initial offering was the 15-foot Aljo trailer, which could sleep five in

WINNEBAGO D-22

FUTURISTIC MOTOR HOME CONCEPT

WINNEBAGO GRAIN TRAILER

WINNEBAGO HELI-HOME

In 1995, Winnebago celebrated its rich and diverse history with the distribution of a 100-card set that featured all products produced since the company's inception, as well as some that it was planning for the future.

comfort and featured a propane gas stove, a sink, and refrigerator all for just $895. Since then, the company has been a leader in the development of recreational vehicles and, with extensive diversification, pioneered almost every aspect of the market.

In 1964, the company developed a lightweight wall material called Thermo-Panel, which was 30 percent lighter than conventional lumber products. This served as the foundation for the company's newest offering, KD Kaps for pickup trucks.

The first motorhome, F19, the product Winnebago is most often associated with, was built on a Ford chassis and introduced in the spring of 1966. The almost instant success of these coaches and increasing demand of other products gave the company incentive to offer two more models, the F17 and D22 on a Dodge chassis, and initiate expansion. On November 7, 1968, the new facility, which was the world's largest for motorhome manufacturing, began operation.

To ensure that Winnebago products were trouble-free and of the highest quality, the company developed numerous test facilities, including the industry's first test track. In the early 1990s, utilization of a computerized MTS Road Simulator, which allowed for reenactment of the road tests, further aided in the development of durable products.

Diversification has been an integral part of Winnebago's success for more than 40 years. In 1975, the company introduced a full line of grain trailer gravity boxes. Other endeavors have included van conversions, the revolutionary Winnie Wagon II with a length equal to that of the average station wagon, and the EuroVan Camper. However, perhaps one of the more interesting niche-market recreational vehicles was the Winnebago Heli-Home. The Heli-Home allowed outdoor enthusiasts to enjoy the advantages of helicopter access to remote locations, coupled with traditional Winnebago motorhome luxury. It was introduced in 1976.

For those who long for the open road, nothing is better than taking the home along. To this end, numerous visionaries have sought the best of both worlds—the joy found in a road trip while never forgetting that home is where the heart is.

Show Cars
Practicality born from pure art

For the auto industry's first few decades, automobiles were really just stagecoaches with engines, and thousands of American car companies came and went in a frenzy that makes the dot-com era look like a church service. By the mid-1920s, the herd had thinned, demand had gone up, and the nature of competition had changed. All cars ran well, so reliability was no longer the main focus. Automobile buyers were no longer shopping by price alone, and Ford's Model T, which was outdated by 1915, was finished.

Cars would be marketed by following the popular images of changing times, and Art Deco and the Jet Age would have more to do with how cars were designed and sold than oil pressure or differential gearing. Eventually, car companies contracted design houses to create concept cars designed as purely art forms. The industry designers drew ideas from these sculptures and adapted them to practical cars.

Locomobile began its 30-year life in 1899 and immediately offered the buyer more than just transportation. Locomobiles had bodies designed by Tiffany and interiors devised by the leading interior decorators of the time.

In the late 1920s, General

The GM Motorama of the 1950s was a highly anticipated event that drew huge crowds in any city that it appeared. The Corvette made its debut at the 1953 Motorama.

SHOW DATES: New York, January 21 to 26 • Miami, February 6 to 14
Los Angeles, March 6 to 14 • San Francisco, March 27 to April 4

Motors established its Art and Color Studio with designer Harley Earl in charge. The department turned out blockbuster designs through the 1960s, taking the design themes of each era and adapting them beautifully, even to the corporation's lowest-priced cars.

The Chrysler Airflow was an accidental concept car. Its sloping lines, filled-in spaces, reconfigured mechanical geometry, and scientifically tested engineering were radical when it came out in 1934, but by 1940, all American car companies had drawn from the Airflow. The car, which was held up as a misunderstood failure, actually influenced an entire generation of car design, and the flowing fastback sedans of the 1940s owe their souls to the Airflow.

When World War II ended, the car-hungry public flooded dealership waiting lists to replace their worn-out, badly maintained prewar cars, which had been ravaged by the war's shortages. By 1950, the rush was over, the hunger had been satisfied, and the public got more choosy.

The contrast-colored side indentations on GM's 1955 LaSalle II concept car appeared on production Chevrolet Corvettes from 1956 to 1962. **Bortz Auto Collection**

Buyers rewarded the car companies that offered designs looking forward into the Jet Age with ornate optimism. Cars were matters of fashion by this time, and the car companies were racing to stay ahead of public taste. Artists had designed the cars for decades, but artistic influence could now make or break a car company. The American car companies contracted Italian design houses like Ghia and individual Italian artists like Pinin Farina to create new designs. Auto industry designers, like GM's Henry Lauve and Chrysler's Virgil Exner, attended the high-end fashion shows in Paris to see what fabrics and colors were popular, to predict what America's growing female customer base would find new and chic. GM's traveling Motorama show introduced Mr. and Mrs. America to the corporation's new lineup every year, but the concept cars were the show-stoppers, and they sparkled from the turntables and foretold a superhighway future.

Concept cars from the 1950s rarely had comfortable seats, doors that opened far enough, or windshields that could be seen through safely. Many did not even have functioning drivetrains, but the auto manufacturers lifted design themes from the concept cars and adapted them to practical cars the public could actually buy.

The single most direct adaptation from concept car to practical car came from Buick when nearly all of the design elements of Buick's 1953 Wildcat I concept car appeared on the production 1954 Buicks. The 1955 and 1956 Chrysler Imperials' open wheelwells and stand-up taillights came from Virgil Exner's cooperative efforts with Ghia concept cars from the early 1950s. The side indentations on the 1956–1962 Chevrolet Corvettes came from GM's 1955 LaSalle II Motorama car. Chrysler produced a concept car called the Falcon in 1955, and the Falcon's front clip appears amazingly intact on the 2004 Chrysler 300, proving that a great concept never gets old.

The 1952 K-310 had more than just futuristic styling, it also showcased Chrysler's latest innovations, including a fully automatic transmission, electric power windows, power steering, and electric seats.

115

Ambulance

A brief history of portable hospitals

For most of the past two decades, there has been a certain uniformity to the American ambulance. This uniformity is due to a narrowing field of companies that specialize in the conversion of vehicles for niche markets, and regulation that has made a box- or van-type body on a truck chassis the most practical. In years past, however, a number of manufacturers specifically focused on transforming stock vehicles into automobiles that met the unique needs of ambulance companies and mortuaries.

On occasion, even original manufacturers handled this work in-house. This was especially common with smaller companies like Checker and AMC in the postwar era, and automakers with subsidiary companies in general prior to World War II.

Quite often all that remains of these earlier efforts are tantalizing clues such as catalogs, brochures, memories of former employees, and factory photos, with little in the way of concrete evidence to prove that they were ever built at all. When was the last time you saw a 1931 Checker MU6 Suburban Utility or a Rambulance, an intriguing factory conversion of a Rambler station wagon?

The concept of transporting wounded individuals from battlefields most possibly dates to the birth of organized armies. However, the modern concept of the ambulance can be traced to the reign of Spanish monarchs Ferdinand and Isabella, who took a deep interest in the welfare of the wounded during the battles against the Moors in the fifteenth century. Under their guidance, surgical and medical supplies were brought together in specialized tents labeled ambulancias.

The next stage in the evolution of the ambulance came in 1792 as a result of the carnage Dominique-Jean Larrey witnessed in the Austrian/Prussian war. Under his tutelage, small, lightweight wagons were built in which surgeons could work with the wounded soldiers on the field of battle. His concept was improved upon during Napoleon's Italian campaigns.

In the American Civil War, battlefield ambulances were most often operated by civilians. There was no uniformity in vehicle design or operation. Even more appalling, however, was the fact that many ambulances were not operated by medical professionals, but by thieves who preyed upon the wounded and the dead. In 1864, this resulted in the Congressional passage of the "Act to Establish a Uniform System of Ambulances in the Armies of the United States." Almost immediately after, the Geneva Convention of the same year reached an agreement where hospitals and persons connected with relief services would be regarded as neutral during time of war.

By the dawn of the twentieth century, ambulance construction had developed into almost universal uniformity; they featured removable floors that could be pulled out to serve as a stretcher and box compartments beneath the driver's seat that contained brandy, bandages, tourniquets, sponges, splints, blankets, and assorted surgical instruments. With the increased usage of automobiles, this configuration was adapted to bus or taxi chassis.

The first use of motorized ambulances in the military was at the urging of President McKinley. Ironically McKinley, after being shot by an assassin, became the first president to be transported in a motorized ambulance, an electric-powered vehicle produced by F. S. Wood of New York.

The modern ambulance made its debut in 1937. One of the world's oldest builders of ambulance bodies, Hess and Eisenhardt of Cincinnati, Ohio, had designed a unit that was to serve as a pre-hospital emergency room complete with medicine cabinets, roof lights, and even air conditioning.

As the units became better equipped, they also became heavier. Then as a result, a sturdy chassis and power became two prerequisites. For these reasons, from about 1950 to 1975, the vehicle of choice for conversion was a Cadillac, with Pontiac being a close second choice. As these manufacturers abandoned rear-wheel drive, and the weight of required equipment such as defibrillators and monitors increased, truck chassis were adapted. Another factor for these changes

"When seconds count..." count on Miller·Meteor ambulances for 1975

Built by Wayne — Powered by Cadillac.

"An inside look at the 1975 Criterion"

Roof compartment for scoop stretcher and fracture board. Optional, extra.

Huge dispensary cabinet with see-thru, sliding plexiglas doors.

Action wall for telemetry equipment. Modura rail, optional, extra.

Easy access storage for fire extinguisher.

Built-in linen compartment over each attendant seat.

Underfloor compartment stores 2 large stretchers.

Walk-thru partition.

Bumper step with non-skid grille.

Squad bunk with wide, hinged cushion.

Underfloor compartment for piped oxygen from "M" or "H" tank; swivel cradle; sight glass.

"D" or "E" oxygen tank storage area.

First aid compartment inside this door and rear door.

About Wayne.

Wayne Corporation is the nation's leading single source for all ambulance needs. Three plants produce five lines of ambulances: Miller-Meteors, Cotner-Bevingtons, Vanguards, Medicruisers and Care-O-Vans. And all, produced under strict quality controls, are certified to meet Federal Motor Vehicle Safety Standards applicable to ambulances. Each Wayne ambulance is backed by warranty coverage, plus service via a nationwide network of experienced ambulance distributors.

Leasing and Financing

Your Wayne Ambulance Distributor can arrange an installment financing or leasing program to meet your requirements. Through Wayne Sales Financial Corporation, your program can be planned by professionals who can time the payments to fit your operation.

Note: Wayne maintains a continuous program of product improvement. We reserve the right to change specifications and prices without notice. Features shown herein are not necessarily standard unless described as such.

Criterion and Lifeliner are trademarks of Wayne Corporation.

Wayne Corporation
An Indian Head Company
125 Clark Avenue
Piqua, Ohio 45356
(513) 773-3824

This brochure represents the end of an era, as regulation was about to require equipment that would only be feasible in ambulances built on truck chassis.

were the federal regulations enacted in the 1970s that governed minimum width, headroom, and equipment levels in ambulances.

Today vintage ambulances represent an oft-overlooked chapter in American automotive history. However, future generations have a better chance than ever to catch a glipse of these forgotten relics, thanks to the efforts of a few enthusiasts and collector societies.

The Last Ride

Going out in style

In automotive industry, the hearse, as well as ambulances, limousines, and any vehicle custom bodied for a specific industry, is loosely defined as a professional car. Initially these conversions often were made to meet two or more needs, such as ambulance/hearse. However, what they all have in common is that their construction requires extensive individual handcrafting.

The hearse has almost always been representative of the special occasion for which it was designed, the last ride. Depending upon the culture, the hearse has been either somber or ostentatious.

In the United States, for the mortuary that could afford the investment, the funeral coach of the nineteenth century was often an ornate vehicle of glass and hand-carved wood. With the introduction of automobiles, more than a few enterprising morticians had the body of the horse-drawn hearse transferred to an automotive chassis. Only large urban funeral homes could afford the first commercially built horseless hearses, which often cost $4,000 or more—this at a time when a horse-drawn version could be had for $1,500!

Crane and Breed of Cincinnati, Ohio, had a long reputation as one of the country's premier hearse builders. In 1909, Crane and Breed joined forces with Cunningham, a custom coachbuilder of Rochester, New York. The two companies began introducing a complete hearse on a variety of chassis, including Locomobile and Peerless. Superior Coach was another pioneer in the industry and was one of the more well-known manufacturers of hearses in the country. This company initially began operations in 1915 under the name Superior Body Company, which was a subsidiary of Garford Motor Truck Company. In 1925, Superior introduced a full line of ambulances and hearses built on the larger Studebaker chassis. A year after the 1928 acquisition of Pierce-Arrow by Studebaker, the company began offering professional cars on these chassis as well. In 1936, Pontiac was introduced as a substitute line.

By 1920, the automobile had almost entirely replaced the horse-drawn coach in the realm of hearses. Likewise, metal had almost completely replaced wood in the vehicles' construction. As a result, the more modern configuration of limousine-styled hearses began to proliferate. There were, however, exceptions in regard to styling.

A few companies such as Cunningham continued to offer hearses with extensive wood carving well into the 1920s. In 1929, Sayers and Scovill took the concept to a more practical level by offering carved panels for hearse sides. Another somewhat practical option was the stamped-aluminum raised-relief panels.

Nine years later, this company would effectively close the era of the carved hearse with the introduction of the first Victoria-style, also known as landau, hearse. The styling features of these coaches included heavily padded leather roofs with blind rear quarters decorated by S-shaped irons that were reminiscent of those used for raising or lowering the roofs in the nineteenth century.

The limousine type of coach had been introduced with the highly successful Meteor Model T of 1915. This company was a true pioneer in the development of hearses. In late 1913, it became the first company to offer a chassis incorporating mechanical components from a variety of suppliers designed and built exclusively as a hearse or ambulance. This chassis was also sold to a number of other coach builders.

Combination coaches (hearse/ambulance), especially in smaller rural communities, became quite popular, as they enabled mortuaries to operate the funeral home as well as serve the community. Another factor in their popularity was cost, as they often were the coachbuilders' lowest priced models built on Chevrolet or Ford chassis. Federal ambulance regulations pertaining to minimum width and height enacted in the 1970s brought an end to this type of vehicle.

Henney and Eureka, another leader in the construction of hearses, introduced in 1928 the first casket table that moved along a Y-shaped track, which allowed for either side or rear loading. This provided an edge of safety and kept pallbearers from the mud that was common on many streets. An additional advantage to this configuration was an increased loading height, which made unloading an easier operation.

Above: *This hearse is relatively unique in that the company utilized an Oldsmobile chassis instead of the more traditional Cadillac foundation.*

Left: *The interior of the hearse represents the craftsmanship that was once common in much of the automobile industry.*

The disappearance of open touring cars presented another opportunity for the custom coach-building companies that built professional cars. As a replacement for the touring cars often used for the transport of flowers and such, these companies began offering what has loosely become known as flower cars and are often confused with pickup trucks.

Superior Coach, with almost a century of experience, now dominates the professional car business in the United States. As with the auto industry in general, the day of the independent has now passed from the stage.

Similar to ambulances, vintage hearses are now viewed as more than a surf wagon or a vehicle with ghoulish overtones. They are viewed as a historic milepost in the development of the automobile and the culture it has created.

Gremlin
Something new, something old

This is the other model: Gremlin with fold-down rea[r] storage and a flip-up rear win[dow] access. Its list price is less th[an] other production car made i[t] for the 2-seater Gremlin.

To say the very least, the AMC Gremlin was unique. Its styling, like that of the Volkswagen Beetle that it was designed to compete against, made confusing it with anything else on the road impossible. In addition, like its chief competitor, the Gremlin soon acquired a surprisingly large base of loyal owners.

Even though it was introduced on April Fool's Day in 1970, the diminutive little car was no joke. It represented a bold and innovative approach to resolving a pair of looming crises in the American auto industry: an alarming increase in the sale of fuel-frugal imports and the tightening of gas supplies. For AMC, it also represented a small triumph; it had beat both GM and Ford to the punch by several months. Both competitors had been planning to introduce a small car as a 1971 model.

AMC also continued a long tradition of small, independent manufacturers creatively utilizing available resources to produce an all-new vehicle within the parameters of a very limited budget. In the case of the Gremlin, the company created the foundation for the truncated hatchback by cutting 12 inches from the wheelbase of the recently introduced Hornet.

The Gremlin's first-year sales exceeded the company's projections, and for a brief time orders outpaced production capabilities. For the following year, in an effort to ensure strong sales, AMC introduced a lengthy options list that included sporty trim and appearance features as well as a performance "X" package. In the years to follow, other notable option packages, like the Levi's interior, complete with blue denim, rivets, and pockets, were available.

In spite of a small price increase from a base price of $1,899 to $1,999, sales continued to increase. Demographics showed that the car was most popular with younger adults, who viewed the car as both practical and hip.

For 1972, rather than invest in sheet-metal modifications, AMC chose to focus on mechanical improvements. The hopelessly antiquated vacuum windshield wipers were replaced with two-speed electrical units as standard equipment. The front suspension was updated to a new one-piece ball joint, and the old-style BorgWarner transmission was replaced with the Chrysler TorqueFlite.

The options list was also greatly expanded. Among the items now available were front disc brakes, a folding sunroof, an inside hood release, and a 304-cid V-8 engine as well as two types of six-cylinder engines.

When new, the Gremlin represented an alternative to import models for consumers in search of an American-built economy car. When it first began to appear on used-car lots, it was an excellent car for the first-time buyer on a tight budget. In light of rising gas prices, today it represents a practical alternative to muscle cars and the American land yachts of its era—especially if you lean toward the eccentric.

The simplicity of the 1970 introductory brochure for the AMC Gremlin, a car with truly original and unique styling, left little doubt as to who the targeted market was.

And look in the open door. You can have optional vinyl buckets when you order custom trim including carpeting, sports style steering wheel, a glove box that locks and a parcel shelf that runs the full width of the instrument panel.

Nobody's going to push you around in any Gremlin.

The Gremlin is not only 7 in. lower, but also 10 in. wider and some 800 lbs. heavier than a VW. Which gives the Gremlin possibly the smoothest, most stable ride you

can get in a car of this size.

Its turning circle is 32 ft., 8 in., about 3 ft. less than VW's. Which makes it about the world's easiest car to park and handle.

The optional rooftop luggage rack you see is a useful extra.

The Gremlin X for 1972 was a rather successful attempt at giving the Gremlin a sports option package.

Pacer

A failure?

Should a car that sold a quarter of a million units over its first three years be called a failure? On March 1, 1975, the United States was pulling out of Vietnam, heading into a deep recession, and still reeling from the gas crunch of a year before. Against all these odds, American Motors introduced the Pacer—yes, the goldfish bowl, the moon buggy, the space module, the pregnant guppy. People called it names, but people bought 72,000 of them the first year and over 117,000 of them in its second year. Pacers were common enough to be held up decades later as a 1970s icon, right up there with disco and leisure suits.

Sales fell sharply between 1978 and 1980, and the Pacer said goodbye. Why is the Pacer called a failure? Could it be its advanced aerodynamic styling? Could it be its trademark acreage of glass and great visibility? Could it be the dashboard, which was 10 years ahead of its time? Could it be the wide, comfortable body that was the length of a Pinto but the width of a Cadillac? Probably not, it was just different. AMC was born from a merger between Nash and Hudson in 1954. Beginning with its innovative strut-style suspension in the 1930s and its aerodynamic bodies in the late 1940s, Nash had a habit of thinking outside the norms. Sometimes it paid off, and in the recession of 1958, AMC's Rambler was the only American car with increased sales over previous years. Other times, AMC became a laughing stock, and Gremlins, Hornets, and Pacers from the 1970s still receive cruel jabs.

The Pacer's faults were not in its engineering. It was originally designed to carry the innovative, powerful Wankel rotary engine with front-wheel drive, but the deal with GM to supply the engines fell through, and the Pacer hastily received the standard, proven AMC 232-cubic-inch six-cylinder engine and rear-wheel drive. Pacer bashers might not have laughed quite so hard if they had been blown off the road by Pacers with Mazda RX7 performance. The Pacer's rounded corners were laughed at in the 1970s, right when car enthusiasts were beginning to seriously collect 1940s and 1950s cars that were defined by their sleek, rounded shapes. New-car buyers who laughed at the Pacer in the 1970s couldn't wait to buy Ford Thunderbirds in 1983 and Chrysler K-cars in 1984, when rounded corners were suddenly cool after 20 years of creased rectangles. People who ridiculed the Pacer's optional Levi Strauss interior package now drive around in SUVs with fashionable Harley-Davidson interiors or shuttle their kids to school in Warner Brother's minivans with Bugs Bunny on the tailgate.

The Pacer's failings were basically due to quality. Used-car dealers report that Pacers had flimsy interiors, weak weather stripping, and poor upholstery. The door handles came off in their hands, and the window mechanisms jammed. While the engines were fine, everything stuck to the engine caused problems.

The Pacer has a small but enthusiastic group of followers. They, like Chrysler Airflow fans, wear satisfied grins as they see the Pacer's rounded corners, sleek shapes, and glass area peeking out of twenty-first-century cars.

The much-maligned AMC Pacer was the length of a Pinto but the width of a Cadillac. Originally, the Wankel rotary engine was to provide its power. The Pacer's interior quality and engine accessories were iffy in quality, but at its root, the Pacer was a good idea and a great design.

When Four Wheels Aren't Enough or Are Too Much

And now for something completely different

Initially the automobile was seen by almost everyone as little more than a novelty, hence the billing given a Duryea Motor Wagon by Barnum and Bailey Circus in 1896. There were, however, a number of visionaries who saw a promising future for the fragile looking "horseless carriage." A few were seeing profit in this future, while others saw a world transported to utopia by these amazing vehicles. A few others lived in their own world.

By 1889, Uriah Smith had become convinced the primary reason automobiles were not more widely accepted was because they scared horses. As he saw it, this was easily resolved by simply mounting a sculpted or stuffed horse head

and neck onto the front of automobiles. As an added plus it could be hollow, allowing for placement of the gas tank inside it.

By 1910, the basic configuration of the automobile had been settled by manufacturers throughout the world. A few people, such as Milton Reeves, still felt that the four-wheel concept was incorrect.

In 1896, Reeves made his first endeavor into the production of a horseless vehicle, as a means to promote the variable-speed transmission he had designed for his pulley company. While the vehicle has been relegated to historical curiosity, a device he designed to quiet the engine noise and appease the neighbors, the muffler, hasn't.

For the next 10 years, Reeves involved himself with a number of automobile-related endeavors, including the production of air-cooled engines. He also designed a bus with axles that were 7 feet long and rear wheels that were just less than 6 feet tall. It was powered by an air-cooled engine of his design, and the rugged little car was labeled the Go-Buggy. All of this experimentation led him to believe there was a direct correlation between the number of wheels a vehicle had and its riding comfort.

To prove his theory, he stretched the chassis on a 1910 Overland and added two more sets of wheels. The resultant Octauto was completed in time for display at the first Indianapolis 500 in 1911. With that grand entrance, Reeves began marketing the concept as something that was adaptable to any vehicle. Apparently the idea of a vehicle with a 180-inch wheelbase and 248-inch overall length wasn't appealing, for there is no record of any vehicles being produced other than the original prototype.

Reeves was not one for throwing in the towel just because a project wasn't well received. In 1912 he decided the same result could be achieved with six wheels instead of eight. At least two Sextautos were built. The first was the Octauto, revised to single front-axle design, and the second was a modified Stutz. When these vehicles also failed to attract customers, Reeves withdrew from automobile production.

At the opposite end of the spectrum was the automobile envisioned by Cadwallader Kelsey, which would be a vehicle that sold for less than the Model T Ford but be even more durable. The result was the diminutive Motorette, a three-wheeled (two in the front and one in the rear) vehicle with a wheelbase of 74 inches, a 56¾-inch front tread, and a total weight of just 900 pounds. The selling price of just $385 was half that of a Model T in 1910. Unlike the products devised by Reeves, the Motorette actually went into production, was well received, and showed great promise until an act of sabotage caused a massive failure rate for the engines.

Since its inception, the automobile has attracted visionaries and eccentrics. Both have made great contributions to the advancement of the motorized vehicle, and a few have provided comic relief.

Above: *The Horsey Horseless epitomizes the confusion about what the automobile even was in the years before the dawning of the twentieth century.*

Opposite: *Even in a time when cars were built of laminated papier-mâché, were popular with just one Cyclops-type headlight, and were sold profitably with just rear-wheel brakes, the Octauto stood out as being truly unique.*

Alternative-Energy Vehicles
Shattering the myths

A press release dated November 10, 2004, heralded the opening of the world's first hydrogen dispenser at a retail gasoline station. Once again, the buzz was the gasoline engine was about to go the way of the Edsel. Further fueling this talk is the relative success enjoyed by the Honda Civic Hybrid and the Toyota Prius.

However, while the names and the technology may have changed, the subject has remained just below the surface for more than a century. After all, alternative energy vehicles are at the very foundation of the automotive industry.

"Steam is reliable and easily understood," is the heading on a 1903 advertisement for the Jaxon, produced in Jackson, Michigan. This succinct statement encapsulates the reason for the dominance of steam engines during the infancy of the automobile.

Almost every pioneering auto manufacturer began with steam engines. Steam-powered vehicles set the earliest speed and hillclimbing records. In many urban markets, electric vehicles, cars as well as trucks, were the ones that spearheaded the movement to replace the horse.

Studebaker launched its automotive endeavors in 1902 with an electric automobile designed by Thomas Edison. The first vehicle built by Ransom Olds in 1887 was a three-wheeled steamer. In 1906, Theodore Roosevelt became the first president to drive an automobile; the vehicle was a steamer built by White.

While at Ormond Beach (now known as Daytona), Fred Marriott established a world's speed record of 127.6 miles per hour driving a steamer built by Stanley in 1906. The following year, he unofficially topped 150 miles per hour—in a vehicle rated at less than 30 horsepower. The year before, Webb Jay had driven a special racer built by White nicknamed Whistling Billy to a world's mile record speed of 73.75 miles per hour. More than 124 American automobile manufacturers produced steam-powered vehicles during this formative period.

Between the years 1900 and 1915, 25 American companies specialized in the production of electric-powered automobiles. Quite often the target market for the electric vehicles was women, for these cars were usually easy to operate and did not require the effort of cranking.

The introduction of the first practical electric starter on the 1912 Cadillac and the inherent flaws and shortcomings of both electric- and steam-powered vehicles provided a solid foundation for the dominance of gasoline-powered automobiles that has continued to this day. Today, the hybrid vehicle is heralded as the next successor. Here, too, there is historic precedence.

A manufacturer of electric vehicles since 1899, Woods Electric introduced the Woods Dual Electric in 1916. At speeds less than 15 miles per hour, the gasoline engine merely idled as the electric motors propelled the car, but the gas engine overcame the limitations of range and speed associated with electric vehicles. It seemed like an ideal combination, but a number of factors prevented the car from gaining wide exposure. As a result, in 1918 the company ceased production.

Today, electric or hybrid vehicles are trumpeted as the wave of the future. In spite of our technological advancement, many of the initial shortcomings associated with these vehicles still exist. Nevertheless, the greatest factor to overcome is not scientific but social, for the American people have made it clear that if they cannot go first class they will not go at all. The demise of the Volkswagen Type 1 stands in mute testimony of this fact.

Above: *Steam-powered vehicles were the speed-record setters in the first decade of organized automobile production. This vehicle built by White was a famous racer nicknamed "Whistling Billy " by fans.*

Left: *Since the inception of the automobile, alternative-powered vehicles have been heralded as the wave of the future. This vehicle, the Electric Shopper, was built in 1960.*

Checker

An urban legend

The Checker, like the Jeep and Harley-Davidson, is an American icon recognized throughout the world. For decades these no-nonsense sedans dominated the taxi industry in many American cities. Their rugged durability and simple, brawny design gave them a brand loyalty without equal in the American auto industry and spawned countless urban legends.

These incredible accomplishments are even more amazing in light of the fact that in 60 years of production beginning in 1922, seldom more than 8,000 units rolled out of the Kalamazoo, Michigan, factory annually. Of these, only a small percentage were the widely recognized four-door sedans. The company also produced niche-market vehicles like the six- and eight-door Aerobus, the Medicar, and stake-bed trucks. An intriguing model known as the MU6 Suburban Utility was manufactured during the early 1930s. It was advertised as a ton-plus station wagon that could be quickly converted from a nine-passenger vehicle into a delivery car, hearse, or ambulance.

Checker's reputation for endurance was a cornerstone of the company from its inception. A 1925 industrial survey noted that many Checker cabs were still on the road after an astounding 250,000 miles.

On numerous occasions, retired cabs were refurbished and resurrected to be sold to taxi companies in Europe. Advertisements form the early postwar period offer additional hints that Checker cabs were in service from Tahiti to Japan, and a blurry photograph from a Swiss auto show is all that remains of a one-off custom convertible.

A Checker was never really retired; as long as it could still move, it had a purpose. More than a few, as evidenced by a recently discovered Model C, were converted to trucks. All of this, as well as limited production, have made some models particularly scarce. As of 2003, only 14 pre-1958 Checkers were known to exist. Of these, fewer than half were roadworthy.

Perhaps the most fascinating aspect of Checker is the many enigmatic chapters of the company's offerings, of which there is almost no concrete material available to separate rumor from fact, or myth from legend. At the Gilmore Museum near Kalamazoo, a Jeep prototype appears to be one of the originals produced by American Bantam, but with modifications made by Checker that include the addition of four-wheel steering. In the closing days of World War II and the months that followed, an unknown number of front-wheel-drive prototypes rolled from the factory for extensive testing, but nothing more than a few photographs remain as mute testimony to their existence.

The Model A of 1940, of which there is one known extant model, was so revolutionary with its numerous safety features and unique sliding rear-quarter landaulet roof that the body was patented. The legendary Ray Dietrich was associated with Checker during this period, leading some to suggest his hand was in its design, but this as well as other contributions he may have made to the company are but another shadowy chapter.

Dietrich's is not the only famous name to have been associated with Checker throughout its colorful history. In a complicated series of stock swaps and proxy acquisitions, E. L. Cord gained control of the

From its inception, Checker produced niche-market vehicles with a certain degree of success. The Aerobus represented one of the most recognizable of these vehicles. **Checker Cab: A Photo History by Iconografix**

company from a consortium that had made the acquisition in a similar manner just a few years previously. Almost immediately he returned Morris Markin, the founder of the company who had been ousted in the original takeover, to the position of president. At this juncture, Checker began using Lycoming (another Cord company) engines, and Auburn began marketing Checker-built Saf-T-Cabs. This complicated deal and the resultant profit realized from stock sales sparked a Securities and Exchange Commission investigation.

Surprisingly, this little company was also a leader in automotive concepts. In the late 1960s, the Perkins diesel engine was made an available option. Checker became the first American manufacturer in almost 30 years to offer an alternative to gasoline propulsion in a production automobile. Another period of experimentation with diesel engines came in the late 1970s during the short period when Ed Cole, a legend in the history of General Motors, had control of the company. In this endeavor, the experiment was with Volkswagen diesel engines.

The history of the company's association with diesel power provides an excellent example of how difficult it is to separate fact from fiction, as well as how many chapters are yet to be written about this fascinating company. A few years ago, research in the International Harvester archives brought to light an intriguing memo from 1956 that indicated a new International diesel was being tested in Checker cabs as well as some light-duty trucks in the New Orleans area.

Although Checker vehicles have been off the streets for more than a decade, internationally Checker is still seen as an inseparable part of the urban landscape that is New York City. Perhaps an even more amazing testimony can be found in the fact that the reputation of these legendary automobiles and the loyalty of proud owners remain undiminished more than 20 years after the last car rolled off the line in Kalamazoo.

Promotion for the non-commercial version of the Checker, as evidenced by this brochure from 1962, emphasized many of the features that had made the cabs so popular. Checker Cab: A Photo History by Iconografix

40th Anniversary CHECKER

COMFORT and ELEGANCE ARE ADDED TO THE BRAWNY, BUILT TO LAST CHECKER

1957 Chevy
Icon of the car-show circuit

The 1957 Chevrolet represents one of the more enigmatic chapters in modern car culture. While new, it was a rather anemic seller because the general body styling was rater dated, especially when compared with the offerings of Ford and Chrysler. Then there were the quality-control problems. Nevertheless, as a used car it proved to be a hot seller, especially among young adults. Today, two generations later, it is a favorite among middle-aged car enthusiasts looking for a reminder of their "glory days."

In spite of its shortcomings, the 1957 Chevrolet hardtop or convertible is today one of the most sought-after postwar collector cars. Is it even possible to attend a basic car show without finding at least two or three models?

There was another, shadowy side to Chevrolet in 1957. In the fall of 1956, Vince Piggins was quietly added to the Chevrolet payroll. Piggins was the former chief engineer for Hudson's racing program during the late 1940s and early 1950s, when the company dominated the racing circuit. His first assignment was to travel to Atlanta and set up the Southern Engineering and Development Company (SEDCO). Officially, even though it was funded by $750,000 from the Chevrolet budget, this company was created as a division of Atlanta's Nalley Chevrolet in an effort to limit the manufacturer's liability.

In 1957, Chevrolet still produced a "utility sedan" with a plywood shelf where the back seat would normally be and absolutely no frills. This was the lightest Chevrolet available that year. In limited numbers, these vehicles were shipped to Piggins at SEDCO.

The cars were then given "slight" modification, including dual shocks as well as replacement of the front spindles and rear axles with those of the half-ton pickup truck. The engines were swapped for fuel-injected 283-cid V-8s. The finished products, dubbed Black Widows, were given identical black-and-white paint jobs.

The exact number of SEDCO Chevrolets produced or still existing is anyone's guess. To date, no official records of production are known to exist. But it is known that the Atlanta shop maintained cars for at least nine stock-car drivers. There must have been another 40 or so available to support the factory teams. Adding to this confusing story and providing another Holy Grail for fans of the 1957 Chevy, dealers were encouraged to construct replicas for short-track racing in their districts.

So the next time you're cruising a car show or special car event, don't be so quick to pass by the row of 1957 Chevrolets. After all, lurking out there somewhere may be something you've never seen: a Black Widow.

The quintessential 1950s cruiser, a 1957 Bel Air convertible, in turquoise and white.

This dealer postcard portrays the '57 Chevrolet at its most basic, a "Two-Ten" sedan in colonial cream and laurel green.

Minivan

Station wagon for the modern era

At the time of its introduction in late 1983, many in the automotive industry viewed the Plymouth Voyager as an innovative vehicle. But in spite of record first-year sales, few realized just how influential this new miniature van from Chrysler would be.

For decades, the station wagon had been the symbolic centerpiece of the suburban household. However, with the introduction of the new "Magic Wagon," as the Voyager was advertised, the decline in the popularity of station wagons that had begun in the 1970s increased dramatically. By the end of the decade, most manufacturers had either suspended or dramatically curtailed production of them.

A large number of the Plymouth Voyager's innovative features soon became industry standards, giving a clear indication of the vehicle's revolutionary nature. Among the standards were: front-wheel drive, power rack-and-pinion steering, dual-path Iso-Strut front suspension, interchangeable or removable rear seats, and an optional 50,000-mile or five-year warranty.

Because of computer-aided design, the Voyager also featured the lowest drag coefficient of any wagon or van produced that year. The initial production facility for the Voyager in Windsor, Ontario, was one of the most technologically advanced production facilities in the world, and it included 120 robot welders.

However, these innovations in production and design are only one example of the influence the Plymouth Voyager exerted. With its introduction and subsequent popularity, the American vocabulary was expanded to include a new term: minivan.

The Plymouth Voyager, introduced in 1984, represented a quantum leap in the evolution of the station wagon and became a milestone vehicle in the American automotive industry.

Voyager LE, shown in Saddle Brown Crystal Coat with optional styled road wheels.

One flexible system to move people and cargo with ease.

Voyager's exceptional roominess and 125 cubic feet of cargo capacity (with seats removed) are made possible by its front-wheel drive design and by the "flexibility" of one of the most advanced passenger seating/cargo carrying systems ever conceived.

Voyager's standard seating is for five people—two low-back bucket seats in front, and a three-passenger rear bench seat with fixed armrests. Front reclining high-back buckets with integral headrests are standard on Voyager LE.

Maximum flexibility comes with the optional Seven-Passenger Seating Package available on SE and LE models. The second seat position is a two-passenger, fixed-back bench seat with fixed left outboard armrest and right outboard fold-down armrest. It's positioned slightly to the driver's side, permitting easy entry to the third seat and cargo area through Voyager's sliding side door and rear liftgate.

The third seat is a unique three-passenger bench seat with a seatback that can fold flat, with a hard backing for package storage. The seatback can be locked in either the upright or folded position with a convenient recessed latch. An adjustable track provides 6½ inches of travel, allowing the third seat to be moved up against the second for additional luggage space. Color-keyed track covers give a clean appearance at all times.

What makes this seven-passenger system so flexible is the quick-release floor attachment provided for each rear seat. One or both seats can be easily removed for approximately 40 percent more cargo space (125 cubic feet with both rear seats removed) than a full-size conventional wagon with rear seats folded down! These seats—with attached seat belts—can be replaced just as easily, to accommodate four, five or seven people.

Voyager's low, flat floor gives passengers 47.6 inches of walk-through space and makes loading and unloading much more convenient.

47.6"

81.9"   48.2"

Voyager's standard five-passenger seating lets you remove rear seat for cargo.

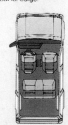

Voyager's optional Seven-Passenger Seating Package gives you interchangeable, removable rear seats you can arrange to suit your needs.

Convertible

Top-down fun

With the introduction of the Ford Tudor sedan in 1915 and the Essex closed-sedan models in late 1919, the practicality of the all-weather car was made available to even the most budget-minded consumer. For the first time, ownership of a convertible became a matter of preference.

Even though the demand for open models ebbed and flowed throughout the coming decades, few manufacturers suspended their production entirely. In fact, quite often manufacturers chose the open models as their show cars. It was during the immediate postwar years, an era of unprecedented optimism and prosperity, that the convertible's popularity peaked. As a result, it is largely the classic chrome-bedecked, tail-finned land yachts of the 1950s that most often come to mind when conversations turn toward convertibles. Internationally, these cars have come to symbolize the romantic era of Route 66, road trips, poodle skirts, jukeboxes, and Saturday-night cruising under the neon.

The upper-end models of this group, like the 1958 Eldorado Biarritz and Imperial, transcend mere transportation; in some circles, they have even been described as rolling sculpture. However, even more plebeian convertibles like the 1957 Chevrolet and 1955 Ford Skyliner are recognized as classics without equal.

Like the fascination with Route 66, the present-day popularity of the 1950s convertible doesn't accurately reflect how it was perceived in its own time. These cars often leaked, were frequently

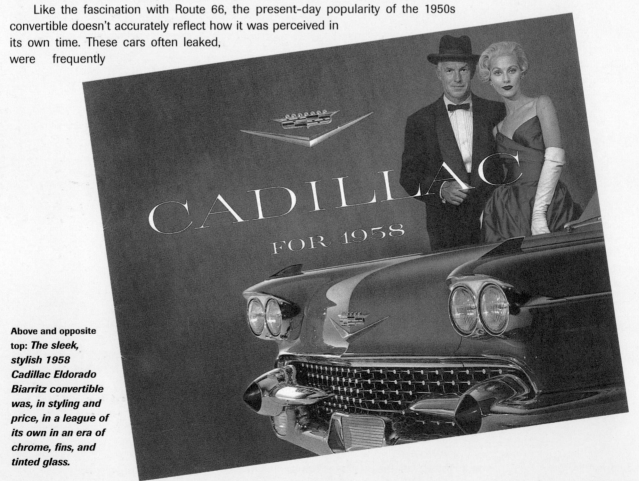

Above and opposite top: The sleek, stylish 1958 Cadillac Eldorado Biarritz convertible was, in styling and price, in a league of its own in an era of chrome, fins, and tinted glass.

cold in the winter, and, as secondhand cars, became ragtops if the owner was not in a position to pay for new canvas.

For 1957, Ford introduced a car that seemed to offer the promise of both worlds. The Skyliner retractable hardtop provided the all-weather comfort of a hardtop and the wind-in-your-hair, top-down fun for those sunny summer days. Nevertheless, buyers never materialized in the numbers envisioned, so 1959 was the final year for this unique automobile.

After almost two decades of limited popularity, the convertible is back in vogue. A new generation is experiencing the open road with the feeling of unbridled freedom, with the warmth of the sun on their faces and the wind in their hair.

Convertibles, such as the 1939 and 1940 Buick, may have been stylish but seldom enjoyed brisk sales. Interestingly enough, the convertible today is often one of the more sought-after body styles.

Corvette

America's sports car

The 1953 Motorama held at New York City's Waldorf-Astoria Hotel was full of surprises. However, few of these would have as much far-reaching impact as a prototype roadster boldly named Corvette, the result of a last-minute change from Corvair.

The response was so intense that General Motors management authorized production to commence immediately. Just over six months later, on June 30, 1953, the first production Corvette was completed. At the rate of about five units per day, an additional 299 soon followed.

For those who had been following the automotive trends of the postwar years, the excitement stirred by the new Chevrolet roadster came as no surprise. European sports cars had been the focus of a rapidly expanding niche market for several years before the Corvette's introduction. In 1952, 11,000 sports cars were registered in the United States, which marked a dramatic increase from the few 100 reported just five years before.

Initially, the Corvette was planned to be a steel-bodied vehicle. But fiberglass (at GM the new material was known by the name GRP, or glass-reinforced plastic) proved to be a viable and cost-effective material for low-production specialty cars, such as the Kaiser Darrin built in Jackson, Michigan, in 1952.

All 300 Corvettes produced in 1953 were white. The options list was succinct: signal-seeking AM radio, heater, and whitewall tires. With a base price of $3,498—more than that of a Jaguar—and a drivetrain that was little more than a modified version of what could be found in a four-door sedan, the expected rush never really materialized. Amazingly, today 255 of these original Corvettes are still in existence.

By December 1953, GM's Corvette production facility was completed in Saint Louis, Missouri, with plans for annual production of 10,000 units for the new model year. But the optimism soon gave way to reality. At the end of the following year, dealers were holding 1,000 unsold units, almost 1/3 of the first year's total production.

Many in General Motors management were in favor of pulling the plug on the project. Almost as quickly as serious discussions to do so commenced, an emergency in the

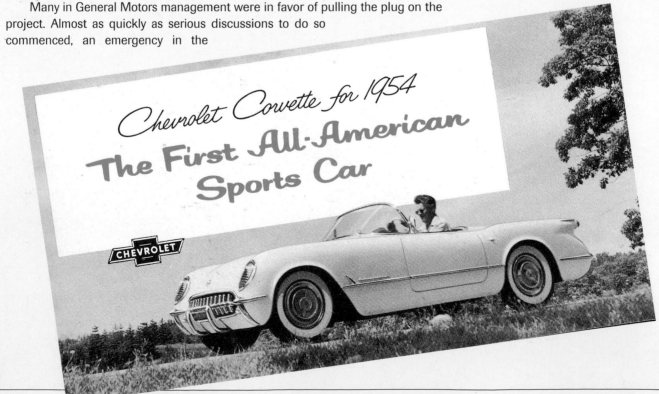

Chevrolet Corvette for 1954
The First All-American Sports Car

CHEVROLET

*Opposite and right: **In 1954 the optimistic advertisement and promotion for the Corvette did not match the reality of sluggish sales or a sports car that was one in looks only.***

It's fun to drive a Corvette

If you're young in heart, you'll like the Chevrolet Corvette. It's a joy to own and thrilling to drive.

Designed for sports-loving, fun-loving people, it combines the sensational performance of the sports car with the luxury of the modern passenger car. The Corvette sets the standard for a coming field
—THE AMERICAN SPORTS CAR.

form of a competitor arose. In late 1954, Ford introduced its sporty Thunderbird roadster, and the only competition GM could provide was the Corvette.

The addition of a V-8 engine for 1955 moved the Corvette closer to being what its design indicated it was: a sports car. Yet, there were still serious shortcomings in the car, such as its suspension. For 1955 the Corvette did not share the new ball-joint front suspension employed on regular passenger cars; instead, the old front suspension first introduced in 1949 Chevrolets was utilized. Another determent to the Corvette meeting its full potential was that until the end of the model year the only transmission option was the Powerglide.

A long options list and new array of available colors were not enough to breathe life into the Corvette. Only 700 vehicles were produced for 1955. Obviously, if production were to continue, dramatic and immediate change was needed.

Topping the list of changes made for 1956 were performance packages that included a dual four-barrel carburetor and a V-8 engine rated at 240 horsepower. Finally, sports car enthusiasts had a car to respond to, and production surged to almost 3,500 units. The following year was a replay of 1956: an increased number of performance-option packages, improved styling, and increased sales.

The rest, as they say, is history. The Corvette's initial shortcomings have largely been forgotten or overlooked, and the Corvette today is internationally recognized as "America's sports car."

The Kaiser Darrin, a limited-production vehicle produced in Jackson, Michigan, preceded the introduction of the Corvette and pioneered the use of fiberglass in car bodies.

Duesenberg
Monarch of the highway

When the now-legendary Duesenberg Model J made its debut at the New York Automobile Salon in December 1928, the Duesenberg name was already quite well known among racing and automotive enthusiasts. The Duesenberg brothers, Fred and Augie, had been building some of the most advanced racing engines available for nearly two decades. In addition, they had also built quality aeronautical engines during World War I, marine engines, and, as of 1920, a limited-production automobile that featured a plethora of technologically advanced features.

The Model J was to be the crown jewel, and the stuff of legend. Its massive chromed and polished straight-eight engine was a mechanical work of art, with twin overhead camshafts and four valves per cylinder, and a drop-forged crankshaft made of heat-treated chrome nickel and aluminum alloy pistons. A gear-driven oil pump provided full pressure with a capacity of 22 gallons per minute. The 8-gallon cooling system kept everything cool. To ensure exceptionally smooth performance, the crankshaft, cradled in five oversize main bearings, was counterweighted and balanced statically and dynamically. A vibration damper with two 16-ounce cartridges of mercury completed the package.

Rated at 265 horsepower, it was the most powerful production car in America. For 1932, perfection was improved upon; the supercharged SJ was made available with a horsepower increase to a conservatively rated 320.

In the months preceding the auto show, E. L. Cord, a master of promotion and publicity, had stoked the public's interest with carefully prepared press releases. One of the releases proclaimed that "with a standard touring body and with top and windshield up and fenders on, this car has attained 116 miles per hour, while a speed of 89 miles per hour has been reached in second gear." These feats happened at a time when the latest Cadillac rated at 95 horsepower was lauded for its performance—and the Packard 640 was rated at 106 horsepower!

In an initial speed test of a convertible coupe SJ at the Indianapolis track, the top speed came in just under 130 miles per hour. A few years later, professional driver Abe Jenkins pushed a Duesenberg to 152.1 miles per hour and set a 24-hour-record average speed of 135.5 miles per hour at Bonneville.

But the Duesenberg was not just a car known for its incredible "go." The coachwork offered was some of the finest available. Still, many buyers chose to personalize their cars and hired the finest craftsmen on both sides of the Atlantic to transform them.

Even in an era of opulent automobiles and classic styling, the Duesenberg was in a league of its own. It was massive in scale: wheelbases ran from 142 1/2 to 153 1/2 inches. With custom coachwork, it often tipped the scale at 5,000 pounds. The cost of the Model J—$8,500 chassis price—was nothing short of astounding in 1930, when $530 could get you a shiny, new Ford coupe.

As a result, the mighty Duesenberg was truly the car for the discriminating few, and the list of owners reads like a who's who of the period: Frank Morgan, who played the Great and Powerful Oz in the film version of *The Wizard of Oz*; Greta Garbo; Jackie Coogan; and Colonel Jacob Schick of Schick Shavers. A fortunate few chose to own several: Philip Wrigley, the chewing-gum king, owned five; Gary Cooper had two, but not at the same time; and Clark Gable also owned two.

Few automobiles have combined speed, performance, and luxury in one package as successfully as the Duesenberg. Even fewer have become a metaphor for something without equal: "It's a Duesey."

The many superlatives these now legendary vehicles represented are not found in this rare advertisement for what, arguably, is the finest American automobile ever built—the Duesenberg.

THE PHAETON

Duesenberg

265 HORSEPOWER

"THE WORLD'S FINEST MOTOR CAR"
WORKS: INDIANAPOLIS, IND.

Edsel
Lemon or lemonade?

The Edsel, conceived to fill the market gap between the Mercury and Lincoln brands, would be a sure winner, according to Ford Motor Company marketing surveys, design teams, and management. In January 1957, Richard Krafve, general manager of the Edsel Division, said, "The new Edsel line of cars will surpass the originally announced first-year sales goal of 200,000 units." As it turned out, they were all wrong. The result was a loss in excess of $250 million dollars and a face for the term "flop."

Introduction for the new line, named for the son of Henry Ford, had been initially planned for 1957. However, production delays and other associated problems resulted in the car's introduction as a 1958 model on September 4, 1957, just in time for a major economic downturn. The recession that year was so severe that Dodge sales were off by 47 percent, Pontiac sales by 28 percent, and Mercury sales by 48 percent. Then there were the issues regarding quality control and glitches with "futuristic" components, such as the push-button shift in the center of the steering wheel.

As a result, sales for the first year were dismal and barely topped 60,000 units. For 1959, the number dropped to under 44,000. The Edsel was given a facelift for 1960 in the hopes that the project could be salvaged. The Edsel's now-famous grille was replaced with a more conventional design, more reminiscent of that used on GM's Pontiac. The "horse-collar" grille theme was retained only on the tail lamps. But the revamp was to no avail; fewer than 3,000 vehicles were produced before production ended with little fanfare.

Today, the Edsel enjoys a small but devoted following. Some of the rarer versions such as the Bermuda wagon and Corsair and Citation convertibles command premium prices in the car collector market.

A proud couple takes delivery of their pink-and-white Edsel at the dealership in Kingman, Arizona.

THIS IS THE EDSEL
never before a car like it

newest expression of fine engineering from Ford Motor Company

This introductory brochure for the Edsel reflects the hopes and excitement the company had for this vehicle. Unfortunately, the public did not share in the enthusiasm.

American LaFrance

America's fire truck

Among the nation's firefighters, the name American LaFrance has been synonymous with the fire truck for more than a century, and for good reason. This company has been a leader in the development and production of fire-fighting equipment since 1873, and it has roots all the way back to 1832.

Truckson LaFrance was blessed with an innovative and visionary spirit. Within 15 years of joining the Elmira Union Iron Works in Elmira, New York, he had obtained several patents for improvements to rotary steam engines. With these patents as the foundation, the company now added the manufacture of fire-fighting equipment to the long list of products, including rail-fence machines, cotton pickers, and locomotives, that rolled from the factories.

In April 1873, a consortium of local businessmen bought the company, purchased 100 acres of real estate, built a modern manufacturing facility, and began serious production of mounted steam engine–powered pumps as fire engines. Organized as LaFrance Manufacturing Company, the new enterprise centered on the genius of Truckson LaFrance as its mechanical engineer.

In 1878, the company built a new-style fire engine. Hoping for international sales, LaFrance shipped the unit to the Paris Exposition, but the boiler thickness did not comply with French law, so the engine was never demonstrated. The failure of the venture, as well as expense incurred in its construction and shipping, nearly brought the company to ruin.

Thomas Hotchkiss, an Elmira businessman, offered to finance the construction of another engine provided it was named after his wife. The resultant Jeanie Jewell was displayed and demonstrated at numerous trade shows and expositions with great success. To exploit this success, better focus company resources, and capitalize on the new rotary nest tube boiler invented by Truckson LaFrance, the firm instituted reorganization under the name LaFrance Steam Engine Company in 1880.

In the decades that followed, the company developed innovation after innovation. In 1882, an arrangement was made with Daniel Hayes, inventor of an extension-ladder truck, to manufacture the ladder trucks conjoined to LaFrance steam-engine pumps. Two years later, the company introduced piston steam engines. In 1894, the company became the first to offer chemical units for fire fighting.

These innovations made the development of high-rise structures more practical. As a result, the skylines of America and the world were forever changed.

The company introduced its first self-propelled unit in 1907. Interestingly enough, the company's first motorized vehicles were introduced in 1903 as "chief's cars." Another slight deviation from the construction of fire engines came in the form of a powerful sport roadster in 1911; this was the last automobile produced by the company.

After deciding that conventional gasoline engines were inadequate for the needs of fire trucks, the company designed its own six-cylinder engine in 1910. In addition, the company manufactured and marketed a front-wheel-drive conversion unit, which converted the horse-drawn steam engines and ladder wagons into gasoline engine-powered fire trucks.

In 1912, the company closed the door on the steam-powered era. It would, however, continue to produce steam engines for several more years with the introduction of a motorized pump truck. The truck was the only vehicle to receive a perfect score from the Underwriters Laboratories test that year. This tight focus on the development of vehicles for a single purpose enabled the company to continue into modern times as an industry leader.

Over the years, the engines developed or adapted by the company have become as legendary as the vehicles themselves. Of particular note were two V-12 engines, the first, introduced in 1931, which increased the capacity of its pump trucks to 1,500 gallons per minute and was used to power Greyhound buses as well as generators on electric trains. Auburn/Cord/Duesenberg had designed the second engine for use in a second-generation Cord. As this car never materialized, this engine was used by Auburn in its Custom and Salon 12s during the early 1930s. The engine was then modified by American LaFrance and used into the mid-1960s.

Adapting its equipment to a variety of chassis has also enabled the company to garner a larger share of the fire-fighting apparatus market, including those items built for specialty applications such as aircraft-crash and all-terrain rescue vehicles. During the teens and early 1920s, the smallest versions were fitted to the light-duty Model T Ford. At the other end of the spectrum were the massive General Motors diesel units so familiar in larger cities during the 1950s and 1960s.

The company, still operating in Elmira, New York, recently expanded facilities and is still a world leader in the development and production of fire equipment. Vintage fire trucks are a cherished piece of American history, and those produced by American LaFrance are the crown jewel of any collection.

The American LaFrance type 75 combination pumping engine and hose car represented state-of-the-art technology in fire-fighting equipment in 1915.

The Big Rig

The heavy hauler; a brief history of trucking culture

If the astronomical rise of the public embrace of the automobile between 1900 and 1920 was an amazing phenomenon, the acceptance of trucks was nothing short of miraculous. Initially the replacement of the draft horse or team by the truck was limited to urban domains. Then the success of trucks used in World War I prompted a grand experiment: the First Transcontinental Motor Train, which launched an industry and finalized the demise of the horse's dominance.

The Autocar U70 series introduced in the early 1950s represented the culmination of more than half a century of truck development for the company.

The First Transcontinental Motor Train was a caravan of 81 vehicles (loaded trucks that included complete machine shops that weighed in excess of 10 tons, scout cars, and motorcycles) that left Washington, D.C., on July 7, 1919, bound for San Francisco. A few days short of two full months later, they arrived in San Francisco and had covered a total distance of 3,250 miles.

In spite of deep mud, cloying sands, inadequate bridges, intense desert heat, and brutal roads, the convoy, with the exception of six vehicles, completed the epic journey. The viability of

HOME OF FINE FOODS AND GOOD SERVICE

THE P-K TRUCK STOP RESTAURANT

MEALS AT ALL HOURS

ON U. S. 30 & U. S. 25 (CROSS ROADS OF AMERICA) BEAVERDAM, OHIO

In the era of the two-lane highway, this rule of thumb applied when it came to finding good food on the road: eat where the truckers do.

long-haul trucking had been proven, provided the roads were improved, and this added momentum to an ever-growing cry for road improvements.

However, the life of the truck driver in the formative years of the industry was not an easy one. What is today a six-hour cruise across the Mojave Desert between Los Angeles and Kingman, Arizona, just east of the California line, was at least a 12-hour run in 1938. Steep grades often dropped speeds for loaded trucks to less than 10 miles per hour. This prompted frustrated motorists to take daring chances, which in turn resulted in white-knuckle near misses.

The vehicles themselves required men, and occasionally women, to be as tough as the trucks they drove. The convoy of 1919 largely consisted of trucks that rolled on solid rubber wheels, with power from the engine transferred to the rear wheels via chain drive. By the late 1930s, truck drivers were labeled "gear jammers" for good reason. Many trucks had four-speed transmissions; a three-speed "brownie box," also known as a gear splitter; and a two- or three-speed rear end.

In the early 1950s, a first-seat, or solo, driver was paid about $160 per round-trip load. "Cruise control" was a two-by-four stump jammed between the seat frame and accelerator. The new Kenworth, in 1949, cost $15,200, and a gallon of diesel cost 14.9 cents. By this time, diesel-powered trucks were rapidly replacing the less powerful gasoline models.

Manufacturers of heavy-duty trucks often found that their products developed strong brand loyalty. Macks, REOs, and Freightliners, Kenworths and Federals, Whites and Peterbilts became legends of the highway heralded in song and tall tales told over steaming cups of coffee. Some companies built unique and even bizarre vehicles that allowed the operator or trucking company to diversify for greater profit. One of the most unusual has to be the "Bruck," a combination bus and box truck, built by Kenworth in 1949.

Businesses such as the Dixie Truckers Home on Route 66 in Illinois were created to meet the special needs of the long-haul trucker and became a key component in the mystique of the road. This particular establishment became an icon of the highway encapsulating the development of long-haul trucking. It opened its doors in January of 1928, weathered the hard times of the Great Depression, became a haven for weary transported troops during the war, survived a devastating fire in 1965, and held on even though its lifeline, Route 66, was severed in 1984. On July 31, 2003, the Dixie Truckers Home passed into corporate hands, and another legend of the highway succumbed to the conformity of the modern era.

Now, times have changed. The two-lane highway is in many locations a thing of the past. The rough-hewn truck stop of old has given way to the family-friendly travel plaza with video arcade and mini-mart. The trucks now have many of the comforts of home, from television to air conditioning. The equipment available, from automatic transmissions to power steering, is a far cry from the days of strong-arming the steering wheel, cranking open the windshield for ventilation, and climbing grades at speeds so low they didn't register on the speedometer. But while much has changed, one thing over the years has remained consistent: the life of the long-haul trucker is still a rough and lonely one requiring days at a time on the road.

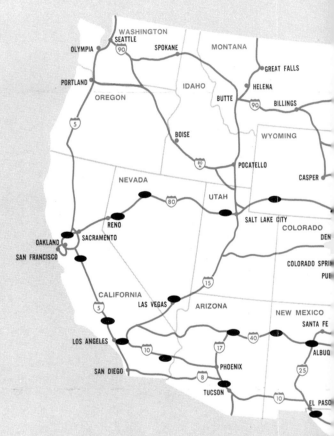

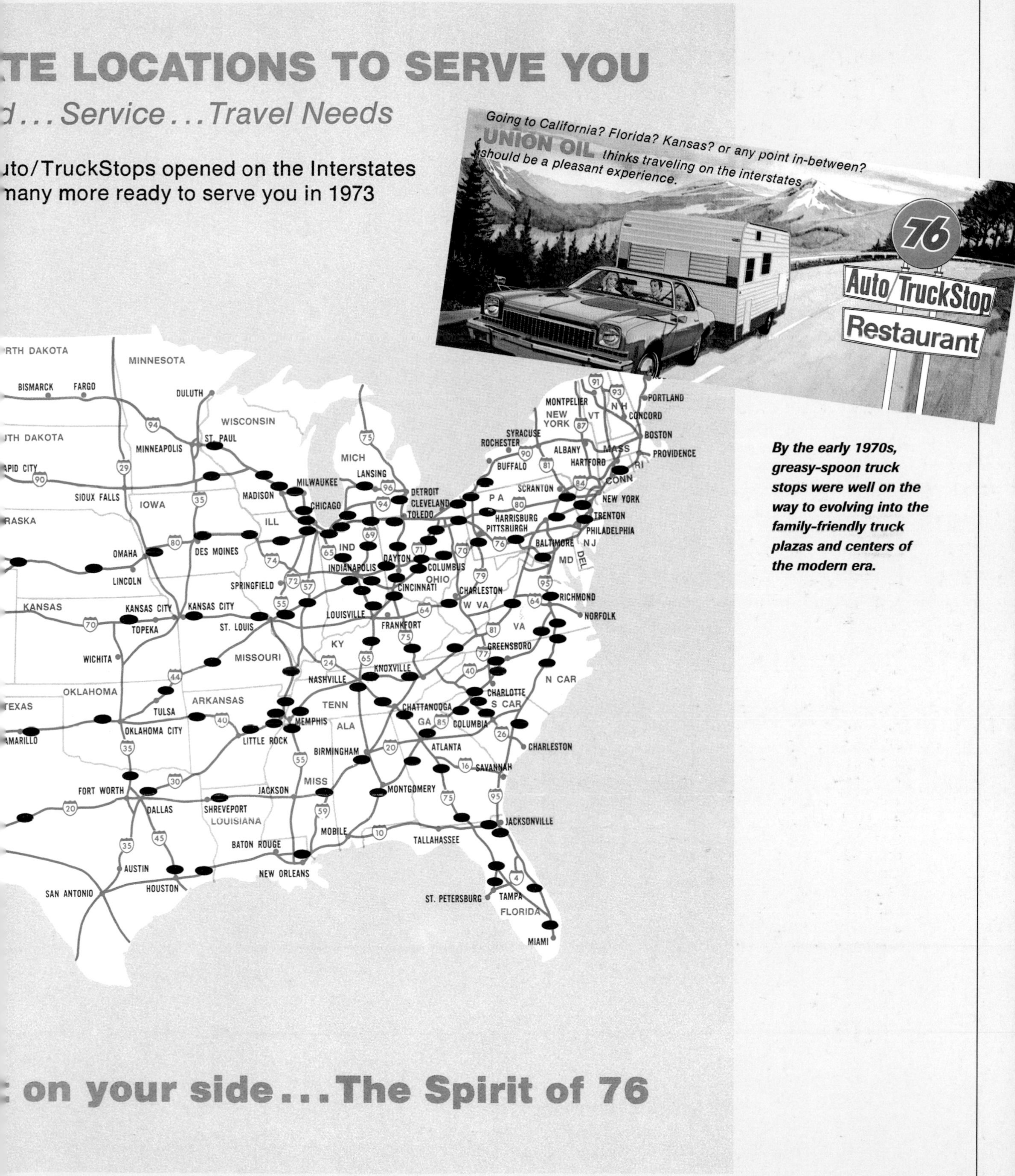

TE LOCATIONS TO SERVE YOU

d...Service...Travel Needs

uto/TruckStops opened on the Interstates
many more ready to serve you in 1973

Going to California? Florida? Kansas? or any point in-between?
UNION OIL thinks traveling on the interstates
should be a pleasant experience.

76
Auto/TruckStop
Restaurant

By the early 1970s, greasy-spoon truck stops were well on the way to evolving into the family-friendly truck plazas and centers of the modern era.

: on your side...The Spirit of 76

Ice Cream Trucks
A summertime classic

"**I**ce cream! Ice cream! You scream, I scream, we all scream for ice cream!" It's the childhood mantra of summer.

Historic references to this standard summer treat date to the reign of Nero, Roman emperor, who enjoyed ice brought from the mountains and covered with fresh fruit, and King Tang of China, who in about 620 A.D. enjoyed a blend of milk, ice, and fruit.

The American association with ice cream has been a long one. The earliest American reference to "ice cream" is in regard to a dinner hosted by Governor Bladen of Maryland in 1700, and the first ice cream parlor was opened in New York City in 1776.

The edible cone made its debut in America at the 1904 Saint Louis World's Fair. While several vendors sold the ice cream in a variety of edible cups, it was a Lebanese immigrant, Abe Doumar, who receives the credit for being the inventor of the cone. He built the first machine designed solely for making waffle-type cones.

Harry Burt, an innovative confectioner, developed a smooth chocolate coating to top those cones in 1920. In fact, because he wanted to combine the two treats without creating a huge mess, his son suggested he freeze his Jolly Boy Sucker sticks into the ice cream, then cover the ice cream with chocolate.

Now all that was needed was a name for his new treat. After observing customers' response to the new taste sensation, he hit upon the idea of calling them Good Humor bars. Then, to expand the market beyond his small parlor, he hired a dozen chauffeur-driven trucks, with bells, to make deliveries throughout the neighborhood—the Good Humor man had arrived.

This period photograph from the mid-1920s is a time capsule for the origins of an American icon: the Good Humor man. **Unilever Ice Cream North America**

The idea caught the attention of New York investor and businessman M. J. Meehan in 1930. Meehan saw great potential in expanding the business as well as the market for the project. He acquired the national rights to the company by buying 75 percent of the company's shares.

By 1950, the Good Humor man had become an institution, and the fleet of trucks was expanding at a steady clip. Then in 1961, the company was sold to Unilever's U.S. subsidiary, the Thomas J. Lipton Company. By 1970, the bottom line reflected the harsh reality: the Good Humor truck may have been an American icon, but it was not a profitable one.

In 1976, with little fanfare, the company ended its long history of direct selling and focused solely on wholesale to grocery stores. The Good Humor trucks were sold but not forgotten, and to this day a few that have been lovingly restored can still be found at auto shows throughout the country.

This promotional photograph was produced to highlight the lengths to which the Good Humor man would go to please customers. **Unilever Ice Cream North America**

GTO
The legendary goat

The Pontiac GTO is legendary. As with most legends, it often becomes difficult to sort fact from fiction when trying to discover its heritage. Suffice it to say, the developmental origins of the GTO are somewhat murky. The results, however, are crystal clear.

The story, so legend goes, begins in early 1963 with a decision by General Motors' top management to suspend promotion through factory-sponsored racing. This did not sit well with Pontiac General Manager Pete Estes. Estes knew that the Pontiac division's recent rise to third place was largely the result of a performance image that was attracting younger buyers.

The point was driven home in a meeting with Jim Wagners, an avid performance enthusiast, drag racer, part-time product planner for Pontiac, and account executive for the advertising agency that handled Pontiac. But Wagner had what he believed was a solution: a simple engine swap. In other versions of the story, the idea was Bill Collins' or Russ Gee's.

As Wagner saw it, the new intermediate A-body-series Tempest was made to order for a special version that would include the big 389-cid engine, heavier suspension, and a few other tweaks. They even went one step further in the idea of the perfect performance car by devising a name for the series that tied it to the Ferrari Gran Turismo Omologato: GTO. With the basic idea out in the open, the next challenge was to sell the idea to the front office. To further ensure their scheme would fly, they enlisted the aid of Pontiac's Chief Engineer, John DeLorean.

The idea, so the story goes, was met with cautious approval for limited production as a 1964 series. Original production plans called for 5,000 units to test the market.

The response from customers was overwhelming. Sales were stymied at 32,000 units because of the availability of the 389-cid V-8. Fueling the explosion of interest was the release of the song, "GTO," which sold more than 1 million records, and a *Car and Driver* comparison story that pitted the GTO against the Ferrari.

The sales brochure for 1964 encapsulated what would become an American automotive legend: "Pontiac GTO. A device for shrinking time and distance. To be perfectly honest, the GTO is not everyone's cup of tea. Designed as a piece of performance machinery, its purpose in life is to permit you to make the most of your driving skill."

For 1965, the styling was updated, the horsepower of the base engine was increased, and an optional package made it possible to have 360 horsepower at the driver's command. Pontiac truly had a winner with the GTO, and *Motor Trend* named it "Car of the Year." During 1965, its sales skyrocketed to 75,352.

In 1966, the styling was given a sharper new look, and, incredibly, the car now offered even more horsepower. This was also the first year GTO became its own model instead of a Le Mans built with GTO options. However, there were also problems because the weight and girth of the car had been increased. The most pressing problems came from General Motors' management. Halfway through the 1966 model year, top execs initiated a serious crackdown. There would be no more super-performance options, including multiple carburetion setups. In addition, the plug was pulled on all racing-oriented advertisement, and all drag racing of factory-backed cars was to cease immediately.

The 1967 GTO marked a new era for the already legendary model. The 389 V-8 was replaced with a bored-out version rated at 400 cubic inches. Though similar to the 1966 version, the body was cleaner with less chrome to break the crisp lines. In addition, a ram-air option introduced in mid-model year was a concession to the demand for the performance the series had become famous for.

The 1968 models were all new from the ground up. Moreover, even though the cars were given a more sporty appearance and performance was more than adequate, the series had been transformed into a mutant. It had a blend of luxury and performance that would be with the GTO to 1974, its final year.

"The Judge," named after an expression from the popular television show *Laugh-In*, was introduced as a special edition for 1969. Pop-art striping, identification decals, and carousel red paint set this GTO apart.

In 1971, General Motors lowered the engine compression ratios for all models, and the GTO was not exempt. For 1972, the GTO came full circle. It was offered as an option for the Le Mans series. Two years later, the GTO was discontinued, and it joined other legendary models as historic footnotes created by GM sanctions that reduced engine power and resulted in decreased consumer demand.

Then for 2004, Pontiac revived the name with a new sporty coupe that featured rear-wheel drive, a V-8 engine, and a six-speed manual transmission. The verdict is still out, but it looks as though it will take more than name recognition and a glorious history to make this new version of the venerable GTO the "King of the Street."

This dealer post card accentuates the clean lines, aggressive stance, and subdued conveyance of raw power that has made the 1967 Pontiac GTO a modern classic.

1967 PONTIAC
PONTIAC GTO

OUR BEST GET BETTER

THE 1967 PONTIAC GTO

MURPHY PONTIAC, INC.
225-229 North Elm Street
Troy, Ohio

Streamliners

Getting the drag out of driving

Throughout the history of the automobile, there have been certain vehicles that seemed to burst onto the scene without warning and be exactly what the consumer wants, becoming industry trendsetters. However, upon careful evaluation, we find that the appearance of instant success is an illusion whenever a given vehicular concept had been previewed before with disastrous results or was simply too advanced for public acceptance at that time. The Plymouth Voyager of 1984 is an excellent example of a vehicle that was an instant success that had been founded on an earlier, failed concept.

Eliminating the drag caused by wind resistance for faster, more stable, and more fuel-efficient vehicles was manifest in the Chrysler Airflow, but it was not the first. Martin Aircraft

The Stout Scarab received little positive response in 1936, but many of its features came together in the highly successful Chrysler-built minivan of the 1980s.

made an effort to introduce aeronautical concepts to the automobile in 1928 with a fascinating prototype vehicle tagged "Aerodynamic Auto." With a rounded front, recessed headlamps, and an oddly, almost cartoonish, rounded body, the Martin car had to have been a real attention-grabber in traffic.

Before 1940, more often than not, streamlined vehicles served a promotional purpose rather than to advance theories of wind-reduction designs. McQuay-Norris, of Saint Louis, Missouri, produced a variety of overhaul parts for gasoline engines as well as other replacement parts. In 1932, the company contracted Hill Auto Body Metal Company of Cincinnati, Ohio, to build six identical streamlined vehicles on 1932 Ford chassis. These unusual automobiles served as promotion and as vehicles that allowed for the testing of products produced by the company while making deliveries.

Arrowhead Spring Water Company of Los Angeles also chose the streamlined vehicle as a means of promotion in 1936. However, this teardrop-shaped vehicle also represented an exercise in engineering, as it featured a rear-mounted V-8 and a three-wheeled chassis.

However, the vehicle that best combined the attributes of the modern minivan was the Scarab, first introduced in 1932. Designed by William Stout and built by the Stout Engineering Laboratories, the Scarab featured unitized body construction and aeronautical streamlining, and it was powered by a rear-mounted Ford V-8 coupled to a transaxle.

The improved preproduction version of 1935 also featured an interior strikingly similar to that which appeared on the minivan of the 1980s. This included removable individual seats, panoramic visibility, and a collapsible table.

However, it was too much, too soon. Records indicate that only five were produced, plus an improved prototype in 1946. The minivan would have to wait almost 40 years before the world was ready.

The Bus
Leave the driving to us

Intercity bus service is another one of those ideas that so obviously had potential that many entrepreneurs came up with the idea at the same time. In the northwest deserts of Arizona, Arthur Black began offering scheduled service between Kingman and Phoenix before 1920. In Luling, Texas, at about the same time, a Packard was modified to carry numerous passengers between railroad connections. The discovery of oil north of Austin, Texas, after World War I and the distance of the boom towns from established rail lines made the establishment of bus lines a natural next step.

During the same period, Carl Wickman established the Mesaba Transportation Company to transport iron miners between Hibbing and Alice, Minnesota. For 25 cents, or 15 cents for a one-way trip, miners could relax in the comfort of Wickman's Hupmobile and leave the driving to him.

IMPERIAL PALACE PULLMAN OF THE HIGHWAY
27 Passengers
WHITE SIX MODEL 54 CHASSIS
THE BENDER BODY COMPANY
CLEVELAND, OHIO

M67—Greyhound Bus Depot, Minneapolis, Minn.

City of Lakes and Parks

7A-H2100

By the late 1940s, bus stations were well on their way to supplanting railroad stations as America's primary mass-transportation terminals. This linen post card is of the former main terminal in Minneapolis, today the home of the renowned First Avenue music venue.

"RIDING TRAILWAYS THROUGH THE LAND OF THE LONG LEAF PINE"

This linen post card captures the colorful buses of the Trailways system, which was Greyhound's chief competitor during the 1940s and 1950s.

The increasing popularity of intercity, as well as intracity, bus service spurred established manufacturers to begin building a variety of coaches. The most popular design was the Safety Coach, with seven rows of seating for four people each. Buses, as with vehicles in general, were rapidly being developed with improved safety and comfort features.

By 1926, more than 4,000 small independent lines offered intercity service. As William Durant had done by combining several carmakers into General Motors, two men, Carl Wickman of Mesaba Transportation Company and Orville Caesar, did by joining forces to form a new company, Motor Transportation Company, to offer expanded service. Four years later, after the acquisition of numerous smaller companies, the company was once again reorganized under the name Greyhound Corporation.

In the fall of 1928, Pickwick Lines introduced special "Nite Coaches" built on GM chassis. These massive double-decked buses had capacity for 53 passengers and were the first to feature restroom facilities. Two years later, Pickwick was absorbed by Greyhound.

Opposite: The railcar influence on the development of buses built for intercity transit is seen in these promotional catalog shots produced for the Bender Body Company.

The railroad influence on buses could be found on many early coaches. Most notably, was the observation platform found on the rear of many buses during the 1920s.

By 1936, Greyhound was close to dominating the intercity bus business. It had implemented a highly successful advertising campaign that promoted the scenic and historic wonders to be found throughout the country, as well as the advantages of leaving the driving to someone else. The only competition on a national level was the National Trailways System, a company that had absorbed many of the railroad-owned bus systems. The year 1936 also marked the end of Greyhound's use of buses with conventional hood and engine in front, and GM's first offering of diesel power for its buses.

World War II was to be the high-water mark for passenger bus service. In the immediate postwar years, airline service and an increase in private automobile usage began to take their toll. The addition of highly advanced coaches such as the now legendary Scenicruiser (which seemed to fore-shadow stylistically the Olds Vista Cruiser station wagon) in 1954 did little to stem the flow. Even though the bus remained a popular means of travel, especially for those on a budget, by 1980 the number of riders was but a fraction of what it had been in 1942.

The Greyhound, a true legend of the highway, lives on in spite of the changing times. Yet in light of the decline of the past decade, the question remains as to how much longer the dog will run.

This brochure from 1949 reflects the growth and transition of intercity bus travel from mere transportation to tour bus, and the foundations of Greyhound's eventual domination of the market.

Hummer and Jeeps
The king is dead, long live the king

Over the years, numerous manufacturers and innovators have applied the principle of four-wheel-drive to vehicles. While racing spurred many automotive developments, four-wheel-drive advancement owed a great deal to the needs of the military.

In 1907, Otto Zachow and his brother-in-law, William Besserdich, invented the double-Y universal joint encased in a ball-and-socket joint. This invention allowed for power to be transmitted to the front wheels, while retaining a modest turning radius. An outgrowth of this innovative idea was the formation of the FWD Company to produce four-wheel-drive vehicles.

Initially the company simply modified two-wheel-drive vehicles into four-wheel drive. The company began construction of trucks built and designed from inception to use all-wheel drive in 1912. The first customer was the British army, which ordered 50 trucks. Interestingly enough, the orders came about as a result of tests conducted by the United States Army in which British observers were present. The United States Army, however, did not begin purchasing these trucks until World War I.

The two decades following the cessation of hostilities saw a dramatic decline in the scope as well as size of the United States Army. Only a few farsighted individuals, such as Colonel Arthur Herrington, a former officer and cofounder of the Marmon-Herrington company, saw the need for a modern mechanized army.

The company had been founded with the sole purpose of developing four-wheel-drive trucks, with a primary market target being military application. The first trucks built in both 4x4 and 6x6 configuration were solely for heavy-duty application. In November of 1936, the company received a unique order from the United States Army to build a vehicle for testing that was smaller than the half-ton Ford 4x4 pickup truck, which was the company's smallest vehicle at the time. The vehicle was to be durable, maneuverable, and have hauling as well as towing capabilities.

By late 1939, the project had resulted in several test vehicles, and none of them were satisfactory. It was becoming increasingly apparent that the United States would soon be drawn into the conflicts that were spreading through Europe and Asia. The Army Utility Vehicle Technical Committee gave the matter priority status, drew up a set of proposed specifications, and in June of 1940 sent them as well as requests for bids to 135 U.S. manufacturers and related companies. The deadline for completion of a prototype was 49 days.

Only two companies took the project seriously enough to respond: American Bantam and Willys. Even though the Willys prototype was the better performer, only the Bantam version met or exceeded all the criteria save the maximum weight requirements of 1,300 pounds; the Bantam prototype weighed 2,030 pounds.

A compromise resulted in the construction of a prototype that was acceptable. However, the government decided Bantam was too small a manufacturer to meet the projected demand. Therefore, the production contracts were awarded to Ford and Willys.

The vehicle christened "Jeep" saw action in all theaters of operation during World War II and met or exceeded all expectations. A resultant worldwide reputation for rugged durability and adaptability to a variety of applications provided an instant postwar market. The question was, however, who would supply the much sought-after civilian version?

The Minneapolis-Moline Company laid claim to having first used the Jeep name on a four-wheel-drive tractor in 1938, and American Bantam claimed the original design. The matter was brought to a head and resolved in 1945 when Willys trademarked the Jeep name.

Willys quickly launched an advertising campaign that reminded the consumer of the Jeep's wartime heritage and showed its usefulness in the civilian market, from plowing snow or fields, to sawing wood and shelling corn. In addition to its reputation, the Jeep afforded the company another advantage: there was no need to retool from wartime production. As a result, the civilian CJ version began rolling from the factory 10 days after VE Day.

THE LEGENDARY H1

As with many of the smaller independent manufacturers, Willys was accustomed to making the most from what was on hand. In 1946, the company offered a two-wheel-drive station wagon that utilized many of the Jeep's mechanical components. A pickup truck in two- as well as four-wheel drive almost immediately followed.

In subsequent years, production of the Jeep continued with little change, as the consumer who wanted a Jeep wanted it for a purpose. The initial civilian version was officially designated as the CJ-2A. In 1949, the CJ-3A was introduced; it featured minor mechanical changes and a one-piece windshield.

In 1952, the CJ-3B with an F-head engine became its replacement. To accommodate the higher-profile engine, the cowl was raised four inches. In an effort to present the same profile, the windshield was lowered by the same amount as compensation. Production of this model continued until 1964. In 1955, the CJ-5 was introduced as a companion model, and production ran through 1975 with little modification. The CJ-6, a longer version of the CJ-5 introduced in 1956, featured a 20-inch longer wheelbase, but maintained the same front clip; the CJ-6 continued to be produced after the CJ-5 was discontinued in 1975.

Now produced by Chrysler, the Jeep's popularity shows no sign of waning. However, its days as king have now passed. In the 1990s, a new breed of off-road vehicle rose to prominence and even replaced the Jeep's role as the military equivalent to the mule: the Humvee or Hummer.

However, the Hummer is more than just an update; it represents a dramatic societal change. The Jeep was no-frills simple, while its replacement is mechanically complicated. The Hummer is a status symbol for the well heeled, while its predecessor was an everyman's vehicle. The Jeep represented the America of World War II; the Hummer, for better or worse, represents the new era.

The Jeep and the Hummer, from promotional materials as seen here to the vehicles' costs, represent two distinctly different concepts in rugged, durable, and adaptable off-road vehicles.

These Soldiers
Go Up in the Air to Prove They Can Take It,
Camp Hood, Texas

PHOTO BY U. S. ARMY SIGNAL CORPS

The American Microcar

Ghost of Christmas future

There has been a great deal of speculation as to why American consumers have most always gravitated to large vehicles. It is almost as though our national psyche has been developed around the romanticized image of the frontier, with its wide-open spaces and larger-than-life heroes.

Even gas shortages, rising costs, and guilt (the result of increased awareness about environmental impact) have not been able to fully break the hypnotic hold of land yachts. As evidence, consider the SUV craze that includes the Hummer, Lincoln Navigator, and Ford Expedition. Also, let us not forget the Chevrolet Suburban.

Over the years there have been a few visionary individuals, home-grown as well as foreign-born, that dared to question the rationale of using a battleship when a rowboat would suffice. But until recent times, these efforts have been met with limited success at best. Even today, when small cars actually compose a respectable share of the market, companies that established themselves by producing diminutive vehicles have been forced to also produce more full-size offerings such as the Nissan Titan.

Even during the hard times of the Great Depression, Americans just couldn't seem to accept the idea of a compact car. The struggles and eventual demise of American Austin (American Bantam after 1938) stand in mute testimony to this viewpoint.

Introduced in 1922, the Austin proved to be a brisk seller in England from its inception. A similar success was achieved in France when the car was built under license as the Rosengart. Ditto for Germany, where the car was sold as the Dixi. So for Sir Herbert Austin, it seemed only logical that America represented a great untapped market for his Lilliputian cars.

Apparently, he was relatively naïve about the American automotive buyer. Saxon had almost met ruin with its miniature version. Even the successful Model T Ford, a relatively large car compared to the Austin, had been replaced by something bigger and more powerful.

Initially, the American Austin introduced in late 1929 as 1930 models were little more than English Austin Sevens with different bodies. The miniature automobiles (credited with being the first American automobile to feature under-the-hood battery placement) were 16 inches narrower and a full 28 inches shorter than any American-produced vehicle. Nevertheless, a guarantee of 40 miles per gallon was not enough to generate sales, especially as the factory list prices started at $445, which was $5 more than a Model A Ford.

However, the diminutive Austin did enjoy a great deal of publicity. Al Jolson, Buster Keaton, and Our Gang, among others, often utilized the cars as a part of their comedy routines; the Austin was seen as little more than a joke. The company went into receivership in 1932 and bankruptcy in 1934. It ceased production in 1935, and was revived in 1937 as American Bantam.

In spite of valiant efforts, surprisingly fine styling, and catchy names like Boulevard Delivery and Hollywood, sales never really materialized for American Bantam. However, there

was one final chapter to be written. In record time, the company designed and built the original Jeep prototype in 1940.

In an intriguing and complicated twist, Austin reappeared on the American auto scene in the 1960s. In 1952, English automobile manufacturers Morris and Austin merged to form the British Motor Corporation. An oil shortage precipitated by Egyptian President Nasser's seizure of the Suez Canal provided a catalyst for European manufacturers to produce fuel-frugal microcars. The BMC version was labeled as the Mini-Minor, which was imported into the United States. By the early 1960s, the cars had evolved into fuel-efficient performance machines. In the decade that followed, the cars also became an icon of the counterculture movement. This was followed by a period of decline and then renaissance with the BMW-produced New Mini in 2004. As with its predecessor, this version has proven to be quite popular among an eclectic range of consumers.

A few entrepreneurs saw the failures of companies such as American Austin as merely opportunities to learn from their mistakes. One of those entrepreneurs was Powell Crosley. The Crosley fortune had been established by making the radio portable and with the addition of features such as a radio built into the door transformed the refrigerator into more than an electric icebox. His dream was to build a truly practical car for the majority of applications: namely, quick, short, local runs.

The extremely short-lived Marathon Six, built in 1909, and a cycle car, the DeCross, built in 1913, marked his first endeavors into automobile production. These vehicles were successful only in the sense that they ran. Undeterred in his quest to popularize the small-car concept, Crosley simply tabled the idea while he made a couple of fortunes in the production of radios and appliances.

Introduced in 1939 at the Indianapolis Speedway, the miniature cars with the Crosley name barely registered on the scale of market shares. By the end of the year, just 2,017 vehicles had

The Crosley Hotshot offered no serious competition for the postwar sports-car market but by 1950 did represent a zenith for the Crosley company.

been produced. In 1946, *Time* magazine summarized the entire small-car concept for the American market when, in a piece on the Crosley, it noted that "the U.S. Motorist has never cared enough for an undersized car to make it profitable to builders."

In June 1939, the car made its official debut at the New York World's Fair. With an anemic 12-horsepower Waukesha engine, an 80-inch wheelbase, and a vehicle weight of 924 pounds, the car was easy to overlook. This was in spite of colorful banners that proclaimed the Crosley to be the "Car of Tomorrow."

Any store that sold Crosley appliances, including Macy's, could be a Crosley car dealer, making the sales network as novel as the cars themselves. Even though the entire concept behind the little cars was decades ahead of its time, the public wasn't ready. And when that was coupled with a plethora of manufacturing defects, failure was assured—for 1940 only 422 cars were produced.

Crosley was not a man accustomed to giving up. In 1941, he launched an astounding publicity campaign, with the culmination being daredevil driver Cannon Ball Baker driving a soft-top station wagon around the United States on a 6,517-mile odyssey with an average fuel economy of 50.4 miles per hour. Amazingly, this campaign, coupled with the correction of many of the initial flaws, resulted in sales of 2,289 for 1941 and 1,029 in 1942 before government-mandated suspension of civilian automobile production took effect.

But the Crosley's stingy use of fuel was not enough to enamor it to the American people, even though the gas rationing of World War II made the cars relatively popular. With the cessation of hostilities, Crosley hit the ground running, hoping to build the Model T for a new generation.

With the intention of developing a vehicle for the commercial market, Crosley expanded the line to include quarter-ton pickup trucks for 1946. In 1948, panel deliveries were added. Since the company could not benefit from the cost savings of large-scale production, the only other option

162

was cutting corners, which on occasion resulted in bizarre features. As an example, left front-suspension springs featured six leaves while the right had only five to offset driver weight.

In spite of the numerous shortcomings of Crosleys, the immediate postwar years were a sellers' market. During 1947, there were 22,526 buyers who chose Crosley. Predictably, sales began to slide in 1948. In 1949, the company finally began to address many of the shortcomings that had been a problem for the company since inception: namely, it replaced the extremely corrosion-prone engine with a highly advanced cast-iron version, and added hydraulic brakes.

But it was too late; sales had already began a precipitous slide. Still, Crosley refused to throw in the towel. Instead he offered two new and very unique models; for 1950 there was the versatile Farm-O-Road, a miniature version of the Crosley that was designed to be a multipurpose utility vehicle, and the Hot Shot sports roadster. However, even Crosley had his breaking point; in 1952, production was discontinued.

It could be said that the Crosley was in its time the ghost of Christmas future. Three decades later, necessity and competition forced the American auto industry to reconsider the small-car concept. And, as had happened with the Crosley, cost cutting and a tendency to address problems as they arose destined these endeavors for failure. Or have we already forgotten the Chevette Scooter, Vega, or Astre?

The new-generation Mini Cooper, as with its predecessors, enjoys strong brand loyalty, and with mild customization is appearing at a variety of auto shows.

The Microcar Invasion

Comic relief

Since the inception of the automobile, almost every generation has had a vehicle that seems to have been introduced solely as comic relief. The 1930s had the American Bantam and the 1940s had the Crosley. For the modern era, there was the Yugo. But no list of diminutive vehicles would be complete without inclusion of the BMW Isetta.

The little bubble car with a front door that also served as the front of the car and a swing-away steering column to facilitate entry is not to be confused with anything else on the road at that time or since. The body was constructed of pressed steel over light tubular steel framing and featured a great deal of glass for excellent visibility. The mechanics of the car, which had a curb weight of just 800 pounds, were as unusual as the car itself.

The drive axles were operated via a series of chains and sprockets. The air-cooled engine with a displacement of just 295 cc provided excellent fuel economy, an average of 40 miles per gallon, but was more than just anemic in performance. The top speed advertised was an optimistic 45 miles per hour, and with just the driver on board, acceleration was in the vicinity of 0 to 40 in 40 seconds.

In addition to having the distinction of being known as one of the most easily identified vehicles in the world, there is another intriguing distinction for the little bubble car. It is the only car to have been built in five countries, on two continents, and yet never became a success. Estimates place the total number of vehicles produced between 1955 and 1965 at less than 250,000.

Today the BMW Isetta stands as testimony to thinking outside the box. It also provides a touch of comic relief in an industry that is taken a little too seriously on occasion.

The diminutive BMW Isetta couldn't be confused with anything else on the road when new; the same is true today.

Lincoln Continental

End of an era

The Continental began as a one-off custom designed by and built for Edsel Ford. It received so much attention that limited production started for the 1940 model year. Available in coupe or convertible form, the V-12 Continentals are true classics in spite of their many shortcomings.

New size, new styling, but unmistakably Continental: the classic profile has been   lengthened to prov

For 1946, the Continental was once again the center of attention when a convertible was selected as the pace car for that year's Indianapolis 500. With little modification, production of the Continental continued through 1948, after which it was discontinued until 1956.

However, upon its resurrection, the Continental was an entirely separate division of Ford Motor Company. Looking like a large, luxurious Thunderbird coupe, the new Continental carried an astounding price—$9,538 compared to $5,381 for a top-of-the-line Lincoln Premiere convertible that ensured limited production.

For 1958, the Continental once again became a part of the Lincoln family and represented the top of the line. This status continued in 1959 and 1960. Then the Continental to end all Continentals, four-door models in hardtop and the convertible series made famous as the car in which President Kennedy was assassinated, was introduced for 1961.

The convertible was intended initially as a showroom drawing card. As a result, it should be no surprise to learn production and sales were quite anemic for 1963 just 3,138 units were sold.

For 1964 and 1965, only the two-body styles were available. The rear doors were still hinged at the rear, the grill and trim received a facelift, and the overall length was stretched to 216.3 inches. For 1966, these mammoth road kings were enlarged 5 inches in length and 1 inch in width.

Also new for 1966 was a two-door coupe and a new 462-cid V-8 engine that developed 340 horsepower and 485 foot-pounds of torque at 4,600 rpm! *Motor Trend* tested the coupe, and at 5,200 pounds, it was the lightest of the three models. The testers came away impressed with a 0 to 60 time of 10.8 seconds and a top speed that hugged 125 miles per hour.

u with greater interior space and comfort.

However, the tradeoff was in fuel economy. Good mileage was almost non-existent with a best average of 13 miles per gallon. If the buyer could afford $6,500 for a car when a new Chevy truck could be had for under $1,700, then they probably weren't concerned with the cost of fuel.

The true beauty of these cars is that they harkened back to an earlier era when luxury cars were built with exacting craftsmanship. An advertising brochure for the 1962 Continental highlights the meticulous attention to detail that went into every vehicle.

Special gauges and testing equipment were developed so some parts could be machined to tolerances of one-millionth of an inch. Each coat of primer was hand-sanded. Every electrical circuit was individually tested, both for operation and insurance of correct current draw. Each engine was individually tested up to 100 miles per hour on a test stand before it was installed. Transmissions received similar testing. Then each vehicle was test driven for 12 miles by an engineer/mechanic.

Although impractical in today's world where fuel-efficient vehicles are king, the Continental is a car without equal. But if you want to truly ride in style, if you really want to experience the open road in comfort, if you like the feel of the wind in your hair and want to take five or six friends along in comfort, there can be no choice other than the Lincoln Continental.

The Lincoln Continental of 1964 hearkened back to an earlier era when a luxury car was a luxury car, without concern for pretense, and even promotional brochures such as this left little doubt of the vehicle's pedigree.

Mack
King of the road

When the Mack brothers produced their first bus in 1900, who could have known that this simple beginning was the launching of an American legend? For eight years before it was converted into a truck, "Old #1" transported passengers through Brooklyn's Prospect Park. Incredibly, by the time of its retirement from service, it had logged almost one million miles—or so it was claimed. The durability of a Mack had been firmly established.

The B series trucks introduced in 1954 were a worthy heir to the Mack legacy for rugged durability that dated to the company's inception in 1900.

Bus production continued to be an important part of the company through 1960. In addition, it also produced locomotives and motorized railcars from 1905 to 1930. Railcar production was resumed briefly between 1951 and 1954.

During the Great Depression, the company was expanded to include a series of light-duty (at least in comparison to traditional heavy-duty models) pickup and panel trucks. Produced between 1936 and 1938 in conjunction with REO, and then from 1938 to 1944 (post-1941 models were all for military application) exclusively as Mack models, the Mack Jr. and ED series are among the rarest vehicles ever produced by the company.

Innovation was also an integral part of Mack's initial success. In 1905, Gus Mack patented a revolutionary constant-mesh gear system to avoid the damaging clash of gears. The 1905 Manhattan trucks featured cab-over-engine (COE) design for better driver visibility. Mack marketed its motorized trucks under the Manhattan name to differentiate them from the horse-drawn equipment the company produced.

However, the truck that firmly established Mack as a leader in the production of durable high-quality equipment for heavy-duty application was the now-legendary AC Bulldog, one of the longest-running truck designs in history. Initially introduced in late 1914, with full-scale production beginning in 1916, this series ran through 1938.

These trucks proved to be almost indestructible throughout years of service on the Western Front during World War I, and they won the respect of everyone who encountered them. According to legend, the term "Bulldog" was bestowed upon the durable, pugnacious-appearing trucks by British engineers. After lengthy investigation about the legalities of using the generic description for a trade name, the company adopted the moniker in late 1920.

By this date, another chapter in Mack durability had been written. The First Transcontinental Motor Train was a coast-to-coast military epic that involved traversing 3,250 miles between Washington, D.C., and San Francisco during the summer of 1919. Axle-deep mud, cloying sand, desert heat, steep grades, and city traffic tested the mettle of each vehicle, but the Mack trucks never failed.

For all intents and purposes, the American chapter of Mack drew to a close in 1990 when it became a subsidiary of Renault. But this, and its more recent acquisition by Swedish automaker Volvo in 2000, has done nothing to lessen the legend of Mack.

MODEL
B-61S

RECOGNIZED for its exceptional diesel economy with maximum capacity loads, Model B-61S has been developed and refined upon sound fundamentals. Power is supplied [by] Thermodyne diesel engine offering performance ability consonant [with requirem]ents of dumper,

MODEL B-61S
CHASSIS DIAGRAM

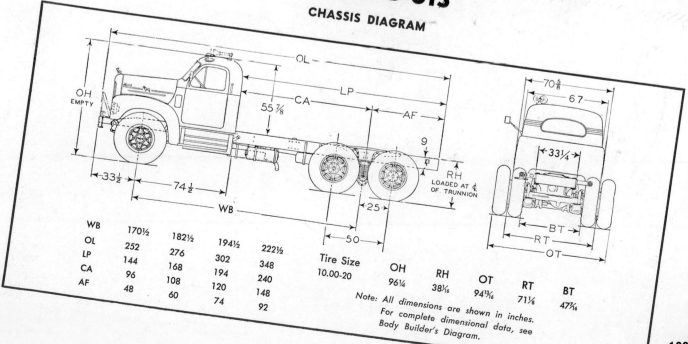

WB	170½			
OL	252	182½		
LP	144	276	194½	222½
CA	96	168	302	348
AF	48	108	194	240
		60	120	148
			74	92

Tire Size
10.00-20

OH	RH	OT	RT	BT
96¼	38¹¹⁄₁₆	94¹³⁄₁₆	71⅛	47⁷⁄₁₆

Note: All dimensions are shown in inches.
For complete dimensional data, see
Body Builder's Diagram.

FEDERAL OPEN BODIES IN MANY COMBINATIONS FOR MANY USES

One-ton No. S-12 stake body with No. 45 coupe cab 50" wide.

No. 81 one-ton utility body with half screens and half doors.

THE line of open bodies—express, stake, and screen—a few of which appear on this page, give you some idea of the wide variety of bodies built exclusively for Federal chassis in the big Federal body plant.

Every one of these models may be obtained in a great number of varieties which make it possible for you to obtain a body exactly suited to your individual needs.

If none of the standard bodies suit you, the body department at the Federal factory is in a position to build special equipment from your own design. In this special work, the highest quality materials and workmanship, which are so evident in the bodies illustrated, are used.

In addition to the full door cowl cab, Federal also builds a "Coupe" cab with half doors and curtains operating

No. 170 two-ton utility express with half doors.

No. 160 two-ton stake body with No. 45 coupe cab 50" wide.

The Federal Motor Truck Company was but one of the many competitors of Mack during the 1920s. This company was unique in that it would continue building heavy-duty trucks as well as pickup and panel trucks into the late postwar era.

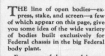

FEDERAL

Trucks that are Trucks

All Sizes Fours and Sixes

Federal Motor Truck Company
Detroit, Michigan, U.S.A.

Motor Transport Leaders Since 1910

FEDERAL PANEL BODIES COM[...]NGTH AND ECONOMY

No. 78 one-ton cowl panel body with half doors.

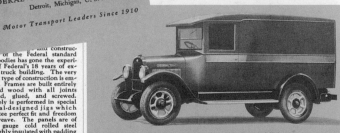

No. 79 one-ton cowl panel body with full doors.

[...] and construc-
[...] of the Federal standard panel bodies has gone the experience of Federal's 18 years of exclusive truck building. The very highest type of construction is employed. Frames are built entirely of hard wood with all joints mortised, glued, and screwed. Assembly is performed in special Federal-designed jigs which guarantee perfect fit and freedom from weave. The panels are of heavy gauge cold rolled steel thoroughly insulated with padding which prevents squeaks.

The Cowl Panel bodies are obtainable with either half doors or full doors. The half door models are equipped with sliding curtains which operate window fashion, while the full doors have glass windows with crank lifts.

These panel bodies may be obtained in four beautiful color combinations, or any special color can be furnished at slight extra cost.

The Utility Panel bodies are available with a number of rear end combinations such as full doors, screens, tail gate, curtains, etc.

No. 95 one-ton utility panel body with half doors.

No. 175 two-ton utility panel body with half doors.

Model T
The legendary Tin Lizzie

In any comparison with its contemporaries, the Model T seems truly primitive, even archaic. Even a decade before production ended, the now legendary Model T Ford seemed to be an anachronism.

Nevertheless, the lowly Model T is arguably one of the most influential automobiles in history. In about 1914, one of every three automobiles produced in the United States was a Model T Ford. A few years later, one out of three autos worldwide would be a Model T.

Henry Ford's insistence that any improvement made to the vehicle would have to be interchangeable with earlier models enabled owners to keep their cars on the road with little expense. The sheer simplicity of the vehicle made it possible for almost anyone to repair any mechanical component. Add rugged durability, and the Model T was the perfect car for the time.

The attributes that endeared many to the Model T also made it the subject of countless jokes. Published in 1917, *Ford Smiles*, a joke book, provides unique insight to the times and the love/hate relationship the Ford fostered, such as these two quips:

"A new device that would be a handy thing on a Ford is a cuckoo clock arrangement on the radiator, to come out, when the machine is going 25 miles an hour, and sing, 'Nearer, My God, to Thee.'"

"The owner of a Franklin contributes this helpful suggestion for tourists: When you find a Ford hogging the road ahead of you, don't try to skirt around it. Just wait until it strikes a bump, and then go right in under it."

Perhaps the most important factor in the sales success and longevity of the "Tin Lizzie," as the Model T was affectionately

An advertisement for the Model T, almost as simplistic as the cars themselves, was as important as the ever-decreasing sales price in ensuring steady sales of the "Tin Lizzie".

known, was its price. Constant improvement and streamlining of the production process enabled Ford to lower the price almost each year of the car's production between late 1908 ($850) and 1927 ($360).

Because of the Spartan simplicity of the Model T, an entire aftermarket industry sprang up to meet the needs of owners. In time, almost every component in the vehicle could be modified

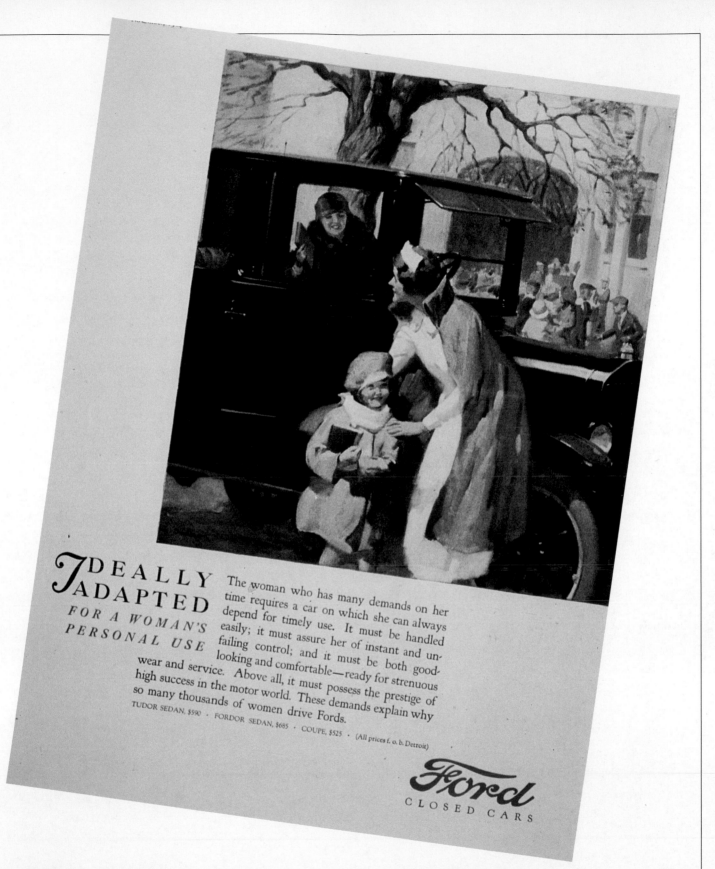

IDEALLY ADAPTED
FOR A WOMAN'S PERSONAL USE

The woman who has many demands on her time requires a car on which she can always depend for timely use. It must be handled easily; it must assure her of instant and un-failing control; and it must be both good-looking and comfortable—ready for strenuous wear and service. Above all, it must possess the prestige of high success in the motor world. These demands explain why so many thousands of women drive Fords.

TUDOR SEDAN, $590 · FORDOR SEDAN, $685 · COUPE, $525 · (All prices f. o. b. Detroit)

Ford
CLOSED CARS

with improvements covering the entire spectrum from the addition of four-wheel drive and speedster bodies to odometers and luggage carriers for the running boards.

By the time production was suspended in May 1927, 15 million Model T Fords had been produced. The Model T, more than any other vehicle, has been credited with putting the world behind the steering wheel.

1965 Mustang

A legend is born

The original concept for the Mustang was a vehicle that would directly target the Triumph/MG-dominated low-end two-seat sports car market. The initial prototype built under contract by specialist builder Trautman and Barnes of Los Angeles had many unique and innovative features. The seats did not adjust, but the pedals and steering were mounted on a sliding box member, so it was possible to adjust to almost any size of driver.

Four-wheel independent suspension as well as rack-and-pinion steering represented state-of-the-art technology. The mid-engine was a revolutionary 1,927-cc V-4 with single-barrel Solex carburetor. The transmission was a specially designed four-speed transaxle. The brakes were disc on front and drum on rear.

America's Favorite Fun Car

A curb weight of just 1,200 pounds and an overall length of 154 inches (90-inch wheelbase) allowed for astounding performance. The car was tested to 120 miles per hour, and in fuel-economy runs it was found to be capable of 30 miles per gallon.

In spite of enthusiastic response, Lee Yucca, general manager of Ford, decided the project was not feasible. He had noted, "All the car buffs said, 'Hey, what a car!' but when I look at who's saying it—the offbeat crowd, the real buffs—I said, 'That's sure not the car we want to build, because it can't be a volume car. It's too far out.'"

Introduced on April 17, 1964, the now-legendary Ford Mustang proved to be the company's most successful introduction since the Model A in 1929. Improved models were debuted on August 17, 1964. As a result, many collectors refer to the first series as 1964 1/2 models even though Ford lists them all as 1965 models. Additional reasons for collectors to view these cars as separate models are numerous. There are subtle differences such as an alternator instead of generator, chrome-plated rather than color-keyed door-lock buttons, and an increase in the size of the nameplate on the front fender from 4.75 inches to 5 inches.

The most telling difference was the explosion of available options, including engines and transmissions that were made available during this transitional period. Initially, there were but three engine choices: a 170-cid six-cylinder, a 260-cid V-8, and a 289-cid V-8. In June 1964, a 271-bhp high-performance version of the 289-cid V-8 was made available. In addition, a close ratio four-speed transmission was also offered. In July, a modified dual exhaust was introduced.

The engine options made available during the first months exemplified what had been decided in some of the earliest conceptual meetings. In an effort to attract a more youthful

If you thought we couldn't improve on a winner— try Mustang '66!

For '66, we did the nicest thing we could think of— we changed Mustang very carefully. There's smart new ornamentation all around, as you probably noticed on the Mustang Hardtop (cover), Convertible and Fastback 2+2 (opposite). Also new (and standard) are a 5-dial instrument cluster, 14-inch low-profile tires and full wheel covers. But the standard features that give Mustang so much of its potent charm are all here. Plush bucket seats, pleated vinyl trim, sports steering wheel, 3-speed floor shift, frisky 200-cu. in. Six, padded instrument panel and sun visors, full carpeting, heater-defroster*, front and rear seat belts. Plus outside rearview mirror, windshield washers and electric wipers, backup lights, emergency flasher and courtesy lights. And, of course, Ford's Twice-a-Year Maintenance (back cover) . . . all *standard* and all wrapped up in the kind of low price tag Mustang made famous.

And Mustang's long list of options—more than 70 of them—are here for '66 . . . with great new ones like the AM Radio/Stereo-sonic Tape System (detailed on page 5). And nearly all these options are available on all Mustangs. More than ever Mustang is designed to be designed by you!

Just mention Mustang and you've set off a lively conversation. All about fun . . . excitement . . . going places . . . doing things. Proof? Over 418,000 on the road in Mustang's first year, an all-time record! Why? Because Mustang is a personal luxury car, family car, performance car, or anything in between.

So don't be content to just talk about Mustang. From the following pages pick your model, pick your options, then head for your Ford Dealer!

Now more than ever designed to be designed by you

By 1966, promotion for the Mustang was being targeted at numerous markets. As such, the portrayal of the vehicle ran the gamut from sedate, sporty transportation car to asphalt-eating GT version.

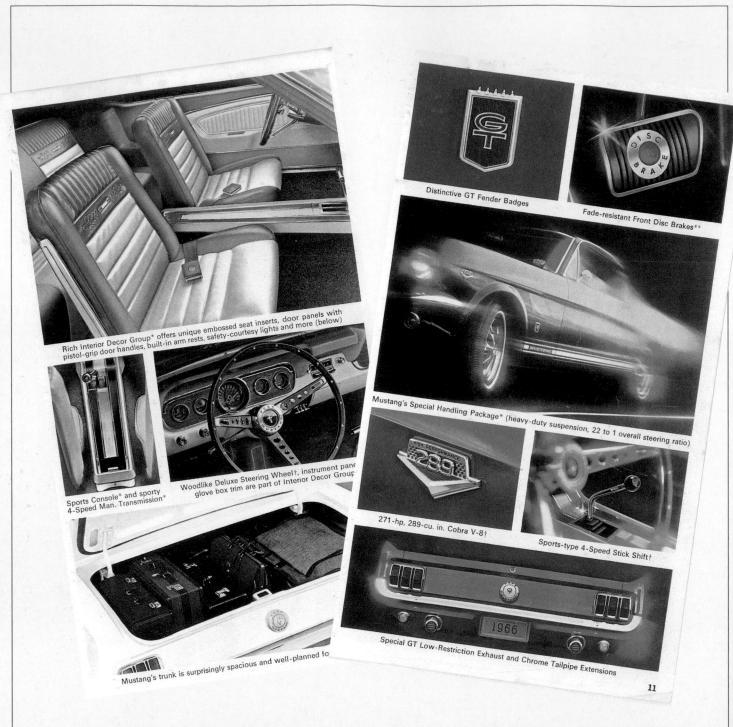

Rich Interior Decor Group* offers unique embossed seat inserts, door panels with pistol-grip door handles, built-in arm rests, safety-courtesy lights and more (below)

Sports Console* and sporty 4-Speed Man. Transmission*

Woodlike Deluxe Steering Wheel†, instrument panel glove box trim are part of Interior Decor Group*

Mustang's trunk is surprisingly spacious and well-planned fo

Distinctive GT Fender Badges

Fade-resistant Front Disc Brakes**

Mustang's Special Handling Package* (heavy-duty suspension, 22 to 1 overall steering ratio)

271-hp, 289-cu. in. Cobra V-8†

Sports-type 4-Speed Stick Shift†

Special GT Low-Restriction Exhaust and Chrome Tailpipe Extensions

11

consumer as well as the more traditional, conservative customer, the Mustang was to have a wide array of options, allowing buyers to customize the vehicle to their specific tastes and needs. As a result, it was possible to order a Mustang that was pure, basic transportation with a sporty flair, a budget version of the Thunderbird, or an asphalt-scorching performance machine.

Then, on September 9, 1964, the 2 + 2, also listed as the Fastback 2 + 2, was introduced. It was painfully obvious to the competition that Ford had a winner in the Mustang; with the average wait for a convertible or coupe at six weeks. With the introduction of the fastback, it left absolutely no doubt that Ford had succeeded and the demand climbed even higher.

In spite of a few stumbles by Ford along the way, the popularity of the Mustang has never waned. Moreover, today, with a new generation of both consumer and car, the Mustang legend is alive and well.

Indian and Harley-Davidson

America's two-wheeled icons

With some certainty, a solid argument can be made for declaring the motorcycle the cornerstone of the automotive age. The first motorized bike was demonstrated at fairs and circuses in 1868. Even though Sylvester Roper's steam-powered wonder failed to rise beyond the status of novelty, he persisted. In 1869, he introduced another version with features that included twisting handgrip throttle. Gottlieb Daimler's initial experiments came together in the form of a two-wheeled cycle in 1885.

By 1900, the bicycle craze had entered a new phase as visionary individuals began attaching engines in various configurations. Two of these pioneering companies became larger-than-life American legends, and one would spawn brand loyalty as well as an entire culture.

In 1901, William Harley and Arthur Davidson began cobbling together a

A postwar advertisement for Harley-Davidson motorcycles focused attention on the freedom and fun of taking to the highways on two wheels.

variety of engines and bicycles. By 1903, their endeavors had reached such a level of both technological advancement and public interest, that they decided production might be a profitable venture.

Oscar Hedstrom was a brilliant, self-taught engineer who designed and built quality racing bicycles. Utilizing a copy of a DeDion-Buton engine with an advanced carburetor of his design, he built the Pacer as a training vehicle for bicycle racers. The little machine was so reliable and practical that Springfield, Massachusetts, entrepreneur George Hendee negotiated a deal to begin full-scale production. In 1902, the first Indian rolled from the factory.

Indian became the leader in innovation with motorcycles like the Hendee Special, which featured a full electric system including a starter and a swing arm-suspension in 1913. Production and sales soared, and by 1914 the company was the largest producer of motorcycles in the world.

Just five years after initiating production, Harley-Davidson was selling 450 bikes a year. Its bikes set records for fuel economy, and were garnering the attention of municipalities wanting to motorize their police patrols. The introduction of the V-twin in 1909 and the subsequent publicity—such as that obtained by a factory rider topping 68 miles per hour at a Bakersfield, California, race—spurred sales.

Throughout the 1920s and the 1930s, Harley-Davidson and Indian battled for dominance of the motorcycle market. Large numbers of bikes built by both companies were supplied to the military during World War II. In retrospect, this was when Harley-Davidson's dominance and international reputation truly began.

Harley-Davidson narrowly edged out the competition in the initial application for government contracts based on certain performance criteria. This victory was followed by a similar win in negotiation for the actual contracts. As a result, Harley-Davidson received its first order for 745 motorcycles in 1940. With the increased need for motorcycles in later months, contracts were awarded to other manufacturers. However, by this time, Harley-Davidson had supplied 540 bikes to every U.S. armored division, in addition to 2,000 for South Africa, 5,000 for Great Britain, and 20,000 for Canada. Small shipments were also made to the Russian and Chinese armies.

With the close of the war, Indian borrowed heavily for expansion of production facilities. Quality-control problems translated to diminished sales, which in turn resulted in the company's inability to meet its financial obligations. In 1950, Indian was broken into separate sales and manufacturing companies, with Associated Motorcycles (the British parent company for Norton, Royal Enfield, Matchless, and AJS) acquiring many of the company's assets.

Still, Indian had a lengthy history and a surprisingly loyal core of buyers. As a result, the reintroduced Chief models of 1950–1953 were a moderate sales success. However, in 1954 there was a dramatic change, and the motorcycles that bore the Indian name did so in name only, because the bike was in large part an amalgam of components produced by various companies. In the late 1950s, even this pretense was abandoned and Norton was the only survivor.

In recent years, there have been numerous attempts to resurrect the legendary marque. However, to date, none of these efforts have succeeded.

While Indian was fading into the sunset, its longtime nemesis was about to skyrocket to prominence. Unfortunately, much of the culture that rose up around the Harley-Davidson mystique was founded on an unsavory element. While a great deal of the outlaw-biker image was fostered by media excess built on actual events and films such as *The Wild One,* many chose to ride solely for the freedom and exhilaration.

Today the biker mystique has spawned legendary events that annually attract fans of America's motorcycle from throughout the world. Many gather for the bikes, but others come for the opportunity to pretend for a day and cut loose from a button-down life. As a result, more often than not the tattoos may be as fake as the female anatomy displayed.

Rental Car
Wheels on demand

Much like the livery business that preceded it, the rental car business was initially a local affair. More often than not, both of them operated from the same stables. In addition, because there was a wide variety of automobile types, many with conflicting gear patterns, starting procedures, and the like, a rental car often came with a rented driver.

A variation of this theme developed in the 1920s when car lots began equipping vehicles with taxi lights and meters, and then rented them to independent operators. In some cities this, as well as drivers who simply adorned their cars with signs and lights, put more cabs on the streets than could be operated profitably.

Compounding the problem were the hard economic conditions of the 1930s, which encouraged operators to take to the streets. In turn, rental car companies that specialized in the renting of vehicles for use as taxis flourished. More often than not, these vehicles were older models in poor mechanical condition. Often possessing little or no experience and driven by the adage that time was money, the drivers often logged 20 hours at a stretch. This resulted in sheer carnage. A study conducted in New York City at the end of 1931 found that of the 23,000 motor vehicle accidents within the city that year, 21,000 had involved taxis. Due to this study, increased and stringent regulation effectively closed this particular aspect of the rental car business.

The man to whom credit is given for the modern concept of rental cars is John Hertz, an innovative businessman who began his career in 1905 as a salesman for the Walden W. Shaw Livery Company. His business acumen and hard work resulted in promotion to full partner in 1908.

Hertz brought the company into the modern era in 1910 by purchasing nine Thomas touring cars, painting them a bright yellow, and establishing a sales division. The cars sold quickly, and in the years to follow the company became one of the more profitable dealerships in the Chicago area.

In 1915, Hertz expanded the company's original business by transforming a selected number of vehicles to taxis, painting them accordingly, and establishing Yellow Cab. This venture proved to be so profitable that the company then expanded into the production of assembled vehicles built specifically for use as cabs: the Yellow Taxicab Manufacturing Company.

In September 1918, Walter Jacobs of Chicago, with just 12 Model T Fords, opened a local car rental agency. It was an idea that was long overdue, and within just five years the company was nearing $1 million in annual sales. In 1925, Hertz sold his cab manufacturing business to General Motors, shortly after selling 30 percent of his holdings in Chicago Yellow Cab to Morris Markin, founder of Checker. Hertz used the proceeds of these sales to buy out Jacobs' rental business, which became the Hertz Driv-Ur-Self System.

During the same period, a consortium of railroads created the corporation Railway Extensions. In addition to the franchise of local car rental agencies, the group promoted car rental use by allocating space for these agencies at railroad stations and the subsidization of telegraph service for passengers to reserve cars at one station for pickup at another.

By the mid-1950s, the company John Hertz had founded some 40 years earlier for the production of taxi cabs and the establishment of taxi franchises had become the nation's leader in rental-car operations.

Back so soon? (He's got The Hertz Idea)

Who's *he*? He's a smart businessman. Leaves his car at home, takes a plane or train, rents a Hertz car at his destination.

That's The Hertz Idea! He's found you can make more calls, save more time, get home earlier, when you reserve a sparkling new Powerglide Chevrolet Bel Air or other fine car at over 1,000 Hertz offices. Drive it as your own. Your driver's license and proper identification get you going with no delay.

Cost? The national average rate is only $7.55 a day plus 8 cents per mile (lower by the week). All gasoline, oil and proper insurance included. And Hertz honors air, rail, most all hotel credit cards; Diners' Club and Hertz charge cards. Next time or *any time* you need a car . . . *call Hertz.* We're listed under ''H'' in phone books everywhere. Hertz Rent A Car, 218 South Wabash Avenue, Chicago 4, Illinois.

More people by far...use
HERTZ
Rent a car

Hertz has new Powerglide Chevrolet Bel Airs (or other fine cars)—just like your own!

Shortly after World War II, the airline industry began to supplant the railroad for passenger service. Emulating Railway Extensions, Hertz began opening franchises at airports, with the first two in Milwaukee and Atlanta. Avis was founded on an expansion of this premise, including almost exclusive centering of operations at airports and aggressive marketing through the airlines themselves.

The 1960s witnessed an explosion in the expansion of rental car franchises, formation of new companies, and subsequent price wars. The rental car business today has become inseparable from the airline industry and is now a vital ingredient for keeping a car culture rolling.

Station Wagons
Long roofs and woodies

Initially known as a depot hack, the station wagon predates the concept of the automobile by several decades and was initially just what the name implied: a station wagon. In essence, it was a vehicle used to transport passengers as well as their luggage from the railroad to their hotel or other destination. Often they were owned by the hotel and were used as a customer service vehicle.

In time, more attention was given to customer comfort, with the addition of tops, extra padding for the seats, and side curtains to hold inclement weather at bay. However, regardless of improvement or modification, the basic configuration and construction remained the same. By 1900, the basic body design, including drop-down tailgates, had been standardized.

Initially, the advent of the automobile did little to alter the design of station wagons, and only the means of propulsion separated the predominately electric-powered coaches from the horse-drawn variants. Many of the companies that had built the horse-drawn versions, such as Brewster and Parry, simply continued with business as usual and only changed the vehicles' power source.

Slowly, however, things started to change for these utilitarian vehicles. First, companies began to apply names that attempted to give them a more modern image. Second, the vehicles were now marketed for uses other than simply depot transport.

By about 1915, the station wagon body had two basic layouts: those with passenger seats that faced forward and those with passenger seats that faced inward. Nevertheless, the construction techniques remained almost unchanged.

During these formative years, the individuals or manufacturers special ordered the station wagon bodies, and they were built by the small, independent firms that had specialized in this type of work for decades. However, there were larger companies that operated on volume, such as Martin-Parry, which had large plants in York, Pennsylvania; Indianapolis,

The Rambler station wagon for 1958, as with most station wagons produced during the 1950s and 1960s, has only recently become sought after by collectors.

SMARTEST, MOST ECONOMICAL STATION WAGON ON THE ROAD

Rambler
Super 4-Door Cross Country for 1958

Indiana; and Lumberton, Mississippi, as well as 60 subassembly plants located throughout the country. In short order, several established auto manufacturers were evaluating the profitability of keeping some of this outsourced production in-house. Chevrolet literature and catalogs for 1920 indicate that a Model 490 station wagon and light delivery wagon were available. But sales were so poor that the project was dropped almost before it had really begun.

In 1923, Durant Motors Company began offering a station wagon in the lower-priced Star line, which is generally acknowledged as the first factory-built station wagon in the United States, even though the majority of body components were actually supplied by Martin-Parry. Surprisingly, the vehicle enjoyed relatively brisk sales.

Still, the market was largely dominated by independent manufacturers such as J. T. Cantrell and Company of Huntington, New York, which began in 1903 with a blacksmith and carriage repair shop; T. F. Scudder; and Hercules-Campbell Body Corporation of Tarrytown and Waterloo, New York. Joseph Cantrell built its first body for automotive application as a depot hack to fit a Model T chassis on special order. The quality of the work quickly resulted in additional orders, and soon the company was fitting its bodies to chassis by a number of manufacturers, including Dodge, Franklin, Ford, and even the Wolverine.

Salesmen representing the company were kept busy during the mid-1920s visiting dealers throughout New Jersey, New York, and Connecticut. At the factory, the incoming chassis were handled by make. When a new model came out, Cantrell designed a body for it and drew up full-size blueprints, which were sent to dealers and given to the salesmen.

Throughout the 1930s, the chassis arrived at the railroad station minus the body from the windshield back. Each unit was assigned to one man who undertook all aspects of the construction. In addition to this volume work, the company also built numerous one-off bodies for the likes of Marshall Field. During World War II, a history of performing this type of custom work served the Cantrell well. The War Department contracted the company for the conversion of sedans into station wagons.

Shortly after the cessation of hostilities, Cantrell was forced to update production to an assembly-line format. However, the era of the handcrafted woody, a throwback to the time of the horse and carriage, was drawing to a close and sales began to slide. In January 1950, Cantrell retired and sold his interest in the company to his brother Albert. Under Albert's command, the company continued limited production through 1957.

Beginning in 1929 and running through 1940, Ford was the largest major manufacturer of factory-built station wagons. Ford initially contracted companies to build the components, but in mid-1935 Ford opened a plant in Iron Mountain, Michigan. The plant manufactured them, but the assembly was still contract work. Beginning in 1939, the entire production process was handled in-house. The popularity of Ford-built wagons and the hard economic times of the Great Depression resulted in the closure of many independents.

In 1935, Chevrolet introduced a vehicle that represented a revolutionary step in the evolution of the station wagon: the all-steel-bodied Suburban Carryall. However, the primary problem with the Suburban was that it was built on a half-ton truck chassis.

Built to meet the needs of postwar families, the first all-steel wagons were sold at prices that were much lower than those of the hand-built wooden models in late 1946. The two available models were as different as night and day, and they

The Olds Vista Cruiser with glass skylights and imitation wood-grain sides has come to symbolize the American station wagon.

represented a marked departure from the traditional concept of the station wagon. The Crosley was a diminutive version, while that offered by Willys Overland had a more rugged appearance because of the shared front design with its cousin, the Jeep. However, both station wagons had Di Noc wood-grain decals as an option, hinting at their heritage.

The prosperity of the postwar years, the baby boom, and the birth of suburbia sent the demand for station wagons soaring. As a result, by 1952 almost every manufacturer offered a station wagon model. With the exception of custom bodies or special orders, they were all steel-bodied. Throughout the 1950s the wagon gained popularity, even though many of the styling features of the time, including hundreds of pounds of chrome trim and tail fins, didn't wear quite as well on the long-roofed cars.

The next major milestone for the station wagon came in 1964 with the introduction of the Oldsmobile Vista Cruiser and the Buick Sport Wagon. With a raised rear roofline accentuated by narrow skylights, much like the GM-built Scenicruiser buses, there was enough headroom for both rear seats to face forward. The Vista Cruiser series came to represent the modern station wagon and, as with wagons in general, is now sought by collectors who want something both stylish and practical in their vintage car.

The Vista Cruiser also represents the final chapter in the full-size wagon story. With the fuel crisis of the early 1970s and the trend toward smaller families, the wagon began to fade from favor. Even attempts to downsize it with Pinto wagons and such were not enough to stave off the inevitable. The final nail in the coffin came with the introduction of the Chrysler-built minivan in 1982.

In smaller numbers, the American station wagon continued in production through the 1980s and early 1990s. With the increasing dominance of the minivan, American-built station wagon sales continued a precipitous slide through the 1980s and 1990s. Surprisingly during this period, some of the finest wagons ever produced were built, including the Ford Crown Victoria Country Squire and the Buick Roadmaster of 1996 powered by a 260-horsepower, 5.7-liter LT1 V-8 as standard equipment. However, by the turn of the century, the Chevrolet Suburban and imitators produced by competitors represented the last of the breed. With the introduction of the Dodge Magnum in 2004, a new era for the American station wagon began. Its popularity has encouraged many to hope that the station wagon is about to make a return.

U-Haul
Moving to a higher level

The development of the rental car business paralleled that of the transportation industry as a whole. As a result, the boom came with the development of travel by airline, most notably for business, which often necessitated an automobile upon arrival. But what if the need was for something larger?

Companies that leased trucks date to at least 1915. However, these services were in large part to meet local commercial needs only. The consumer in need of a truck for a cross-country move was usually left to his own creative talents: in other words, buy one or make one from a car. In the years immediately following World War II, America began to move in record numbers. An American entrepreneur stepped in to fill the perceived void, and a legend of the highway was born. More importantly, an entire industry was created.

In the fall of 1945, L. S. Shoen, with the help of his wife, the Cartey family, and a $5,000 loan, began building trailers in the garage on their Ridgefield, Washington, ranch. In an effort to establish an identity, they painted the trailers bright orange. The company's name, U-Haul, was stenciled onto the sides and back with the notice, "Rental Trailers—$2 per day."

To expand the business into something more than just a local operation, U-Haul devised a unique franchise system. Service stations in select locations were approached and solicited with a lucrative commission structure. Additional recruitment was done through the customers, who could receive a sizable discount on their rental by agreeing to establish an outlet for U-Haul at their destination location. Coupled with a customer-financing plan initiated in the early 1950s, the company skyrocketed.

By the end of 1952, it was possible to rent a trailer city to city in almost every region of the nation, and trucks were soon added to the U-Haul fleet. Today, U-Haul equipment can be rented through 15,500 independent operators and 1,342 company-owned moving centers.

But U-Haul no longer has a monopoly on the move-it-yourself business, and numerous companies, most notably Penske and Budget, have nudged the pioneering company from its position of dominance. However, this has done little to keep U-Haul from being the first name that comes to mind when it is time to pack it up and move on.

The brightly colored murals on modern U-Haul trucks are common sights on U.S. highways.

Tow Truck
The Samaritan of the highway

Mechanical things break. Accidents happen. These two axioms are an integral part of the motoring experience, so there is and has been a need for resolution. If it won't move under its own power, then it has to be moved with power from another source. If it's badly broken because it met an immovable object or another moving object, pieces will need to be moved. Enter the tow truck.

Who exactly devised the concept of the tow truck is not known. Nevertheless, it can be said, with some assurance, that the launching of the industry began on the banks of the Tennessee River in Chattanooga, Tennessee. The need for a tow truck was recognized in 1916, after Ernest Holmes, Sr., and several associates spent a long night using a block and tackle to recover a friend's overturned Model T Ford from a creek.

Credited with opening the first independent automobile repair facility in the city, Holmes set about finding a better solution for such projects. The result of these efforts was the invention of the reversing winch and the development of a twin boom mounted on a cut-down Locomobile.

On-the-job experience resulted in near-constant improvement, and an ever-expanding reputation made production a profitable venture for Holmes. By 1920, Holmes equipment had become the mainstay of the fledgling towing and recovery business to such a degree that almost any recovery unit was referred to by that name.

Then came the introduction of the Holmes 485, and an industry standard was set. The unit was built in a heavily constructed box that could be mounted on almost any sturdy chassis. At each front corner, there was a stabilizing outrigger jack that was topped by a vertical mast. A boom, which could be used separately (one side to stabilize while the other lifted) or together, over the rear center was attached to the mast. Winches contained 100 feet of cable and were hand operated, but an electric winch powered by storage batteries was offered as an option.

Holmes was not the sole producer of wrecker equipment, but their innovation and dominance resulted in the application of the name to most towing bodies. This unit was manufactured by E. F. Wegner Company of Cranbury, New Jersey, in 1975.

WRECK - MASTER
MODEL 800
8 TON

Here are some of the standard features on the new Holmes "440" . . . offered at no extra cost. Examine them in detail. They combine to make the finest power wrecker of its class you can buy . . . Holmes "440."

The varying thicknesses of steel plate . . . the tapers, the angles . . . a new concept in wrecker engineering for the greatest strength and lightest weight.

Five foot telescoping boom extension . . . twice as long as any extension previously available on this size wrecker. Can reach out 7 feet behind . . . Adds versatility and many new profit possibilities.

Action-sequence photo of partially extended boom picking up engine block to lower it into wrecker body . . . an action done completely by power winch . . . no muscle required.

Boom extension lock pin is spring loaded and self-locking . . . you can't lose the pin. Adjustment holes are spaced at one foot intervals for varying length requirements. The square boom tube simplifies boom adjustment and eliminates "hole hunting."

Single lever controls permit effortless rear-end control from either side of the wrecker.

Cable, unhooked from boom, making a side pull through a snatch block, directly from the mast.

An original Holmes feature, the Rapid-Reverse Winch, with its built-in reversing mechanism, completely eliminates the need for awkward truck-clutch controls, reversing P.T.O. or bulky reversing transmission.

Fully enclosed boom winch permits rapid positioning and holding of boom at desired elevation.

The versatility and simplicity of the Holmes 440 made it extremely popular, inspired a great deal of imitation, and made it an industry standard.

While Holmes may be the most famous manufacturer of towing equipment, there were numerous other innovative and successful companies. Weaver of Springfield, Illinois, produced a dual A-frame unit, but it was limited to inline lifting. The company's main claim to fame was a two-wheel dolly called an auto ambulance. Another large share of the market was garnered by Manley of York, Pennsylvania, which specialized in the construction of heavier equipment rated between 2 1/2 tons and 5 tons in 1927.

The evolution of the automobile prompted corresponding changes to towing equipment. In the 1930s, Holmes developed a "Hi-speed towing cradle" designed exclusively for use with autos that had knee-action suspension. Likewise, the construction of modern vehicles is prohibitive to towing in the traditional manner: hence, the rollback truck. The needs of the military during World War II spurred the development of heavy-duty towing equipment, specifically the use of hydraulics, effectively replacing the mechanical lifts.

Ernest Holmes, Sr., died in 1943 leaving the company in the capable hands of his son, Ernest Holmes Jr., who retired in 1973. The year Holmes retired, the company was sold to the Dover Corporation. The legacy later continued through Gerald Holmes, the founder's grandson. In Ooltewah, Tennessee, he built a company, Century Wreckers, to manufacture hydraulically powered wreckers and towing equipment.

Just as the independent auto manufacturers gave way to international conglomerates, so too have the makers of specialized towing equipment. The assets of both companies, Dover Corporation and Century Wreckers, as well as several other manufacturers, were obtained by Miller Industries, which continues production in Ooltewah and is now the largest manufacturer of towing equipment in the world.

For many, the tow truck is simply taken for granted. However, an enterprising group has come together to preserve and chronicle this important chapter in automotive history. Fittingly, the International Towing and Recovery Hall of Fame and Museum have been located where it all began, in Chattanooga, Tennessee.

Whizzer

Two-wheeled wonders

Humble beginnings have been the hallmark of many automotive ventures, and Whizzer was no exception. Introduced in 1939, it was originally an engine kit for bicycles built by Breene-Taylor Engineering Corporation of Los Angeles, California. This company's primary business was the manufacture of aircraft parts, and shortly before the United States entered World War II, the Whizzer Division was purchased by Martin Goldman, an attorney for Breene-Taylor, and Dietrich Kohlsaat, the financier for the project.

The new company, Whizzer Motor Company, depended heavily on subcontractors for many of the individual components of the Whizzer. As a result, many of the early engines, designated D, E, and F, suffered from quality-control issues. In addition, early correspondence indicates there were extensive delivery problems from two of the main suppliers. In spite of these issues, the Whizzer developed a loyal following among those who were too young for a car, but felt they were too old for a bicycle.

While the D and E models sold relatively well, the model F introduced in 1942 launched the Whizzer legend. About 4,250 of these 2½-horsepower engine kits were produced. The company offered a trade-in for older engines with the introduction of the model H in the spring of 1946. This model proved to be even more successful, as evidenced by the sale of 139,000 engines.

Up until 1948, it does not appear the company offered assembled bikes, because advertisements promoted the products produced by the company as "America's Finest Bicycle Motor." After 1948, advertisements often read, "America's Finest Motor Bicycle." The confusion over factory-assembled bikes is a result of bicycle dealers who on occasion purchased the engine kits, assembled them, attached them to a variety of bicycles, and then sold the completed units. Additional confusion stems from the company's practice of shipping engines and bikes to dealers separately to keep the cost down by beating the federal excise tax on complete motorbikes.

Introduced in May of 1948, the J series featured an improved motor and motorcycle-type grips. The following November, the 300-series engine with a high-compression head rated at 3 horsepower made its debut. Now available in two variations, the Sportsman and the Ambassador, and with features such as kick-start, generator, and ignition, the Whizzer was blurring the lines between a kid's bike and an actual motorcycle.

The Whizzer continued through another series and several more years of production. The Whizzer Motor Company, now Whizzer Industries, terminated its motor division in 1970. However, the end for the Whizzer had come many years before, with the initiation of regulation that required drivers of motorbikes to be 16 years of age with a valid license, and a flood of small, cheap bikes imported from Japan.

To capitalize on the perceived nostalgia of a generation that first experienced the wind in their face on two wheels powered by a Whizzer, there was an attempt to market a reproduction in 1992. As with the original, quality-control problems quickly developed and the project was almost stillborn.

In 1998, the Whizzer name, logo, and all patent rights were sold, and almost immediately following the acquisition a new version was introduced. The modest success encouraged other models to follow, and even though they are not the "old Whizzers," those produced today allow a now-graying generation to rediscover a bit of their youth.

Here's Why
WHIZZER
Is America's Leading Bike Motor

AIR COOLED MOTOR
4-cycle design, 2½ rugged h.p. Auto-type carburetor gives 125 miles per gallon. Speeds to 35 m.p.h.

TWIST-GRIP CONTROLS
Motorcycle type, for safe, easy control under all operating conditions.

STREAMLINED GAS TANK
Holds 5 quarts. Made of heavy gauge steel, baked enamel finish.

STEEL CABLE BELT DRIVE
Notched V-belts are reinforced with 5 high-flex steel cables, give extra efficient power transmission.

RUBBER MOTOR MOUNTS
Special three-point suspension, mounted in rubber, soaks up vibration.

HOT-SPARK IGNITION
High tension magneto, coil and condenser for quick starting. No battery required.

ALL-CHROME TRIM
Motor mounts, belt guard and exhaust pipe chrome plated for extra beauty, longer life.

FOR NEAREST WHIZZER DEALER, CALL WESTERN UNION, ASK FOR OPERATOR 25

HEAVY-DUTY BIKE STAND
Adjustable, extra heavy stand supplied with every motor.

COMPLETE WITH ALL NECESSARY ATTACHMENTS
$109⁹⁷
Federal Tax Included, F.O.B. Pontiac, Mich.
Fits any man's balloon tire bike

PRECISION ENGINEERED
Cylinder micro-honed to 5/10,000" tolerance. Drop forged crankshaft, camshaft, connecting rod.

FREE LITERATURE!
WHIZZER MOTOR COMPANY
350 South Sanford,
PONTIAC, MICHIGAN

Send me literature on the Whizzer Bike Motor

NAME _____
STREET _____
CITY _____ STATE _____

MARCH 1949

255

189

Volkswagen Beetle

David spoke, and Goliath listened

In 1949, a little thing that didn't even look like a car appeared on the streets of America—first with a split rear window, then with an oval one. It looked like a crawling insect and sounded like it was rattling apart. It had also been developed in the 1930s by the German government under the leadership of Adolph Hitler, and no American would buy that, right? The Volkswagen didn't look like anything to worry about.

American cars were growing bigger, heavier, and more powerful in late 1950s, but before World War II, many American cars with high-quality engineering were capable of fuel economy over 20 miles per gallon. Efficient overhead-valve Chevrolets, Buicks, and full-size Nashes breathed easily through the 1930s and 1940s. Well-oiled six-cylinder Chrysler products glided along in overdrive. Studebaker Champions, Nash 600s, and Hudson's Terraplanes were underpowered but very efficient for city driving.

After World War II, prosperity reigned from coast to coast, and it was time to replace those rusty, worn-out prewar cars with the sleek new Jet-Age style. Automatic transmissions appeared all over, with varying results. American cars got bigger and bigger, and as racing became televised, V-8 engines began outselling sixes in the early 1950s. Freeways worked their way through cities and across the plains, and big, gliding, American cars hit their zenith. At the same time, so did the Volkswagen.

There were only about 1,200 Volkswagens on American streets by 1954, but the numbers quickly grew, and Volkswagen sold 18,000 cars in 1958. The American car companies must have been watching, because in 1960 alone, GM, Ford, and Chrysler caught up to Rambler, which had always kept an economy make on the road. A herd of Valiants, Lancers, Falcons, Comets, and Corvairs poured out of American auto plants, and they were followed quickly by Tempests, F-85s, Specials, Chevy IIs, and Darts. The bigger-engines-are-better mistake was repeated, and by the late 1960s even these American compacts had V-8s stuffed into them. They were

The optional sunroof gives the little car a greater feeling of space inside and lets the sun illuminate the dashboard's prewar feel.

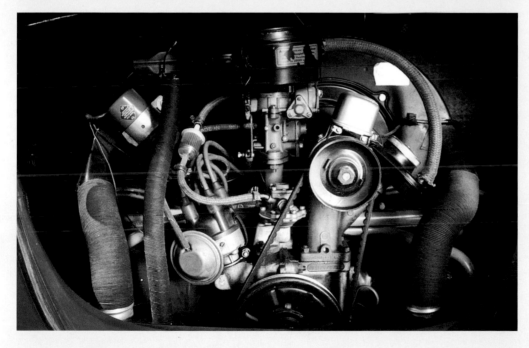

Most Volkswagen Beetles were stripped-down economy cars, but this dolled-up example from 1962 has been in the same family since new, and it shows that even a humble Beetle could be accessorized into campy, pint-sized luxury. The fender skirts increase the aerodynamic look, while the gravel shields, headlight eyebrows, and whitewall tires carry the torch of Jet Age American cars from a decade before.

soon to be replaced by Pintos, Vegas, and Gremlins in the 1970s.

The Volkswagen could be remembered for what it caused as much as for its actual qualities, but they were fun cars. The small engines were underpowered, and the wind blew the cars around on their bias-ply tires. After the addition of larger engines and the advent of radial tires, the Beetle became a car of choice among errand-running mothers, college students, urban commuters, and long-haired flower children who held grudges against their fathers' Dynaflow Buicks.

Volkswagen stopped production of the Beetle in Germany in 1978, but the Beetle rang in the twenty-first century still in production in Mexico. The very last Beetle left the plant in 2003 to the sentimental strains of mariachi music, destined for a museum in Germany. It left behind a family of over 21,000,000 cars rolling on the streets worldwide.

Americans tended to misuse their Beetles, forcing 1,100-cc models up Rocky Mountain grades in the summertime, just as they had misused their big American road cars to run to the store for a bottle of milk. Each car had its place and purpose, and the Volkswagen can be remembered for reminding the American car companies to build efficient cars in the late 1950s when they were forgetting how to do it.

Hot Rods and Customs

The personal touch

Personalizing an automobile, making it something that is truly reflective of the owner, most likely began with the second car ever produced. By 1920, an entire industry had developed to meet the growing needs of automobile owners who wanted to give their cars the personal touch. However, during this early period, a great many of the custom touches were in actuality the addition of items that made the car safer, more practical, or more comfortable. Advertisements for a few of these add-ons proclaimed, "Broken Arms Prevented From Ford Cranking–Non-Kick Device Company" and "The Hunter Starter for Ford Cars–Hunter Auto Supply Company."

The roots of the custom car and hot rod culture of the 1950s can be traced to these formative years. Advertisements such as "Arrow–Racing Body for Fords–$69–painted free in Stutz Red, Blue, or Brewster Green" and "Make Your Ford a $3,000 Car–Roof 16 Overhead Valve Equipment" beckoned owners to customize.

Even though there were sparks and pockets of customization during the 1920s and 1930s, it was the postwar years when the fad gained its cult following. It was in 1946 that Ed "Big Daddy" Roth acquired his first car, a 1933 Ford coupe, a vehicle that came to symbolize the golden age of the hot rod. Before joining the Air Force in 1951, he had transformed the little coupe to something quite different from what Henry Ford had envisioned.

In the years before the introduction of the small-block engine, and now with an interest in recreating classic street rods, the flathead Ford V-8 was the engine of choice for hot rodders.

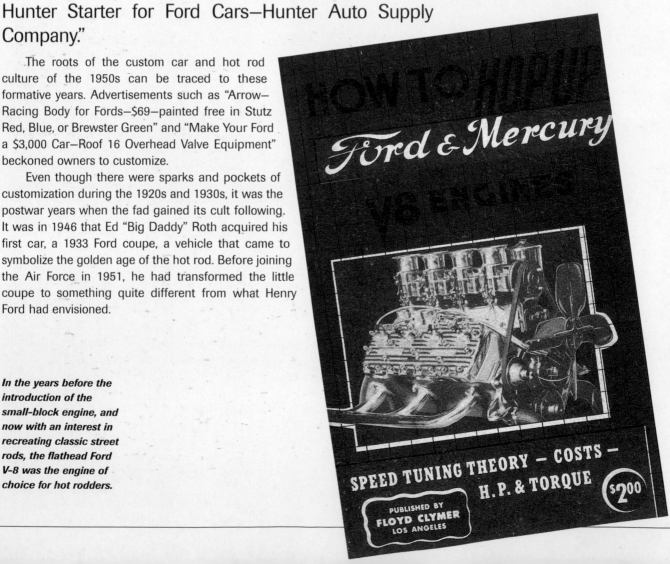

HOW TO HOP UP
Ford & Mercury
V8 ENGINES

SPEED TUNING THEORY – COSTS – H. P. & TORQUE

$2.00

PUBLISHED BY
FLOYD CLYMER
LOS ANGELES

Good Luck to my friend Jim
Charlie Ryan

Charlie Ryan with the original
"Hot Rod Lincoln," a modified Ford coupe
that came to symbolize hot rods in the 1950s.

By the late 1950s, the custom car craze had spawned an entire subculture, and countless publications were established to capitalize on this market.

In 1938, Harry Westergard, a Sacramento, California, garage owner, ignored the need for speed that was already becoming the trademark of the hot rod set and set his sights on truly customizing his ride, a 1935 Ford. He began with severe modification to the suspension, which resulted in a vehicle so low it seemed to hug the ground. Next he chopped the roof, further lowering the profile. Then he removed the chrome and filled the body seams. His partner in this endeavor was a young piano player by the name of George Barris, another legendary pioneer in the custom car culture.

By 1950, what would become two distinct cultures, the hot rodders and the low riders set out on distinctly different paths. The hot rodders focused on go, with the show being in wild paint schemes, stripped fenders, big tires, chopped tops, and painted flames dominating the front clip. The low riders focused on slow, low vehicles built for show with plush interiors. The former were born from the economic postwar boom, the latter in the hardscrabble of barrios in places such as East Los Angeles and El Paso.

The hot rod scene and the car that inspired it was encapsulated in one song, "Hot Rod Lincoln," written by Charlie Ryan, and his car had started life as a 1941 Lincoln Zephyr four-door sedan. A couple of years after purchasing the used car, he decided to hot rod it. Step one was the removal of the Zephyr body, and the second was to cut 2 feet from the frame to shorten the wheelbase. Next a Model A Ford coupe body was mounted on the chassis. Power was supplied by a Lincoln V-12 and transmitted to the rear wheels by way of a 1948 Lincoln three-speed transmission and overdrive unit. Cut-down Zephyr bumpers, a Lincoln greyhound radiator ornament, and a Lincoln emblem on the grill were the most noticeable modifications to the front. Inside, the instrument cluster was pure Lincoln, housed in a cut-down Zephyr dashboard.

The song "Hot Rod Lincoln" was first recorded in 1955. Since that time, it has been recorded for each succeeding generation: by Johnny Bond in 1959, Commander Cody and the Lost Planet Airmen in 1972, Asleep at the Wheel in the 1980s, and by Jim Varney for the film *The Beverly Hillbillies* in the 1990s.

An ironic twist to the hot rod and custom story is made manifest at car shows everywhere. At some juncture, the individuality of the movement that was so apparent in the creations of the Ayala brothers of Los Angeles, Ed "Big Daddy" Roth, and Harry Westergard was being replaced with a wave of conformity.

Collector cards issued by custom-car magazines, such as this one by Car Craft Magazine, *and cards included in bubble-gum packages were a hot commodity among schoolboys during the 1950s and 1960s.*

Ford coupes were fitted to 350-cid Chevrolet V-8 engines, 1957 Chevrolets were all given "flame jobs," and the V-8-powered Model T roadsters known as buckets came to dominate the scene. The low rider scene has not been immune to the conformist movement of the past 20 years or so either.

There are rays of hope that individuality will once again reign. There is a growing movement to recreate hot rods of the 1950s that are powered by highly modified flathead Ford V-8 engines. Recently, with the help of a computer stylus and modern fiberglass, a Tucker was recreated and outfitted with a full Cadillac Northstar drivetrain.

Pedal Cars
In the beginning

Juvenile cars, as some companies initially called them, have served as an introductory vehicle for countless generations. The majority of early toy cars were made of tin, with body designs that merely mimicked the basic design of those being produced for the adult market. Pedal power often served as the means of motivation.

However, some manufacturers graced their showrooms with intricately outfitted scale-model recreations of the full-size models. The resultant pedal-powered LaSalles, Packards, and other miniature luxury cars with glass windshields and nickel-plated chrome trim and grills are highly sought after by collectors today.

Cars were not the only mode of transportation rendered to Lilliputian scale and powered by the pedal. Airplanes and boats also proved to be quite popular.

A few companies decided to forgo pedal and illusion, with the result being operational "junior" cars. To say the very least, the American Motor Vehicle Company of Lafayette, Indiana, was a diverse manufacturer. In addition to a cycle car, a small 1,000-pound panel truck for light delivery use, and a two-passenger roadster, they also produced the American Junior in 1916. The company insisted the $160 car was not a toy—this in spite of the fact that it had a 70-inch wheelbase, a single-cylinder engine most often used to motorize bicycles, a weight of just 225 pounds, and promotional material that left little doubt it had ostensibly been designed for children.

This was not the only example of attempts to encourage a desire for things automotive in the younger generation. In 1906, the Juvenile Electric built by the American Metal Wheel and Auto Company of Toledo, Ohio, was marketed as an operational electric car for adolescents.

Today pedal cars and other junior automobiles are highly sought after collector's items that on occasion bring prices at auction in excess of a full-size vehicle from the same period. Perhaps the reason can be found in the fondness one has for his first set of wheels.

With their diversification in 1907, manufacturers of children's cars, often pedal powered, mirrored the automobile industry of the period.

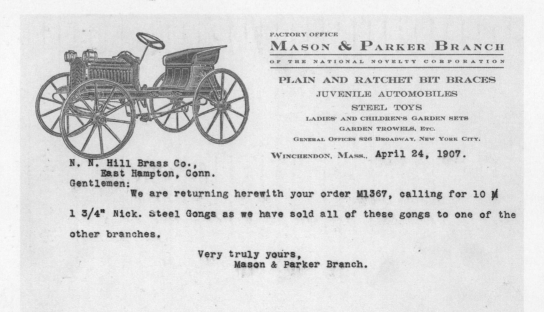

FACTORY OFFICE
MASON & PARKER BRANCH
OF THE NATIONAL NOVELTY CORPORATION

PLAIN AND RATCHET BIT BRACES

JUVENILE AUTOMOBILES

STEEL TOYS

LADIES' AND CHILDREN'S GARDEN SETS

GARDEN TROWELS, ETC.

GENERAL OFFICES 826 BROADWAY, NEW YORK CITY.

WINCHENDON, MASS., **April 24, 1907.**

N. N. Hill Brass Co.,
    East Hampton, Conn.
Gentlemen:
            We are returning herewith your order M1367, calling for 10 M

1 3/4" Nick. Steel Gongs as we have sold all of these gongs to one of the

other branches.

                    Very truly yours,
                    Mason & Parker Branch.

School Bus

Hate me now, love me later

Three guys have been working all day. They're tired and punchy, and they've given up appearances. They're riding at highway speed in the back of a big stake-bed truck on a Los Angeles freeway with a big portable stereo, dancing up a storm like the front row of a George Clinton concert. They're being watched. Approaching from behind are 80 witnesses in a Crown Supercoach, many of whom stand, strike a pose, and join their freeway neighbors in a round of funky dancing.

The sleek lines of California's classic Crown Supercoach wearing its best school-bus yellow.

REO SAFETY SCHOOL BUS

SCHOOL BUS

REO SAFETY SCHOOL BUS

SEATS 55
STANDEES 11

REO

SCHOOL BUS

• SPECIFICATIONS •

The guys in the truck see the high-schoolers, and they begin to laugh, point, and out-funk them. For the next 20 seconds, the laborers in the truck and the high school band on the bus are friends doing the same dance, over enraged admonitions from the bus driver and band director.

Not all bus-bound memories are so wanton. One boy glances back, out of boredom, and sees a girl staring out the window. She's completely lost in her own thoughts and mouthing the words to "Sweet Home Alabama" as it crackles out of the radio.

A beautiful girl, who doesn't know she's pretty, gets sleepy on a long trip and falls asleep with her head on the shoulder of a shy, unpopular boy who sits as still as he can in order to not wake her. He wants to savor the moment. Another shy, unpopular boy is watching and nods his congratulations.

Maybe school memories are overly romanticized, but it's also undeniable that people go to reunions to see the schoolmates they knew in a place they hated. School buses may be fondly and bitterly remembered for the first kiss, the first fight, making lifelong friendships, making school-time enemies, being greeted by friends, or being given the don't-you-dare-sit-by-me glare. They remember the pretty girls, nerdy boys, the quiet ones, and the bullies. Most of the time, the school bus was about waiting impatiently in freezing weather to be taken to someplace we hated to go. School was drudgery, and the bus took us there. Most of the morning bus rides are remembered years later as a blur of diesel engines, rough shifts, hissing air brakes, and loud voices. Then, one day, we realize that the model of bus that took us to school

REO was just one of many truck manufacturers that produced school busses during the immediate postwar years.

SAFETY TROPHY
Reo Safety School Bus was 1946 winner of Safety Engineering Magazine's annual award for outstanding safety in motor vehicle design — the first since 1941.

Wide, comfortable seats spaced at 27 inches and covered with genuine leather, generous aisle width and roomy book racks are features. Note that seat handholds permit a good grip. Other seats and spacings are available.

REO SAFETY SCHOOL BUS
equipped with LIFE GUARD TUBES

Reo has provided additional protection for America's school children. To prevent the tragedies that so often follow tire blowouts Reo has adopted the Lifeguard Safety tube as standard equipment. No other bus offers this and all the other Reo safety and quality features.

ORDINARY TUBE
Blowout completely deflates single air compartment frequently throwing vehicle out of control.

LIFEGUARD TUBE
Only outer chamber blows out, inner chamber supports tire while vehicle is brought to safe smooth stop.

The instrument panel is as neat as an automobile's. At left is the light switch panel with independent switches. At far right is a glove compartment for log book and reports. Two fire extinguishers and an axe are within easy reach.

Above, This unique driver's seat is a safety factor. Adjustable — forward or back, up and down — to put driver within easy reach of all controls, it also swivels for quick accessibility. Unusually comfortable, seat can be removed from bus in a jiffy.

Left, The wide, folding entrance door, with vertical closing edge equipped with large, soft rubber snubber to protect children's fingers, permits quick, easy entrance and exit of children. A metal guard is between the loading well and right front seat.

decades before has disappeared from the roadways, and at the moment of realization, it's too late to see one again.

Some school buses showed their inner roots, and their Ford, GMC, International, or Studebaker truck noses stuck out from under the bus body, making what some kids called the "dog-face." Others were all bus, and they were not identified by their chassis makers but, rather, by their body makers: Gillig, Bluebird, Pacific, Thomas, Carpenter. The Gillig looked like a Crown imitation, but it had its own charms and a rich history, and drivers loved its ten10-speed transmission. The Pacific had a memorable second set of horizontal windows under the windshield, and it looked like it was wearing granny glasses as it took kids to school in Oregon and Washington.

The Crown Supercoach was the beauty winner. The sleek, curvy Crowns took millions of Californians and Southwesterners to school, football games, and on field trips. The Crowns took their shape in 1950 and held their form until going out of business in 1991. They've become classics, and they're disappearing fast.

Every American knows what color school-bus yellow is. It was chosen only because it's easy to see against all backgrounds and in all weather, but it's become a deeper symbol than that. Many Americans who love automobiles learned started that love affair on the school bus, where they could get a bird's-eye view of all the cars on the road. They rode more miles on school buses than in their own families' cars, and they feel sad when they notice that it's been a long time since they've seen a classic Crown or a GMC with "cat's eyes" in the hood.

4

The Culture of the Road

In the past century, the automobile and its supportive infrastructure have become such an integral part of our culture it could even be said that car culture is our culture. Our very vocabulary is a cornucopia of automotive-related terminology.

Nearly since its beginnings, the automobile has been the object around which our lives revolve. From the food we pick up at the drive-thru on the way home, to getting to the office, to taking the family on vacation, the automobile has become almost as essential in our lives as air is for breathing.

And yet each generation bemoans the good old days, the glorious time before the minivan, unleaded fuel, gas shortages, the interstates, World War II, and the Great Depression. It would seem selective amnesia: the ability to forget the hard times or at least overshadow them with the good is an integral part of human nature.

Ties to those glory days are tenuous, and with the passing of time the memories begin to fade. But with a little stimulus—an old picture, a cheerful jingle, an advertising slogan or highway sign—they become fresh again. It is almost as though each is a special time capsule filled with sights, sounds, and even smells.

Regardless of your age, try to remember any point in the past without an automotive reference. Watch the memories revive whenever mention is made of. . . .

Bates Motel
"They moved away the highway…"

Everyone in Psycho is looking for something they've lost. Lila Crane's sister is missing, and she wants her back. The real estate company is missing money, and they want it back. Sam Loomis' girlfriend is missing, and he wants her back. Marion Crane's boyfriend kept leaving her to return to his hometown, and she wanted him back. Once Marion stole the money to make it possible to be with her boyfriend, her conscience attacked her, and she wanted her dignity back. Unfortunately, Norman Bates had lost his mother, and he wanted her back.

Marion looks at a pile of money in her office, and behind her on the wall are two paintings, one of the place where a California Highway Patrolman would confront her, and one of the Bates Motel. Marion commits the first criminal act of her life out of desperation and love, and she does the next most logical thing. She gets into her car. She's a beautiful girl with a plain, black, base-model 1954 Ford—a joyless, anonymous car with no describable features, which reflects Marion's life.

Alfred Hitchcock was a master of authenticity, and car and road enthusiasts can accurately follow Marion's drive to hell. She would have left Phoenix and headed west on U.S. 60 all the way to Los Angeles, where she would have turned north on U.S. 99—Interstate 5 today. The rain is pouring, and car lovers smile at the shots through the windshield that show the fender of the 1957 Ford that Marion did not yet have. Marion pulls over and sleeps in her car. She's parked on the old Ridge Route between California Highway 138 and the town of Gorman on the east side of U.S. 99. The Ridge Route in this area is called the Gorman Post Road, and Marion is surprised by a highway patrolman who rolls up in his 1957 Ford patrol car and wakes her. She talks her way out of it, and through her back window, she sees the deliberately back-lit, predatory, beast-like patrol car take the Gorman exit.

"I'm in no mood for trouble!" California Charlie says to the nervous customer on his used-car lot who's also being watched by the highway patrolman across the street. Marion lacks the sociopathic skills necessary to be a good thief, and California Charlie finally says to her, "I take it you can prove that car is yours." Marion strolls past two Edsels with a 1955 Pontiac in the background.

"They moved away the highway," the young motel owner says to Marion at the end of the day near Sacramento. There was a lot of that happening on U.S. 99 in 1960—detours, bypasses, road construction, upgrades to freeway standards, and destroyed businesses. The motel guests have been taken away, but the property tax bills keep coming. The isolated, obsolete Bates Motel is very realistic.

Within 10 miles of her destination, Marion takes Norman's advice and decides to not live in her "private trap." However, at the moment of her repentance, a killer sends her to the bottom of a swamp in the trunk of her 1957 Ford.

Sam Loomis and Lila Crane keep looking for Marion in Sam's 1955 Dodge pickup truck—an honest, decent, working-man's vehicle. The egotistical private eye with the slick turn-of-a-phrase looks for Marion in his flashy, attention-getting Mercury. After the detective meets his violent end, Norman Bates stands smiling in the dark near the swamp where, presumably, the Mercury rests in the mud at the bottom, chrome flashing no more, and attracting no attention. Psycho's cars and its portrayal of travel say so much, and all of it is believable.

At the end, the killer says, "and they'll say, 'Why, she wouldn't hurt a fly,'" and Marion's mud-covered Ford is pulled from the swamp with the same cruelty with which it was sunk. Movie trivia buffs claim this very same 1957 Ford starred in the first season of Leave It To Beaver. What a sweet beginning, and what a terrifying end.

This motel sits bypassed by a later freeway, out of the way and forgotten along the original path of U.S. 99 as it heads north-by-northwest near Fresno, California. In the frenzy of highway improvements, the U.S. Highway system was notorious in 1960, fort the premise of Psycho was even easy for the birds to believe, and Marion would have been better off seeing the Bates Motel getting smaller in her rear window. On the serious side, the dawning of fenced-off, limited-access freeways did make viable businesses suddenly obsolete through the late 1950s and 1960s, and with time, and public began to miss their individuality. Many highway history enthusiasts have referred to bypassed motels as "Bates Motels," immortalizing the believable location in car-culture jargon as well as in the cinematic lexicon.

Billboards and Burma Shave
Signs of the times

Roadside promotion predates the automobile by centuries. There is evidence that the blank sides of buildings that face roadways have been used for advertising at least since ancient Rome. A Tennessee company that had used the same concept with great success served to inspire Garnet Carter's now-famous Rock City barns.

Nevertheless, it took the automobile to make roadside promotion an art form. And few reached the lofty levels attained by the Odell family, with their signs designed to promote their brushless shaving cream, Burma-Shave.

The Odells had some success with their initial product, Burma-Vitas, when they began developing a product that would have wider market appeal. After repeated experimentation and market evaluation, they created the famed Burma-Shave. The next problem to overcome was marketing and promotion.

This challenge was resolved by Alan Odell, who in 1925 received reluctant approval from the company to test-market his sign series along select highways in Minnesota. Initially the signs didn't rhyme, but merely promoted the product. Still, after seeing the signs along the roadsides, travelers began requesting the shaving cream. The company now found itself with another dilemma: meeting the demand.

The success of the advertising campaign soon spread into surrounding states, and humor was added to the signs to promote the shaving cream, as well as impart safety or moral messages. "If daisies are your—favorite flower—keep pushin' up those—miles per hour—Burma-Shave."

To further promote the company, zany contests were added to the signs, and customers were encouraged to send in their jingles. "Free Offer! Free Offer!—Rip a fender off your car—Mail it in for a half-pound jar—Burma-Shave" and "Free! Free!—A trip to Mars—For 900 empty jars—Burma-Shave" were two that received the greatest response.

Incredibly, the company received hundreds of fenders, and in each instance the company honored its obligations even when it came to a trip to Mars (spelled Moers, a small community in Germany). By World War II, the Burma-Shave signs had become such an ingrained part of American culture that GIs created their own version or received the real thing from family members who had removed them from the roadsides, and the ubiquitous signs were soon seen in almost all theaters of operation.

Eventually, higher speeds on interstate highways made the small signs impractical. This, coupled with decreasing sales, prompted the Odell family to sell the company to Philip Morris, which also operated American Safety Razor. With the acquisition of Burma-Shave, Philip Morris discontinued the roadside signs in 1963.

Even if the Burma-Shave roadside jingles had survived the changing times, they would have most likely succumbed to the onslaught of regulation. On October 22, 1965, President Lyndon Johnson signed the Highway Beautification Act, which effectively brought an end to the era of innovative roadside promotion and hid the junkyard from view.

But here and there, vestiges remain. As travelers roll along the plains of the Texas panhandle, for example, they can still meditate on making Tucumcari tonight or in rare instances find the recreated Burma-Shave signs, which were placed a few years ago by *Reminisce* magazine.

New Beauty....New Body Types
LINCOLN - ZEPHYR V·12
for 1938

Foster and Kleiser

The billboard was as much a part of the roadside scenery as trees in the years before the Highway Beautification Act.

12 BOTTLES 50¢

PLUS DEPOSIT

Coca-Cola

ENJOY AT HOME

Burma-Shave JINGLE BOOK

FORTY-FOUR JINGLES *Burma-Shave*

DIRECTIONS FOR USE EXPLAINED

This Burma-Shave jingles book featuring most of the famous slogans was a promotional item that was included with jars of the cream in the mid-1930s.

Test Facilities
To the limits and beyond

In the beginning, automobile manufacturers tested and improved their vehicles in full view of the public through racing, endurance runs, and hill climbs. Quite often the owner of the company was also the chief engineer and driver.

In March 1896, Henry Ford took to the streets of Detroit in his first car. F. E. Stanley, one half of the famous Stanley brothers, kicked off the company that bore his name with a public demonstration of his car's hillclimbing abilities in 1897. The racing prowess and mechanical skills of Louis Chevrolet and his brothers were quite well known before there was ever a vehicle that carried his name.

Once-remote spots on the map—locations like Bonneville, Daytona, and Pikes Peak, where vehicles could be pushed to the limits for both publicity and the advancement of automotive technology—soon became as well known as Washington, D.C. Race tracks such as that in Indianapolis were elevated to shrine status among auto enthusiasts. While places such as these would, and still do, play

This circa-1928 souvenir booklet highlights the many technological advancements in testing utilized at the new General Motors proving ground in Milford, Michigan.

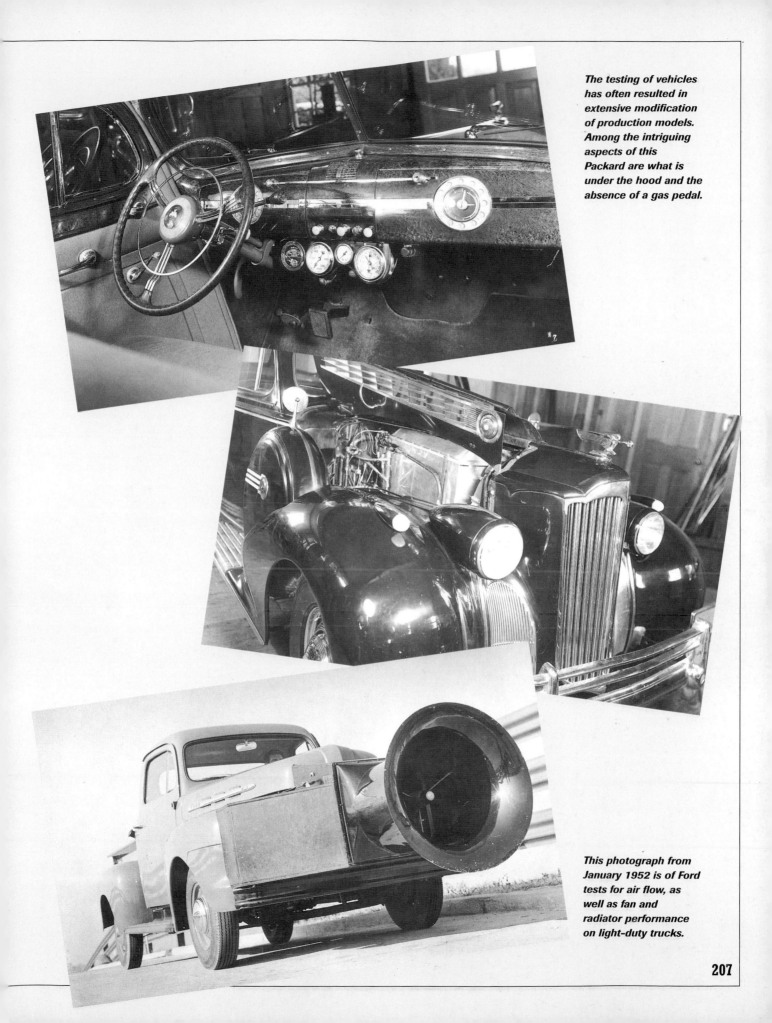

The testing of vehicles has often resulted in extensive modification of production models. Among the intriguing aspects of this Packard are what is under the hood and the absence of a gas pedal.

This photograph from January 1952 is of Ford tests for air flow, as well as fan and radiator performance on light-duty trucks.

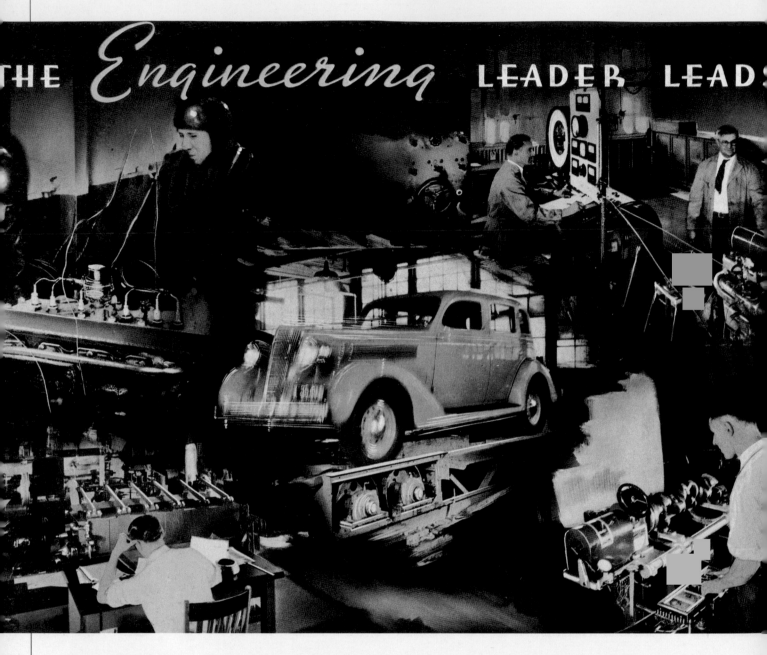

THE *Engineering* LEADER LEADS

By the 1930s, testing of vehicles and their individual components was an integral part of the automobile manufacturing process, as shown in this Chrysler Airstream brochure.

an important part in American car culture, by 1910 it was becoming increasingly important to test vehicles in a more scientific and controlled manner. Of equal importance was the need to beat the competition, which required testing new advancements, including those of competitors, with a little more secrecy.

By the 1920s, most American manufacturers had established extensive high-security proving grounds. Vehicles were subjected to a variety of controlled conditions and could then be tested and dismantled. A lengthy list of tests was often standard, including fuel economy at various speeds over level as well as hilly conditions, vibration and noise levels, acceleration on a variety of grades with variable loads, cold-weather starting, and braking.

Many tests were modified or abandoned as road conditions and consumers' demands evolved. For example, in the 1920s the General Motors facility in Milford, Michigan, routinely tested vehicles on an 11.65-percent grade, with 450-pound load, starting in high gear at 10, 20, and 30 miles per hour. The concrete grades were set at 7.26 percent, 9.7 percent, and a long one at 11.65 percent. A variety of gravel grades ranged to an astounding 24 percent!

Postwar facilities also began to test for corrosion, seat wear, and paint durability under a

variety of weather conditions. By the mid-1960s, increasing concern over emissions resulted in a new era of vehicle testing.

The dynamometer, a device consisting of rollers and plates that vaguely resembled a standard service-station hoist, allowed a car to be operated as though it were on the road while being viewed from any angle. The dynamometer had been a key component in the test facility for many years. But with the advancements in electronics, a new twist was added. Special sensors transferred data from a variety of real highways and roads onto magnetic tape. From the dynamometer control booth, the operator was then able to program the rollers to duplicate specific real-world conditions.

With rapid advancements in technology, automobile testing has greatly evolved. For example, the old method used to gauge turning radiuses involved two men who measured the wet circle created when a vehicle was being turned, while someone lay over the fender pouring water on the tire. Nevertheless, real-world tests are still an integral part of vehicle development, and American manufacturer's proving-ground facilities can be found throughout the United States and Canada.

Postcards and Bumper Stickers

Wish you were here

Post cards and bumper stickers are two of the most widely recognized souvenirs from an adventure on the road, and they are arguably the most cost-effective manner for promoting a roadside business. They are also wonderful time capsules that chronicle the development of roadside America. Moreover, both have come to symbolize America's love affair with the highway and the road trip.

In many circles, credit for inventing the bumper sticker has been given to Lester Dill, owner of Meramec Caverns in Missouri. Promotion for the caverns, located on Route 66, began in a manner similar to that of Rock City, with painted barns in the 1930s. This was followed by well-circulated rumors that the cave was the site of buried treasure, Civil War caches, and Jesse James' hideout. In turn, these stories were enhanced with tour guides "discovering" rusty guns, canvas bank bags, or saddles.

Additional promotion came in the form of heavy cardboard signs with the cave's name silkscreened onto them. These signs were wired to the rear bumper of cars in the parking lot by local teenagers. The next stage in the evolution came with the application of double-sided tape to the cards. But if there was wax or oil on the bumpers, they wouldn't stick. The solution came from 3M, which had recently developed a waterproof adhesive-backed paper.

The use of picture post cards for quick notes to the folks back home, as well for collecting, dates to the late nineteenth century, when post cards became an international mania. Even though the craze had begun in Europe, the

SERPENTINE TRAIL
PIKES PEAK AUTO HIGHWAY

Post cards and souvenir booklets have been an integral part of America's love of the highway from the inception of the automobile, and as such are true time capsules. From right to left: a real photo post card of the Columbia River Highway in Oregon; a card from the Indianapolis Speedway circa 1918; an intriguing Cadillac stretch sedan at the Redwoods in Northern California; and a souvenir booklet from Pikes Peak circa 1920.

folks in America soon jumped on the bandwagon. In 1906, Americans purchased more than 700 million post cards. By 1913, the number had risen to 968 million, but then, because of hostilities in Europe, as well as the growing popularity of greeting cars, sales plummeted precipitously.

Throughout the 1920s and 1930s, the use of post cards remained relatively flat. In the 1950s, as Americans took to the roads in record numbers, the use of post cards once again came into vogue, as did collecting. Today post cards from the glory days of the highway are highly sought-after time capsules from that era, with many actually being reproduced, as a wave of nostalgia spearheaded by an international resurgence of interest in Route 66.

Coffee Shops and Diners
Eating with the locals

The diner and the coffee shop are often confused, and even more frequently imitated. Nevertheless, they were initially as different as the interstate highway was from the Lincoln Highway. According to the American Diner Museum, a true diner is a prefabricated structure built at an assembly site and transported to a permanent location for food service. *Webster's Dictionary* notes that the word *diner* is a derivative of *dining car*, and that a diner is a restaurant that reflects that lineage.

The coffee shop is, well, a coffee shop. Usually it is a small restaurant with limited food offerings, often a hangout for locals, and almost always a microcosm of the community in which it is built.

According to legend, the origins of the diner can be traced to Walter Scott, a teenage pressman who supplemented his income with the sale of sandwiches and coffee. By 1872, he had abandoned his primary job, converted an express wagon into a lunch cart, and started selling food in front of the *Providence Journal* office.

It has been said the greatest compliment one can be paid is imitation. The success of Scott's lunch cart was soon emulated throughout the city. This popularity led several manufacturers to build lunch wagons. A few of these wagons were oversized and allowed customers to stand or sit on stools that were sheltered from the weather. As the carts' popularity spread, so too did their development and improvement. A few were rather ornate, featuring intricate woodwork and leaded, etched windows.

Because of their growing success in some communities, lunch-wagon vendors became subject to stringent regulation of location and areas of operation. During this same period, electric models were replacing horse-drawn streetcars. Enterprising individuals purchased the antiquated cars at reasonable prices and set them up on semi-permanent locations.

However, the diner cars or lunch wagons had from their inception been geared toward clientele on a budget. Likewise, the owners had often begun to run their operations on meager budgets. Many establishments became known as greasy spoons or ptomaine palaces. Nevertheless, reputable owners made sure their establishments were clean and presentable. Fresh paint and flower boxes were often added to improve their image.

In the 1920s, numerous companies utilizing the railroad dining car concept began building the cars with increased dimensions and offered them to operators on credit. But overall, the diners were changed little from the lunch wagon of a generation before.

The streamlining of railroad equipment in the 1930s spurred manufacturers of diners to follow suit. Trolley cars were being abandoned for buses, and once again prospective diner operators had an opportunity to begin an operation with a meager budget through buying old trolley cars. This trend, as well as the hard economic conditions of the time, forced many diner manufacturers to close their doors.

After World War II, the diner once again surged to prominence. Americans were in a hurry and on the road as never before. Soon a new concept in roadside dining, the fast-food restaurant, was appearing along the roadsides. The few remaining builders of diners attempted to counter the threat by producing diners in a variety of styles to replace the traditional look of stainless steel, bright colors, and eye-catching neon. Diners from an earlier era were often remodeled, and the shiny exteriors were covered with brick facades.

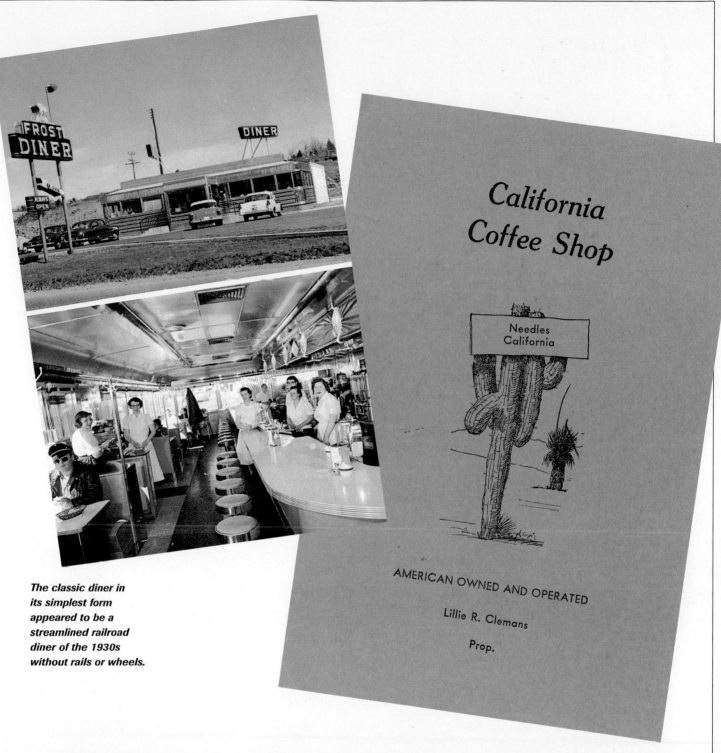

The classic diner in its simplest form appeared to be a streamlined railroad diner of the 1930s without rails or wheels.

California Coffee Shop

Needles California

AMERICAN OWNED AND OPERATED

Lillie R. Clemans

Prop.

Then in the 1970s, a revival of interest in diners spurred the three remaining manufacturers to begin fabrication of new diners. As things turned full circle, a few national chains, such as Denny's, Silver Diners, and Johnny Rockets, began using the diner as part of their marketing strategies.

Today, vintage diners that have survived are being resurrected and relocated, as an international wave of nostalgia for the roadside of America sweeps the nation. The Massachusetts Historical Commission has placed all historic diners that are still in operation on the National Register of Historic places. From Bisbee, Arizona, to the Henry Ford Museum in Dearborn, Michigan, a new generation is discovering a landmark from the glory days of the American highway, the diner.

This menu from the California Coffee Shop features regional and local favorites such as figs, keno sandwiches, and Spanish omelets.

Drive-In Theater
Passion pits and family fun

When one considers the American love affair with the automobile and passion for motion pictures, the success of the drive-in theater should come as no surprise. However, what is surprising is how long it took from inception to widespread acceptance. Moreover, in light of the romanticized view of the recent past and the elevation of highways such as Route 66 to the status of icon, another surprise is that the drive-in theater hasn't enjoyed a revival. In addition, when one considers the fond memories almost anyone over 40 years of age has for the drive-in, all of this becomes even more amazing.

The legend began in the early 1930s, when Richard Hollingshead began showing films in the yard of his New Jersey home using a sheet and a projector mounted on the hood of his car. The explosive success of the endeavor led him to apply for a patent, which was granted on May 16, 1933. On June 6 of the same year in Camden, New Jersey, Hollingshead opened the first drive-in theater.

Incredibly, the concept was relatively slow to catch on. Between 1933 and 1939, only 17 additional drive-in theaters were opened. Then in 1941, the introduction of the in-car speaker developed by RCA sparked an explosion in drive-ins. Within one-year, 95 theaters opened in 27 states. The rationing of tires and rubber during World War II muted this trend, and in several instances theaters closed due to lack of business. However, shortly after the war, the drive-in theater

Drive-ins become a symbol of the postwar era and an increasingly profitable area of the exhibition industry. **Redwood Theatres Collection, courtesy of the Academy of Motion Picture Arts and Sciences**

Mid-century matchbook covers highlight the amenities and architecture of drive-in theatres.
Ross Melnick collection

was rediscovered and the boom began.

By the end of 1949, the number of theaters had risen to 820, and by 1958 the number had skyrocketed to 5,000. With this explosion came improvements and diversification.

In Copiague, New York, the All-Weather-Drive-In opened with an astounding 2,500-car capacity, in addition to indoor seating for 1,200. The complex also featured a playground, restaurant, and cafeteria. Other theaters came to include everything from Laundromats to swimming pools, concession stands, and in-car heaters.

Nevertheless, there was a dark side to the drive-in theater, and soon they were being referred to with disdain by concerned parents and morally minded citizens as passion pits. But this wasn't what brought the reign of the drive-in to a close, nor was it the value of properties for redevelopment, as some have speculated. The drive-in's demise can't be completely blamed on the introduction of the VCR and cable television, either. Though all of these were contributing factors, it was ultimately nudity and adult subject matter in films that hastened the demise of the drive-in.

Throughout the 1990s, there was a glimmer of hope for those who yearned to once again enjoy their films under the starlit sky. Ten drive-ins added new screens and 21 new drive-ins were added to the roster. Further hope was found in the formation of the United Drive-in Theater Owners Association in 2000, and the construction of 3 new theaters in 2003.

Drive-Thru Windows
Service without leaving your car

The drive-thru window represents a near-perfect marriage between the automobile and the fast-paced culture that embraced it. As such, it is most likely that the idea was thought of by numerous enterprising individuals independent of each other.

As with many innovations, there are legends to attest to its origins. The Pig Stand in Dallas, Texas, opened its doors in 1921 to an enthusiastic public and soon expanded to other locations, pioneering the concept of the franchise.

Whatever its origins, the drive-thru window is a mainstay of American car culture. Fast food, a staple of the American diet, wouldn't exist without the drive-thru window. Where would we be if we couldn't use drive-thru windows at banks and pharmacies?

The drive-thru window has also served as a springboard for innovative entrepreneurs. In Las Vegas, some wedding chapels now feature drive-thru service. In 2003, Huntington, West Virginia, opened the first drive-thru-window library, and the first customer was "Elvis Presley" (West Virginia Library Commissioner J. D. Wagner in costume).

The most original concept for incorporating drive-thru service into a business has to be the Climax Gentleman's Club in Delmont, Pennsylvania. Motorists pull up to the first window, show identification that they are at least 18 years of age, and then pay five dollars per minute. In the back of the club, at the second window, they can then watch a nude dancer for their allotted time.

Numerous safeguards against nonpaying viewers were included in the design. The club was built next to a steep hill that was then covered in thick, thorny bushes. A canopy with a wall against the hill blocks a direct view of the window, and partitions on each side of the window allow for the show to be seen only when the motorist is directly in front of the window.

On this note, one wonders: What unique and innovative application will the drive-thru window have next?

The drive-thru window is such an integral part of American car culture that it is difficult to imagine the world without it.

216

Miniature Golf
The big business of a small game

Is it possible to find anyone between the ages of 8 and 80 in the United States who has not seen or played that version of golf that challenges the player with windmills, waterfalls, and grinning clowns? Would it be a fair assumption that miniature golf is one of the most recognized roadside entertainment venues in America?

While the origins of this truly American game are lost in the mists of time, there is little argument as to who was responsible for the first successful course: Garnet Carter, founder of roadside icon Rock City, on Lookout Mountain overlooking Chattanooga, Tennessee. In the 1920s, Carter made plans for Fairyland, an exclusive community high up on the slopes overlooking the city. This development was to feature deeply wooded lots and a deluxe golf course.

Delays in construction, in conjunction with a near-constant clamoring from those who wished to play golf on the promised course, prompted Carter to build a small, challenging putting course in 1927. Much to his surprise, the miniaturized fairway and putting greens were a near-instant hit.

The Great Depression and other financial woes impeded the completion of Fairyland, but it did nothing to alleviate the popularity of the Tom Thumb golf course. So Carter decided to take the show on the road.

He soon began marketing the courses for national distribution under the name Tom Thumb Golf. By 1930, more than 200 employees were involved in the various aspects of the business. An added plus, especially in the early days of the Great Depression, was that the new miniature golf courses created a new market for products that were not in high demand, such as cork and felt.

It soon became apparent to the many owners of roadside establishments that this craze was not going to be a flash in the pan, and that there was money to be made with minimum investment. As a result, miniature golf courses exploded onto the scene throughout America.

By the beginning of World War II, miniature golf had exploded in popularity, and an estimated 40,000 courses could be found throughout the country. Then, in what should have been the sport's glory days, a precipitous slide began. So suddenly, Ralph and Al Lomma of Scranton, Pennsylvania, added a new twist.

In 1955, Al began toying with the idea of mechanical obstacles powered by a variety of motors, gears, and belts. The result was the now famous, or infamous, windmill. The windmill, as well as other such obstructions, gave new life to the sport. The Lommas' course was soon inundated with customers, and they quickly opened two more courses to meet the demand.

The Lomma brothers had found their niche, and soon imagination was put to work at an amazing clip. Among these creations was the placing of a clown's face at the end of the course where the player could win a free game with a shot to the nose. But the real genius was that the last shot also acted as the owners' control by locking the ball inside the obstacle.

Today, the Lommas' company is the largest manufacturer of miniature golf courses in the world, with over 5,000 sold annually. The sport itself, with an estimated 15 million people playing each year, shows no sign of decreasing in popularity.

Garnet Carter, founder of Rock City, built the first successful miniature golf course while waiting out construction delays at Rock City. **Rock City**

Easy Rider
"You know what, Billy? We blew it."

Wyatt and Billy were not career criminals. They just muddled their way through one lucrative drug-smuggling deal to raise enough money to not have to work for a long, long time. They committed one crime to attain the freedom that America promises and hit the road on wildly styled Harley-Davidsons. They were free.

Easy Rider is often misunderstood, even by people who love the movie. It is not a rebellious film about drugs, bikers, and hippies shattering long-standing traditions. The movie's theme is more complex and subtle. The motorcycles are too easily compared with horses, and Wyatt and Billy are too easily compared to cowboys riding the range in search of adventure. These comparisons would be clichés. More importantly, movie cowboys were heading west for adventure, but Wyatt and Billy are heading east—more like cowboys who are trying to find their way back home. They're not riding into the sunset like most cowboys, rather, they're riding east trying to find a new dawn.

Wyatt, played by Peter Fonda, is the intelligent one with high ideals. Billy, played by the movie's director, Dennis Hopper, is far less intelligent, but his instincts are clearer and less clouded by ideology.

After they make their fortune, they hit the road. Their first traveling encounter is with a farmer from Oklahoma who didn't quite make it to California in the 1930s. Wyatt compliments the farmer by saying, "You have a great spread here."

The farmer thinks Wyatt is talking about his many children, and the farmer says with a laughing smile, "Yeah, I sure got a lot of 'em. My wife's Catholic."

The farmer's Mexican wife happily and obediently responds to the farmer's polite request for a cup of coffee. The farmer is the opposite of everything the 1960s counterculture stood for, but he is happy—deliriously happy with his wife, his children, and his horses.

"Where are you from?" Billy later asks the hippie hitchhiker.

"The city," the hippie answers, which is counterculture code for San Francisco. "I'm *from* the city, a looooong way *from* the city, 'cause that's where I want to be right now."

Something has gone wrong in "the city," meaning something has gone wrong with the counterculture. Wyatt and Billy take the hippie to a Taos, New Mexico, commune, where hippies think they're being innovative, while actually failing at living like the traditional farmer. Wyatt and Billy overhear conversations about hash deals gone bad and backstabbing in the commune. Wyatt's ideology wants to believe in the commune, but Billy's instincts know better.

This is *Easy Rider's* theme. Nothing is as it's supposed to be. The traditional, old-fashioned farmer was welcoming to long-haired young men, while the hippies of their own generation viewed them suspiciously as outsiders. The traditional farmer's prayer before lunch is simple, sincere, and joyful, while the hippie commune's prayer before a meal is phony, overly dramatic, and absurd. The police who arrest them for parading without a permit are kind to them, while the ACLU lawyer who joins them is a childish, selfish man. The prostitutes are decent and moral, while the regular folks in a diner serve up threats instead of Southern hospitality. Wyatt and Billy are trying to lead a wild, uninhibited life, but they are so decent and old-fashioned themselves that they can't commit the deed with the prostitutes they've hired, and they take the girls on a long walk and treat them like ladies. Quiet conversations under the stars expand their minds, while an LSD trip is a nightmare.

Easy Rider is a road movie. The famous opening credits blast onto the screen with Steppenwolf's "Born to be Wild" blaring away. The boys are crossing the Colorado River heading east on Route 66, while seen in the background are the white arches of the bridge over which the Joads headed west in *The Grapes of Wrath* a generation before. Later in the opening, the camera pans down from the sky, and Route 66 stretches before Wyatt and Billy in the Aubrey Valley. Just around Chino Point, in front of them is the little town of Seligman, Arizona, where the Route 66 preservation movement was born 20 years later. They stop for gas after picking up the hippie at the Sacred Mountain Trading Post on U.S. 89 north of Flagstaff, Arizona, and spend the night under the stars in Monument Valley. They end up dead on the side of a road in Florida, killed by law-abiding, traditional Americans in a pickup truck.

The motorcycles were indeed horses, but Wyatt and Billy were trying to go home. Ordinary living had been enough adventure for them. *Easy Rider's* promotional tag line read, "A man went looking for America and couldn't find it anywhere." Millions of people sitting in rush-hour traffic want to do the same thing and, maybe, find it.

Neon
Rainbows of the night

"I could see that sign for miles, and I always knew I was getting close to home when I saw it," says retired truck driver Bill Pierce, who hauled cars for decades between Los Angeles and Albuquerque on U.S. 66. He was talking about the giant neon Roadrunner's Retreat sign that glowed huge in the black sky above the Mojave Desert, near the tiny town of Chambless, California.

A high-voltage electric current runs through a glass tub filled with neon gas, and the gas begins to glow seemingly on its own in vivid, cartoonish color. Neon signs came into their own in the 1930s, and in the beginning they were small. Yet, as postwar prosperity spread across America, neon signs became extravagant works of art. Their artists proudly wore the professional title of "benders."

As the 1950s progressed, neon signs went from announcing to screaming, and pulp novels and film-noir movies would describe a city as a "neon jungle." Neon went from flashy to garish and from artsy to sleazy in the American mind. While a single neon sign might be a flashy work of art, many highway-side towns were known for having dozens of gaudy neon signs in a row, all trying to out-shout each other.

"I want to make sure that the America we see from these major highways is a beautiful America," said President Lyndon Johnson in 1965, as he argued for the adoption of the Highway Beautification Act. With first lady Lady Bird Johnson in charge, the law called for the removal and control of certain types of signs. The neon era was coming to a close.

The neon era finished with the energy crisis of the early 1970s. Plain-composition signs that glowed anonymously from the inside with white fluorescent tubes took over the outdoor advertising business, and earth tones swept the continent like a brown plague.

By the 1980s, people were unhappy. They missed the glitter and individual artistry of the neon era. By 1990, Route 66 became one of the gateways to see old neon in its original locations, and the incentive to restore the signs dawned happily on business owners looking for new customers who appreciated their locations' histories.

From mom-and-pop operations restoring their neon to recover from the defeat of passing eras to corporations like McDonald's tearing down 1970s-era buildings and replacing them with McDonald's original 1950s architecture, complete with their neon Speedee logo in place, neon is once again bouncing off the hoods of cars driven by people looking for good food or a place to sleep.

The artful curves of neon signs that illustrate the artist's skill are attractive even in broad daylight.

Used-Car Lot
Tarnish on the crown

The slick-talking loudly dressed used-car salesman has been the mainstay of comedians, the bane of consumers, and an indispensable part of American car culture for generations. His lots, with their multi-colored flags, garish window signs proclaiming "One Owner!" and "Low Miles" and banners proclaiming "Low Monthly Payments" and "Honest Deals," are as much a part of the urban landscape as the pizza parlor and golden arches.

Interestingly enough, while cars and sales methods have changed dramatically over the years, the used-car lot has remained largely unchanged. Attracting the customer's attention with flashy colors and an eye-catching vehicle elevated on a pedestal for all to see has been used in various guises for more than 70 years. In essence, the name of the game has always been to sell the sizzle and not the steak.

As with the automobile industry in general, in the beginning there was little regulation and almost no standards in the used-car business, other than the ethics and morals of the owner. Tricks of the trade came to include the use of sawdust to quiet well-worn differentials; turning back the odometer to give the illusion that the vehicle was a low-mileage cream puff; and a variety of oil additives to eliminate, though briefly, the telltale signs of oil-guzzling engines.

The Kelley Blue Book introduced in 1926 has been a vital tool for the auto dealer since its introduction.

Unfortunately, these practices gave the industry as a whole a bad reputation when the majority of dealers simply sought to make a living, while providing a service to their neighbors as well as the community. In an effort to ensure a level of quality as well as to protect themselves from increasing regulation, dealers often initiated organizations such as the Independent Auto Dealers to give the small dealer more influence.

Standardizing a vehicle's value is a boon to both dealer and customer, and it is now simply viewed as part of operating a used-car facility. Les Kelley worked to spearhead this concept in an era when there were several hundred independent automobile manufacturers. In 1926, Kelley began publishing the *Kelley Blue Book,* a compact guide to automobile values based on numerous factors. The Internet has bought this guide into the modern era, and now consumers can easily access the specific information they need to make the best deal.

Technology has affected every aspect of society, and the used-car dealer has not been exempt. One of the most promising trends in this field is one that protects the customer and also serves as a sales tool. CARFAX provides a history of the vehicle in regard to its use as a rental car, and reveals if there have been any insurance claims or if the car has a salvage title.

The used-car lot today is a vital component in American car culture. The used-car lot is often a reprieve of sorts for an automobile before it becomes simply another item to be recycled, or a donor of parts to keep other vehicles on the road.

REPRINT OF AN ORIGINAL KELLEY BLUE BOOK

Wrecking Yard
End of the line

Until recently, when we deemed them eyesores and hid the treasures behind fences, the wrecking yard was a part of the American landscape. They were silent monuments to the hopes, the dreams, and the aspirations of the common man. These sites are the final resting place for stylish Fords that were once someone's pride and joy, a used car lot's drawing card, and a teenager's first set of wheels. This is where those on a budget come to pick over the remains in an effort to stave off the inevitable for their own vehicles.

The wrecking yard of today is often a far cry from those of yesteryear. Instead of merely putting the vehicles out to pasture, occasionally with some sense of order, regulation requires the removal of fluids that may be harmful to the environment, and profit dictates that cars be dismantled, racked, stacked, and inventoried as soon as possible.

For the vintage car enthusiast, discovering an untouched yard from another time is akin to discovering King Tut's tomb. In many instances, it represents the end of the search for that elusive part needed to bring a classic survivor back from the brink.

The modern, sterile wrecking yard is largely the result of the push to beautify the roadsides of America through the Roadside Beautification Act of 1965. Things do have a tendency to go full circle. Today a yard littered with former kings of the highway, their chrome crowns tarnished and glittering among the leaves, is seen as art and adorns everything from calendars to fine-art prints.

Wrecking yards such as this one was and once a common sight before the Highway Beautification Act. Today, yards like these are increasingly rare relics that are treasured by collectors and restorers for their priceless inventory of parts.

Vehicles as extensively damaged as these would have most likely found their way to a wrecking yard, where they would have been cannibalized or crushed.

Wienermobile
Motorized promotion

Initially, the sheer novelty of the automobile was more than enough promotion. A company merely needed to have one. In 1898, Montgomery Ward had two electric vehicles built to order to use as advertising novelties. The circus drew large crowds by giving one, a Duryea Motor Wagon, top billing.

By 1920, however, the automobile had become a common sight on the streets and highways of America, so something else was needed—unique, creative, and clever vehicle conversions. Beer and soda-pop companies had trucks constructed in the shape of bottles. Zippo Manufacturing Company converted a Chrysler to resemble a larger-than-life version of its product, the famed Zippo lighter. Oscar Mayer had the Wienermobile, the most famous product mobile of all time.

Introduced in 1936, the Wienermobile has undergone numerous transformations, but the concept has always been the same: promoting Oscar Mayer products with a hot dog on wheels. The idea was the brainchild of Karl Mayer, the nephew of the company's founder.

The first Wienermobile was a 13-foot open-cockpit hot dog built on a Dodge chassis by General Body Company of Chicago, Illinois. The $5,000 initial investment proved to be a wise one. Sales soared in the Chicago area almost as soon as the mobile wiener took to the streets. The replacement, which debuted in 1950, was also built on a Dodge chassis, but this vehicle was built by Gerstenslager of Wooster, Ohio.

In 1958, the Wienermobile's signature bubble-nose cockpit design was introduced. This model was built on a Willys Jeep chassis and served as the model for four more. One of these survives and is on display as the Wienermobile Café at the Henry Ford Museum/Greenfield Village complex in Dearborn, Michigan.

By the 1990s, the Oscar Mayer jingle and the Wienermobile were more than mere promotional props; they were internationally recognized American icons that had appeared on posters, post cards, and as a Hot Wheels car. In 1995, the new Wienermobile was created by world-renowned automobile designer Harry Bradley and took full advantage of the latest automotive design technology, including computer-aided design-imaging tools. This was to be the largest Wienermobile to date: 27-feet long, 11-feet high, and 10,500 pounds. It was also the fastest Wienermobile, capable of speeds in excess of 90 miles per hour.

The two most recent incarnations of the Wienermobile took high-tech to a new level. The 2000 model has a sunroof, six relish-colored seats, a ketchup-colored walkway, and state-of-the-art audio visual equipment. The 2004 version even went further in technological advancement by adding a GPS navigation system, a gullwing door with automatic retractable step, and an official wiener jingle horn.

This 60th anniversary commemorative post card documents the evolution of the Wienermobile from simplicity to technological masterpiece.

Route 66 TV Show
Every young man's secret dream

Two young guys, a Corvette, and Route 66, the road most related with cross-country travel. The premise of the TV series *Route 66* promised adventure, fun, excitement, and an attainment of freedom that only the young men understand. Actually seeing the show, though, was a surprise. It was a drama.

Martin Milner was already a veteran movie actor when *Route 66* hit the airwaves in 1960. Milner had acted in movies as serious as the Korean War drama *I Want You* and in frivolous drive-in fare like *13 Ghosts*. He knew what he was doing with the character of Tod Stiles, the educated amateur philosopher who wanted to see the world before settling down. George Maharis was a few years older than Milner, but somewhat new to acting. He had worked in television in the 1950s. For three seasons, he played the role of Buz Murdock, the earthier and more practical of the two travelers. Glenn Corbett and his character, Lincoln Case, replaced Maharis for the last season or two of the series. Many of the episodes were directed by famed movie director Robert Altman, and Stirling Silliphant wrote the dramatic and meaningful dialogue.

The plots revolved around the guys pulling into a town looking for work. They then encounted a grand conflict between people, solved the problem, and drove off into the sunset. Yes, the show could be preachy but it did capture the young American male's secret desire to be a traveling hero—to save a town from the bandits or save new friends from prejudice or drugs.

In 1960, many older American men valued their homes, families, and occupations in a way that's not always understood today. They had grown up in the Great Depression and watched friends die in World War II. To them, a home and a secure job were paradise and protection from the true horrors they had witnessed. Their sons, however, didn't understand that, and saw Tod and Buz's life as ideal.

Every Friday night, Tod and Buz hit the road—traveling much, working little, and saving the girl. Then they looked gravely to the next adventure through the windshield of their Corvette, with the wind in their hair, under a big American sky. In the early 1960s, every young man with a car wanted to do the same thing.

American Graffiti
"The whole strip is shrinkin'…"

"**D**o you want to end up like John? You just can't stay 17 forever!" Ron Howard played Steve in *American Graffiti*, and he was imploring his friend Curt, played by Richard Dreyfuss, to keep his appointment to leave for college the next morning. John, played by Paul Le Mat, has the hottest car in town, but at that moment, he symbolizes immaturity to two smart kids destined to get out of Modesto, California.

American Graffiti is about the end of an era. "Rock Around the Clock" thumps through the opening sequence, but the movie ends with the Beach Boys' harmonious "All Summer Long". The movie's story takes place in a single night in the late summer of 1962, but truly, the movie begins in the 1950s and ends in the 1960s. There's a deep divide no one will acknowledge between the high schoolers who drive their parents' Edsels and hand-me-down Studebakers and the 20-21 year-old hotrodders who are still stuck in the 1950s.

Time is passing, and they're all getting nervous. Time is pushing the teenage high school graduates into the adult world, and the end of this summer is their last cruise night. John with his '32 Ford hotrod, Bob Falfa (Harrison Ford) with his hopped-up '55 Chevrolet, and the "Pharohs" gang with their chopped-top Mercury are out of synch with the younger kids and looking way too old to be acting the way they are.

"The whole strip is shrinkin'," John says. "I remember about five years ago, it would take you a couple hours and a tank-full of gas just to make one circuit. It was really somethin'."

The guys who had been out of school the longest had the hottest cars, but they were rapidly becoming old-fashioned. John expresses his dislike of surf music and says rock just wasn't the same after Buddy Holly died. John knows his era is ending, and his car impresses younger people less than people his own age.

Steve passes his 1958 Chevrolet Impala down to his young, nerdy, unpopular friend Terry "the Toad." Terry hopes the flashy car will make him accepted, but it doesn't help, and he quickly learns he's still the Toad to most people. He finally meets a girl who accepts him, but there's something a little creepy about the way she says, "I just love the feel of tuck-and-roll upholstery" and "I just love it when guys peel out."

All night, Bob the challenger looks for John the Champ, and when the '32 Ford and the '55 Chevrolet finally meet at a traffic signal, it's time for them to size each other up for dominance. The signal goes green, and the two cars scream down the street trailing smoke. The next signal goes red, but Bob and his Chevrolet fly right through it. John's teenage companion says, "Wow, he's fast!" but John knows what he's just seen and says, "Yeah, but he's stupid!" Even hotrodding John has limits to the chances he'll take, but the challenger represents something more than a guy with a faster car. Bob represents a new, more reckless, more ruthless era on the horizon. When they meet again for the big race, the '55 Chevrolet ends its racing career in a horrible rollover accident—another end.

George Lucas directed *American Graffiti* in 1973, and the makers were clearly nostalgic for an era that was only ten years before—an era when the streets were full of cars from the 1950s instead of Pintos and Gremlins, an era when girls could safely ask boys they hardly knew for a ride across town, an era when popular songs dwelled on love and dancing, an era when America still loved itself. The flashing, chrome-laden American cars were smiling beasts that cruised the streets hunting for a good time, and the kids mixed and mingled unafraid, but the time was nearly over. The 1960s per se vomited forth beginning in 1965-1966, and cruising would never be the same.

Much is made of the girl in the white Thunderbird that Curt keeps seeing, but she's a simple symbol: Curt's desparate wish for a good reason to stay in Modesto and live these cruise nights forever, but he knows he'll end up like John if he does, and he smiles a goodbye from the airplane when he flies away the next day.

In 1972 George Lucas, a young filmmaker, begins work on one of his earlier films: American Graffiti. *It is a coming-of-age movie set around the California street scene, circa 1962. One of the featured vehicles in this 1932 Ford Coupe.*
Art-Tech/IMP BW

5
Gasoline Alley

IIf modern America has built its culture on the automobile, the cornerstone is the gas station. However,But like so many things in our fast-paced era, it is often overlooked with little thought given to how much influence it has had and continues to have on our lives. Like the expectation of running water when we turn on the tap, the gas station is just there. Its icons and advertising jingles are familiar friends that make us comfortable when we arewe're miles from home. The neon, brightly litbright neon signs and gas- pump globes are modern lighthouses in a sea of asphalt and concrete.

The Gas station promotional giveaways over the years have enabled us to keep track of the days, helped us gather a set of china when it wasn't in the budget, kept us from getting lost, and provided a distraction for the children in the back seat, if only for a brief time. The Christmas cards and reminders of when it was time for service made the corner station owner almost seem like family.

Quite often, for young men a fascination with cars and things mechanical made the service station a natural for the first job. More often than not, the access to a shop as well as good used parts resulted in the first car, a jalopy, getting the personal touch.

The concept of a service station today is quite different from that of just a few decades ago. But with just a little imagination, it is possible to still hear the bell, see the white- uniformed attendant, and smell the new rubber tires when we here make mention of . . . .

AAA
A century of service

In the infancy of the automobile, one of the primary prerequisites for a motorist was an adventuresome spirit. Regulations varied from state to state, and even from municipality to municipality. Roads, or what passed for roads during the period, especially in rural areas, were little more than mud-filled ruts when it rained and dust-choked trails when it didn't. The ability to repair a tire or magneto along the side of the road was a necessity. Amazingly, in spite of these overwhelming obstacles, ownership of automobiles continued to skyrocket.

There is strength in numbers, and soon automobile owners were forming auto clubs to petition for better roads and more realistic regulations. Auto clubs also offered a network for information on road conditions as well as reputable repair facilities. Yet even these endeavors were largely limited to regional pockets. Then, in 1902, the entire face of American motoring was forever changed when nine auto clubs in the Chicago area joined to form the American Automobile Association.

The organization hit the ground running. Less than nine months after its formation on December 9, it began to throw its weight behind passage of the Brownlow-Latimer Bill, which called for the appropriation of federal funds for the improvement of highways. The organization doggedly pursued this goal until 1916, when its efforts finally bore fruit. President Wilson's signature was then acquired on an AAA-sponsored Federal Aid Road Act.

Initially, automobile racing had proven to be a primary venue for gathering support of automobiles in general. In 1904, the recently installed AAA racing board endorsed the Vanderbilt Cup Race. Contest board members were on hand to supervise the first Indianapolis 500 in 1911. The organization continued to support automotive racing until 1955.

For 1905, the fledgling organization continued its efforts to promote automobile usage as a more practical alternative to the horse with the sponsorship of the first Glidden Tour. Originally conceived to demonstrate the reliability of the automobile as a form of transportation, the Glidden Tour continues to be the oldest annual antique car tour. During that year, the AAA published its first sanctioned map of Staten Island, New York. This was also the year the first reciprocal agreement was reached with a foreign auto club, the Touring Club of France, which extended the reach of the AAA and expanded the benefits offered to its members.

By 1910, just eight years after the organization's founding, the AAA had contracted for distribution among members the *Automotive Blue Book*, a detailed listing of roads and their conditions as well as approved facilities. As an interesting historic footnote, there were two other guidebooks published before the universal acceptance of road atlases and the standardization of maps as well as services.

One guidebook published in 1936 and titled *Negro Motorist Green Book* was "to give the Negro traveler information that will keep him from running into difficulties, embarrassments, and to make his trip more enjoyable." A similar, older guidebook had been published for Jewish travelers.

In addition, AAA authored and supported the Uniform State Motor Vehicle Bill, which called for standardized regulations regarding registration and regulation of motor vehicles. The AAA also cosponsored the First National Good Roads Association. Other milestones included the debut of *American Motorist* magazine, the establishment of a European Touring Bureau in Paris, and the sale of American Express traveler's checks.

Expansion of organizational activities escalated dramatically in the decade that followed, paralleling the growth of automobile ownership and production. In 1911, the organization published its first European maps, as well as select strip maps of American roads. Under the auspices of the Automobile Club of Southern California in 1912, the organization established an insurance underwriters group, thus resolving what had been a major problem for owners who wished to protect their automotive investment. In the same year, the first map copyrighted by AAA, a transcontinental map that sold for 25 cents, was published.

In 1914, again spearheaded by the Automobile Club of Southern California, the National Old Trails route between Los Angeles and Kansas City was designated with the posting of 4,000 road signs. For 1915, the Emergency Road Service (ERS) was made available to members. Initially this service was only available through the Automobile Club of Saint Louis, which sent five men on motorcycles, known as the First Aid Corp, through the streets of the city in search of stranded motorists. By 1920, the ERS was almost universally available to all members.

With the establishment of the National Park Service in 1916, the AAA successfully lobbied for the opening of the parks to automobile traffic. In 1919, the association played a pivotal role in the passage of the Dyer Anti-theft Act, which made the transportation of stolen motor vehicles across state lines a federal offense.

Another revolutionary benefit to members was introduced in 1917: an official directory of hotels with ratings. By 1920, additional publications—a report on road building, a campground directory, and an updated hotel registry—were also made available.

By 1920, with this solid foundation of leadership, AAA launched itself on a campaign for improved safety, improved services for travelers, and improved roads that would span more than 75 years and show no sign of waning. Many of the standards we have in place today for motoring can be accredited to AAA. Safe railroad crossings and school-safety patrols, as well as the introduction of driver's education courses for schools are but a few examples. Other achievements include the promotion of cooperation between Canada and the United States in 1939 for the construction of the Alaskan Highway; the initiation in 1946 of a campaign for the construction of an interstate highway system; the development of conservation programs; and the promotion of seatbelts.

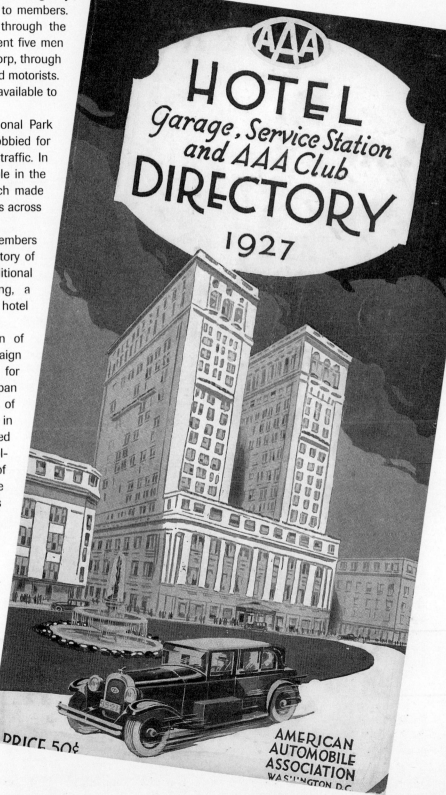

By 1927, AAA members could travel the country with the assurance of finding quality lodging and repair facilities with their official AAA directory.

Auto Mechanic
Heroes and cons, surgeons and laborers

Decades ago, there was good news and there was bad news. The good news was that automobiles were simple enough that men could fix their own cars and problems were identifiable. The bad news was that any ape who could turn a wrench could hang out a sign and declare himself a mechanic.

In the twenty-first century, there's bad news and good news. The bad news is that modern cars are so overburdened with high technology that people can no longer fix their own cars. The problems the cars have can be mysterious phantoms found through expensive trial and error, sometimes resulting in calling in a diagnostics man with a truck full of computers. The good news is that today's competent mechanics have been through years of schooling and have degrees in automotive technology. Usually, today's technician standards filter out the shade-tree charlatans who pretend to know what they're doing.

Allen Davenport is a 1969 graduate of the Rankin Technical College in Saint Louis, and after a stint working as an Oldsmobile service technician, he returned to his alma mater as assistant automotive department chair. Davenport is passionate about returning the auto mechanic's image to that of a respected professional.

"After World War II, all these soldiers came home and went to college on the GI Bill, and this was the era when we started belittling the craftsman," Davenport explains. "Everyone wanted their kids to do better than they did in their jobs, but the parents did not recognize the dignity of their own labor, and they shipped their kids to college. If you didn't go to college, you were a grease monkey. It was a terrible attitude. In the meantime, the automobile was taking off technologically

Mike Shattuck of Hesperia, California, is diagnosing a patient. Today, cars need less repair because lubricants, belts, hoses, tires, and roads are so much better than in decades past. Nevertheless, it can take a bank of computers for a mechanic to know if he's fixed the car, which usually involves him being forced to throw parts away and replace them.

because the cars had more equipment, were more scientifically designed, and the emissions regulations came along. The parents *still* didn't realize the value of the mechanic's trade, and the technical colleges got nothing but the discipline problems from the high schools for a long time, but then, a change took place. As the cars got more technological, auto repair required more analytical thought. The good auto technicians today are like NASA people of 20 years ago. They have tremendous skills for analysis. Analytical skills are more important that manual dexterity now."

Looking back on his start in the business, longtime Atlanta, Georgia, Chevrolet dealer John Smith III fondly remembers the simplicity of mid-twentieth-century cars: "I remember working on the old Chevrolet 216 engines in people's cars. I was a tune-up man one year. The lifters were mechanical, and we had to lash the valves. You could always tell when you had the engine running right because you'd go around the back and feel the exhaust. If the exhaust felt right you *knew* you had fixed the damn car! Now, the computer tells you, and you'd better hope it's right." From the 1920s through the 1960s, when a car broke down, it wasn't always the car's fault. Those autos were tough enough to stand the poor oils, bad roads, crude tires, and weak belts and hoses of the time. When a car had a problem, it was usually one of these culprits. Today's cars routinely run over 200,000 miles without a breakdown because these items are so good. When a problem finally shows up, it's the car's fault and the mechanic can have a devil of a time finding it, often at great expense.

Up until 1970 or so, parts were replaced less and repaired more. A mechanic didn't replace a starter; he put new brushes and bushings in it. A mechanic didn't replace a water pump; he put a rebuilt kit into it. Today, a mechanic will replace an alternator that costs the customer $200 plus labor, when in days past the alternator just needed a set of $8 brushes and a $20 set of diodes.

The old cars allowed good mechanics to be craftsmen. They didn't force the mechanic to replace parts, but allowed him to fix and save them. Mechanics looked like grease monkeys but spoke the language of surgeons.

Above: *Seen here is the San Pedro Street Garage in Los Angeles in the late 1920s. Poor motor oils, roads, tires, belts, and hoses inflicted severe wear on the fine cars of the time, but the mechanics were free to be craftsmen who fixed existing parts instead of throwing them away. They were free to be creative, and they knew by the sound and feel of things if the car was healthy.*

High-Flying Promotion

The illusion of soaring brought to Earth

As early as the 1920s, in some parts of the nation competition among service-station operators was becoming heated. As a result, independent operators as well as some company-owned chains became quite creative in their efforts to ensure their facility received attention and stood out from the crowd.

Perhaps the most novel of these attempts were those that combined air travel with down-to-earth-service. Among the earliest of these was the Airplane Service Station near Knoxville, Tennessee, built in 1928 by the Nickle brothers. In essence, the unique facility was a faux airplane with a wing that served as a canopy over the pumps. In Paris, Tennessee, a second Airplane Service Station facility was constructed. This station was demolished in 1960, while the former has survived and was recently added to the National Register of Historic Places.

Perhaps it was only logical that something this novel would evolve into even grander designs. Bob's Air Mail Service, in Los Angeles, California, utilized a real twin-prop airplane to top its station, with the wings serving as canopies to shade its General Petroleum pumps. In a similar manner, Stop Agan Service (the owner was L. E. Agan) in Texarkana added a World War II surplus Cessna Bobcat to its station roof and a giant rabbit with a saddle out front to ensure that it stood out from the competition.

The most extreme example of utilizing aircraft for the promotion of a service station has to be Art Lacey's Bomber Gas Station in Milwaukie, Oregon. His choice for an attention-grabbing crown was a 32-ton, 75-foot-long World War II–surplus B-17 bomber! Opened in 1947, the station was followed by the addition of the Bomber Diner in 1948. The popularity of the station and its location on Highway 99 resulted in near-meteoric growth. Initially the station had 5 pumps. By 1960, when the station had become one of the largest-volume stores in the country, the number had risen to 40 pumps. Today the Bomber Gas Station and the Airplane Service Station stand as quiet monuments to a time when artistic talents for promotion were limited only by the ambitions of the dreamer.

Gas Pumps
Keeping them on the road

Prior to the invention of the automobile, kerosene was the primary product produced from petroleum. Gasoline was merely viewed as a waste byproduct suitable for little more than stove fuel.

The crowns that topped pumps served to identify various grades of gasoline and ensure brand recognition by way of advertisement.

Both fuels were usually stored in barrels and sold through the local general store in gallon cans or containers supplied by the customer. For obvious reasons, this was a very dangerous way of distributing these products.

However, as early as 1885 there were alternatives, such as a product manufactured by the S. F. Bowser Pump Company marketed as the "Filling Station." This self-contained unit featured a storage barrel, a hand-operated lever connected to a plunger, and an upright faucet lever.

Still, as late as 1903, the majority of motorists carried funnels lined with chamois or cloths to strain fuel into their tanks from 5-gallon cans, which had been filled from barrels via gravity feed. With years of experience, Sylvanus Bowser recognizing the growing need for better methods. As founder of Bowser Pump Company, he developed a new version of his Filling Station for outdoor usage.

The Bowser Self-Measuring Gasoline Storage Pump, introduced in 1905, was a secure wooden cabinet enclosing a metal tank. It was topped with a forced-suction pump that was operated by a hand lever. The pump was quite revolutionary because it featured predetermined quantity stops, a vent, and a hose that allowed for the dispensing of fuel directly into an automobile's gas tank.

This was the same year Harry Grenner and Clem Laessig formed the Automobile Gasoline Company in Saint Louis, Missouri. With nothing more than a gravity-feed tank and a garden hose, they began offering pull-up service for motorists. Thus, they established what is believed to be the first gasoline filling station.

John McLean, sales manager for the Seattle district of the Standard Oil Company of California (SOCAL), is credited for the next stage in development of the service station, which provided incentive for the development of gas pumps and related equipment. Securing a location on a busy intersection next to the Standard Oil Company bulk plant in 1907, he mounted an upright cylindrical 30-gallon tank on a wooden post. A valve controlled the flow through the flexible hose. Other innovations included no-smoking signs next to the tank and shelving to display of Standard's oil products.

However, men like McLean and Bowser were not the first to address the fuel requirements of the growing motorist market. John Tokheim had evaluated the original Bowser system and found ways to improve on it. His first endeavor was a self-measuring visible-register gasoline pump patented in 1901 that became the standard for the storage and distribution of gasoline.

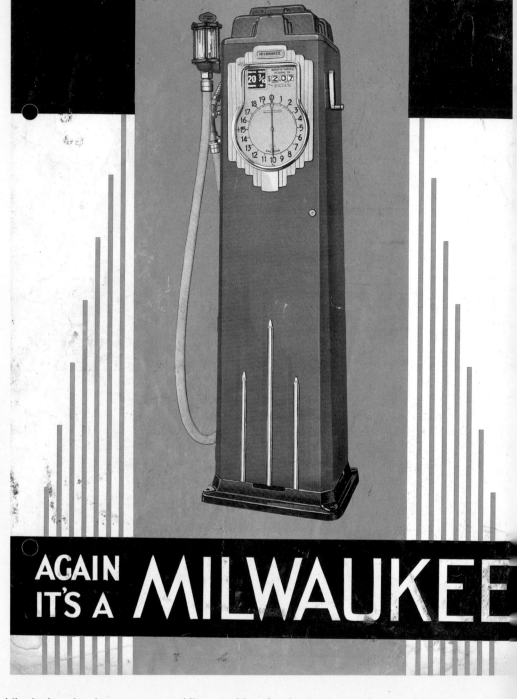

The visible-register pump had numerous advantages. It allowed the consumer to more accurately measure the fuel being purchased. By the 1920s, with the addition of dyes to the underground tanks, the newly formulated grades of gas could be identified on sight. As an example, Gilmore Oil Company sold Blu-Green gasoline brands; other companies used red or blue to designate premium grades and amber for the cheaper grades.

The success of the initial endeavor encouraged Tokheim to organize the Tokheim Manufacturing Company in the same year. Within a decade, curbside pumps were appearing in front of bicycle shops, feed stores, garages, automobile dealers, hardware stores, and livery stables. Any business proprietor could have a pump and storage tank installed and begin selling gasoline.

Between 1911 and 1916, under Tokheim's direction, the company pushed the evolution of the gas pump forward. The innovative products Tokheim manufactured during this period included the Triune Electric Gasoline Pump, one of the first curbside pumps. It was also the first pump to feature metered discharge in combination with an electric street-light post. The Triune Electric Filtered Gasoline Pump was the first known electric pump to use a flow meter and wet-hose discharge nozzle constructed in the form of a curbside electric gasoline signpost.

By the late 1920s, electric meter–type pumps were rapidly replacing the visible-register models. Loosely known as clock-face pumps, Erie Meter Systems first developed these units. There were improved versions of these pumps by Tokheim and other manufacturers, but the overall concept was the same. Two counting dials, one on each side, dominated the faces of the pump. A large red pointer, similar to the minute hand on a clock, measured gallons in fractions. After a complete revolution, a bell would signal 1 gallon. The total gallons pumped were measured by a shorter black hand on the dial. Variations included a numerical counter, which allowed the station owner to keep track of gallons pumped for the day, and a glass instrument called the tele-gauge. The tele-gauge was mounted on the side of the pump to mimic the visible register pumps, which helped customers make the transition to the newer pumps.

The next evolutionary step in the development of gas pumps paralleled the changing face of architecture in business, namely, the Art Deco movement. The first of these pumps with a numeric computer was introduced in 1933. With the exception of the exterior case, this remained the basic design of the gas pump until the introduction of modern computerized pumps with digital faces.

It could be said that the development of the gas pump paralleled that of the automobile. In the beginning, both were the product of innovation and were simple in design. By the 1920s, both had become more sophisticated, and both were now being designed rather than simply built. By the 1950s, flash hid the fact that on the inside little had changed. Today, electronics have made gas pumps simpler, but at the same time more fragile.

When the motorist drives up to a Milwaukee Cash Recording Pump, he can see exactly what is going into his tank and just what he has to pay to a cent. No mental or pencil-and-paper calculation. Not a chance for an over-charge, and no mistake the other way about.

Milwaukee Cash Recording Pumps command customer confidence and satisfaction. They attract new customers, increase gallonage and reduce station losses. Small purchases may now be made of gasoline measured in currency units, rather than in gallons. For instance, an odd figure sale such as 79c or 89c can often be increased to an even dollar, through the mere suggestion of the station attendant. Selling gasoline in even monetary amounts, such as $1.00 or $1.50, has proven a substantial gallonage builder wherever the Milwaukee Cash Recording Pump is used.

ERRORS ELIMINATED

Errors in computing sales and posting prices are eliminated with this new "Milwaukee." Once the recording mechanism is set, the operator cannot post another price not in line with that recorded. The price-changing mechanism is under lock and key, so that only authorized persons can make price changes.

There is no guesswork and no possibility of mistakes. The buyer knows that the correct price of the gasoline delivered to his tank is automatically and accurately recorded by the machine. He never has to check the price, because it is done for him, right in plain view.

ENCOURAGES MORE GALLONAGE

Nothing is left to chance. No need of pencil and paper, to figure decimals or fractional gallons, as in the past, thus removing the obstacle which has always been a deterrent to the practice of completely filling the tank. Now, with this new "Milwaukee," it is a simple matter to "fill 'er up" and, by a single glance at the dial, know instantly the exact amount to be paid without the usual calculation and consequent possibility of error.

For example: It takes 11.3 gallons of gasoline to fill a tank; gasoline selling at 16½ cents per gallon. To determine the exact charge by the pencil-and-paper method involved considerable calculation. As a result, the average attendant would rather stop at an even eleven, or, perhaps, only ten gallons, rather than take the trouble to figure in fractions. Multiply such instances by a reasonable percentage of daily customers, and it will be readily seen that there is a substantial loss in gallonage that might just as well be had.

ALWAYS A STEP AHEAD

The new Milwaukee Cash Recording Pump fits perfectly into the modern picture of progress. In design, efficiency, reliability and accuracy it combines the same measure of advantages that have characterized the pace set by Milwaukee pumps for twenty years.

"Milwaukee" engineers have put into Milwaukee Cash Recording Pumps all the skill and experience gained through twenty years of specialization in this type of equipment.

Accurate Measure of Fractional Gallonage and Automatic Price Computations » » »

In the illustration above, the gallonage dial registers 10 gallons. The price per gallon is posted as 20.7. Thus, with 10 gallons delivered, the automatically synchronized price tumbler register $2.07 as the actual amount the motorist pays. There is no guessing; no chance for human errors in figuring.

Price change targets are so designed that it requires only thirty-nine tags to accommodate the full range of fractional price changes from .08 to 30 in 1/10—⅛—¼-cent computations.

Large gallonage dial gives more accurate control of measurement than the speedometer type tumbling figures, increasing public confidence. Cash and gallonage indicators are of new and improved design. The gallonage indicator will meter sales in twentieths of a gallon.

The Stations
Rise of the oil-company oasis of the highway

The gasoline company we pledge our allegiance to more than likely had its origins in the Standard Oil Trust and the empire of John D. Rockefeller. Before the government mandated the breakup of this massive conglomerate in 1911, it controlled more than 90 percent of the production, transport, refining, and marketing of petroleum products in the United States. Then there were the international aspects to consider.

After the company was dissolved, many of the resultant companies were allocated districts maintaining the Standard name. This was an advantageous move in regard to public recognition, but a terribly confusing one from the standpoint of research. In addition, an added problem for researchers is that many of these companies continued to use popular gasoline, oil, and accessory brands such as Red Crown and White Crown, Polarine and Mobiloil, and Atlas tires and batteries.

Standard Oil Company of New York (Socony) was awarded distribution areas including Maine, New Hampshire, Vermont, Massachusetts, Rhode Island, Connecticut, and New York. By 1930, the company had expanded by purchasing Magnolia Petroleum, General Petroleum, and Eagle Petroleum.

Standard Oil of New Jersey (known as Standard Oil) encompassed New Jersey, Maryland, Washington, D.C., Virginia, West Virginia, North Carolina, and South Carolina. This company also acquired numerous smaller companies, including Humble Oil and Refining of Houston, Texas, in 1919.

Standard Oil of Ohio (Sohio) had been awarded Ohio. However, the company expanded into neighboring states under the name Fleet-Wing. Standard Oil of Kentucky (Kyso) blanketed a large portion of the old Confederacy, but was supplied by arrangement with Standard Oil of New Jersey. The rest of the nation was served by Standard Oil of Indiana (Stanolind), Continental Oil Company (Conoco), and Standard Oil of California (Socal).

In 1930, Standard Oil of New Jersey became known as Jersey Standard, with the main brand of gasoline being Esso. During the initial days of Esso, the company adopted the tiger as its corporate mascot. Jersey Standard acquired Colonial Beacon Oil Company in 1931 to market fuel in Socony territories, and then expanded into Arkansas and Louisiana through acquisition of a portion of Sinclair Oil. As part of the agreement, Sinclair Oil obtained rights to use the Standard name in its remaining territories. These territories also included Indiana Standard, Esso, and Socal.

In 1933, Standard Oil of Indiana purchased American Oil through its Pam Am division. It put the entire package in the eastern seaboard states under the Amoco name, and the Sinclair division was operated as an independent company. This business entity then acquired Richfield of New York in 1935. This brought things full circle, because Sinclair's parent company was Richfield Oil of California. In 1935, Sinclair acquired Richfield Oil of New York but was not exercising its rights to use the Standard name. The parent company of Richfield Oil of New York was Richfield Oil of California.

By 1941, more than a few of the independent Standards had merged with other companies as well as with each other, further clouding the picture. Socony merged with Vacuum Oil Company in 1931 to form Socony-Vacuum, which marketed Vacuum's Mobilgas using Socony's logo, Pegasus. During the same period, Atlantic Refining declined its option to exclusive use of the Standard name in Pennsylvania, and marketed its products as Atlantic.

Conoco chose not to exercise its rights as a successor to the original Standard Oil. Therefore, it distanced itself from the former parent company, at least in name. Conoco formed a travel bureau that in time became second only to AAA in the promotion of leisure travel. Socal introduced the red, white, and blue chevron as its logo in 1931. The company expanded into other western states by purchasing the Standard rights from Conoco.

By the late 1950s, it was becoming increasingly apparent that national marketing was the key to expansion and continued profits. As a result, a new wave of confusing oil-company mergers swept the country. Socony was Standard Oil Company of New York, in 1931 they merged with Vacuum Oil Company becoming Socony-Vacuum; the primary gasoline brand sold was Vacuum's Mobilgas. Socony's Pegasus logo was chosen for the new company. In 1955 the company dropped the Vacuum name to focus on a name that could be marketed nationally. The result was Socony-Mobil marketing Mobilgas. The Socony name was dropped in 1966 and the company became Mobil Oil.

In the late 1940s, Socal began undergoing a lengthy restructuring process that ended with the company being known as Chevron. Atlantic merged with Richfield in 1966, creating Arco.

Logos and trademarks were an important part of these conflicting transitions. As a result, collectors can with reasonable certainty chronicle the evolution of companies by using their products and signage.

Before the breakup of Standard Oil in 1911, all divisions sold gasoline under the brand name Red Crown, and many pumps were crowned by this symbol. For the next 50 years, Red Crown was still used by many Standard-related companies.

During the 1930s, as different octane levels and blends became available, the crowns changed. This began with Standard Oil of Indiana, which used red crowns for Red Crown Ethyl, which later became White Crown, and blue for Solite. For other fuel products, there would be crowns in orange, gray, and green.

For 1947, there was yet another change. Red Crown represented regular gasoline and White Crown was premium. In 1956, White Crown was replaced with Gold Crown premium.

Then there are the glass promotional globes that capped early pumps, and plastic globes in later years. These globes were diverse in design. The Home Oil Company's globe featured a detailed scene of a home surrounded by a grove of trees and rich period farming details. Globe Gasoline used a detailed hand-painted globe, Polar Gasoline featured fanciful polar bears, and Independent had three marching men.

Mascots first appeared in print and signage and then turned up in filmed commercials as television became more prominent. The mascots became a key component in developing brand loyalty and recognition. The Esso Tiger, the flying red Pegasus, and the Union 76 ball all created strong brand recognition

The value of these mascots to each company was inestimable. However, an idea as to how much value the companies place on them can be found in the study of a fascinating bit of litigation over the tiger image as used by Esso and as used by the cereal company, Kellogg's. The orange-and-black striped tiger with the trademarked phrase "Put a tiger in your tank" had by the mid 1960s become an integral component in Esso Oil's marketing efforts. The tiger retired before the end of the decade but was resurrected in 1972 when Esso changed its name to Exxon. The new slogan was, "We're changing our name, but not our stripes." The tiger was again retired in the early 1980s and then revamped in the 1990s. Cereal maker Kellogg's contended that the new Exxon tiger infringed on its Tony the Tiger trademark. The case, Exxon Mobil Corporation v. Kellogg Company, 00-252, is now just another fascinating chapter in American jurisprudence.

Today, even though some motorists swear a particular brand of gasoline is superior to another, the differences between companies have become quite blurred in the last 90 years or so. Like glaring monuments to the transition from individuality to generic that is the American highway today, large plastic-covered fluorescent signs seen from the interstate stand in mute testimony.

Oil companies made great efforts to ensure that their stations were uniform and recognizable in style as well as color. This promotional flyer captures the clean, sterile, futuristic style that was becoming the industrial norm in the 1960s.

A *Hospitality* CASE OF

COCA-COLA
TRADE-MARK ®

WITH OIL CHANGE AND FILL-UP

A FREE *Philcheck* CHASSIS LUBRICATION SERVICE WILL BE GIVEN WHEN EMPTY BOTTLES ARE RETURNED WITH TAG.

179—12-63

Giveaways

"We even have stationery with Bates Motel printed on it, in case you want to make your friends back home envious . . ."

Archeologists have discovered small outdoor kitchens on what were once busy Roman street corners. The unearthed Roman streets were wide and lined with businesses and homes, so these kitchens appear to have been the first fast-food joints. There were many, and the competition must have been fierce. Each one must have had a gimmick—a way to make customers remember the place and return, maybe with friends. The Romans were less technologically advanced than the twentieth-century American burger-joint, gas-station, and motel owners, but they were just as smart. It's easy to imagine the Roman fast-food restaurateur giving away something with his name on it for the customer to remember him by—a wooden toothpick, a wooden fork, a chit for half-off the next meal, or a discount at another local business.

Promotional giveaways and slogans are as old as free enterprise itself, and the Roman fast-food guys surely had some equivalent to "Put a Tiger in Your Tank!"

Twentieth-century promotional giveaways are some of the most popular collectibles in all of automotive Americana and are too numerous to list here. Car enthusiasts collect announcement-day giveaways. Seekers of U.S. highway memorabilia collect motel and café post cards. Some of the promotional items wind up being valuable tools to the commercial archeologist who wants to know when an old motel replaced its garages with more rooms; just look at a vintage post card to find out.

Some of the most serious giveaway seekers collect depression glass, complete sets of dinnerware and drinking glasses that a woman could collect by the piece when she bought her gasoline at the same station every week. These giveaways were popular during the Great Depression, when it was exceedingly difficult for a young wife to gather nice things for the kitchen.

Most people retain a special place in their heart for their childhood possessions. Promotional items for kids were popular when they were new, and they are seriously sought after by people who want a piece of their childhood memories. General Motors was especially generous to women and children on the days when new car models were announced every fall. The women would leave the GM dealerships with bottles of name-brand perfume, and children would ride in a new car with coloring books showing this year's newest cars at exciting locations.

In the twenty-first century, promotional giveaways are at the top of many collectors' lists. With so many different promos, the supply is endless and inexpensive. They are truly a great way for a young collector to begin a collection.

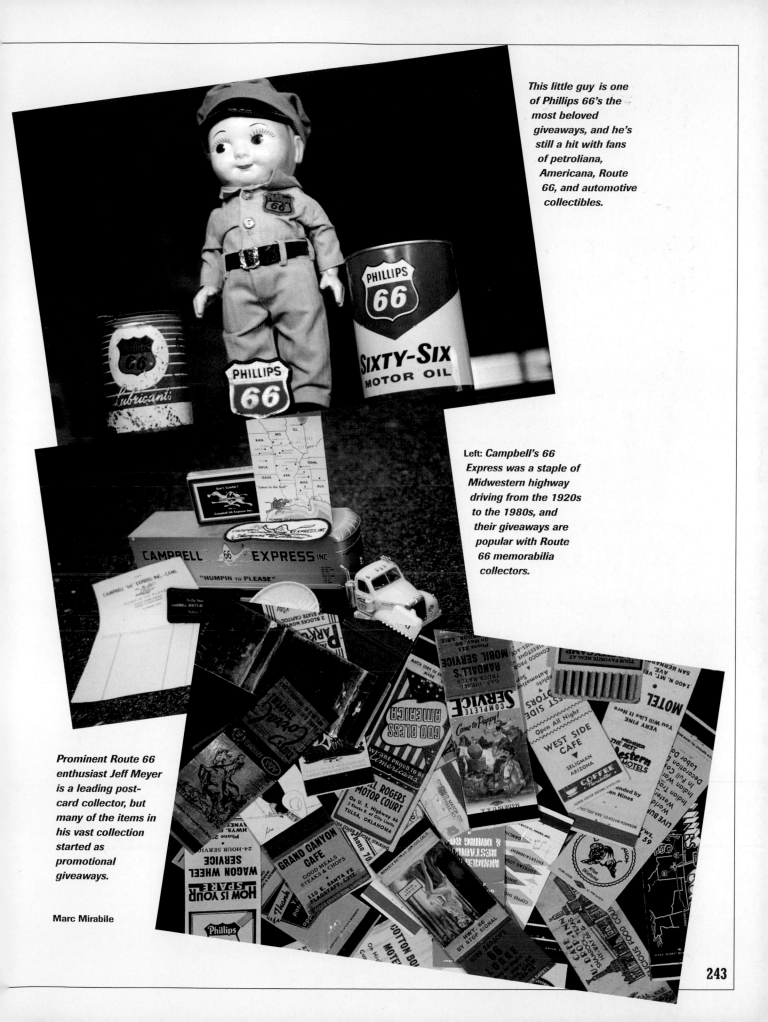

This little guy is one of Phillips 66's the most beloved giveaways, and he's still a hit with fans of petroliana, Americana, Route 66, and automotive collectibles.

Left: *Campbell's 66 Express was a staple of Midwestern highway driving from the 1920s to the 1980s, and their giveaways are popular with Route 66 memorabilia collectors.*

Prominent Route 66 enthusiast Jeff Meyer is a leading post-card collector, but many of the items in his vast collection started as promotional giveaways.

Marc Mirabile

243

Handbook for the Woman Driver

By **CHARLOTTE MONTGOMERY** Automobile Editor of **GOOD HOUSEKEEPING**

PHILLIPS 66

Central and Western **UNITED STATES** and Adjacent Canada INTERSTATE MAP

ESSO

Happy Motoring!

HUMBLE OIL & REFINING COMPANY

CAPTIVATING

RIGHT ON THE CORNER
RIGHT ON THE PRICE
WINSLOW, ARIZONA

ARIZONA US 66

UNION 76

	1939	~JANUARY~			1939	
SUN.	MON.	TUE.	WED.	THU.	FRI.	SAT.
1	2	3	4	5	6	7
8	9	10	11	12	13	14
15	16	17	18	19	20	21
22	23	24	25	26	27	28
29	30	31	Full Moon 5th	Last Quar. 12th	New Moon 20th	First Quar. 28th

Calendars and maps, the former serving as year-round reminders have long been mainstays of service station giveaways. More specifically targeted items, such as handbooks for female motorists and coloring books for children, were also common.

244

Restrooms
Some things just can't wait

Al Clouse is a retired New Mexico State Policeman, and he worked Route 66 for many years beginning in the 1950s. Highway nostalgists are well aware of the towns Clouse worked: Albuquerque, Tucumcari, and San Jon. The New Mexico State Police patrol the highways in the Land of Enchantment, and Clouse was continually enchanted by the creative excuses motorists came up with when they were caught speeding. The favorite excuse for female speeders was that they had to go to the bathroom, and eastern New Mexico's prairies don't offer much cover.

The more luxury travelers have, the more they want. The Mormon pioneers who walked from Iowa to Utah in the 1840s had more to worry about than their peers seeing them squat in the distance. The more technological Americans became, the more they desired privacy. By the time the automobile allowed private transportation, privacy became a highly preferred luxury.

In the 1930s, an automotive accessory company offered the Salesman's Friend. A rubber hose went out through a hole drilled in a car's floorboard, and the other end of the hose went comfortably and discreetly up the driver's leg, and, well . . . relief was his at will. It is not known if the same company produced a Saleswoman's Friend with corresponding anatomical allowances.

The earliest auto courts were really just campgrounds with cabins and communal cathartic pits. The shower scene in *It Happened One Night* with Clark Gable and Claudette Colbert captures the essence of waiting one's turn for the communal facilities. The movie's producers were careful to obey Hayes Office standards for movie morality for the 1930s, but it's also pretty clear the scene applied to purgative facilities as well as the showers.

Traveler-serving businesses were leaving the Stone Age by the 1940s, and big signs touting "Clean Restrooms" at the top of their neon lungs became common. Some

The sun rises over the Mojave Desert, and a lonely restroom in Helendale, California, faces a stretch of Route 66 that was bypassed in 1959, still seeming sadly welcoming.

people will admit it only to close friends who share their traveling interest, but many highway architectural enthusiasts are known to make a beeline for the restrooms to see how well-preserved a vintage gas station or restaurant is. Occasionally they even find that some of the original ornate porcelain hardware is rather beautiful and worthy of comment.

As with everything else, restrooms have become matters of law. California, among other states, has enacted legislation to ensure that gas stations provide clean, working restrooms. Something that was once a matter of good business, once again, becomes a matter of law.

Credit Card
The rise of plastic

In an effort to promote customer loyalty, gas stations often issued credit cards to preferred customers. It was a win/win situation. The customer carrying the card had an illusion of prestige and did not need to worry about being caught without cash. The chain had a steady customer. The local owner/operator could expect additional revenue due to customers from outside his locale seeking him out.

It can be said with a fair degree of certainty that the modern era of the credit card—the birth of the phrase "charge it"—began in 1949 with a business dinner, a forgotten wallet, and an idea. Frank McNamara had just finished a productive dinner meeting at Major's Cabin Grill in New York City when he realized that his wallet was in his other suit. Even though he managed to resolve the matter with little embarrassment, the idea that people should not be limited to what cash they have on hand, but what they can afford to spend, was lodged in his mind.

Selling this thought to businesses and individuals proved to be relatively easy. Merchants saw the brilliance in being able to offer an alternative form of payment as well as attracting customers who may have been somewhat short of cash, yet had buying power. Individuals recognized the advantages and prestige of being able to pay later.

By 1952, the new Diners Club card was being accepted by thousands of merchants. It had become the first international charge card, with franchises in Canada, Cuba, and France. In 1955, Western Airlines became the first carrier to accept a credit card, the Diners Club card, for ticket purchases. Within a decade, the card had become a cultural phenomenon with the 1962 release of the movie *The Man From the Diners Club* starring Danny Kaye, and a board game, "The Diners Club," by Ideal Toys.

Through the 1970s, Diners Club continued to focus on the niche market of business travelers. The first innovation of that decade was the introduction of the corporate charge card, which provided the business traveler with confirmed hotel reservations, automatic air-travel insurance, and rental-car coverage. By 1980, Diners Club was the preferred card for more than 50 percent of Fortune 500 companies. In 1984, the company became the first to offer a rewards program, now an industry standard.

By now, the era of credit had arrived. Nearly every consumer could enjoy the privileges and advantages of carrying plastic instead of cash. By the close of the last century, Visa, Mastercard, and Discover were accepted in more locations than cash itself.

HAS YOUR FLYING A CREDIT CARD BEEN LOST, STOLEN OR DAMAGED?

Do you need extra credit cards for other members of your family, or possibly a card for another car or boat? Enjoy the convenience of a second credit card by filling out the form below—and if you have moved lately and are not sure you have notified us, please give us your new address on the self-addressed, postage free postcard below.

Initially the credit card was issued to select customers in an effort to promote brand loyalty and thus ensure increased revenue for the company. This credit card application is for Tidewater Oil Company's Flying A stations.

Self-Service and No Service
The service behind the station

As regulation and traffic congestion pushed the gas pump from the curbside, the gas station began appearing on vacant lots. Initially, the ability to throw up a building, have a few pumps and a tank installed with little expense or business experience resulted in the majority of stations being little more than ramshackle buildings on trashy lots.

Major oil companies realized that allowing operations like these to dominate the market was giving the entire industry a bad name. As a result, major oil companies initiated the construction of stations that were unified in design and established service requirements, which made it possible for a customer to recognize a company's facilities regardless of city or location.

Shell Oil pioneered the concept with its West Coast stations. A study instituted by the company in 1922 found that of its 1,841 stations, the 200 that were built of common design with standardized paint schemes and graphics accounted for more than 40 percent of sales.

Many oil companies went beyond the call of duty by constructing stations that were designed to promote civic pride in a manner similar to banks or city halls. Atlantic Refining Company went as far as using stylized Greek architecture, complete with Ionic columns.

This period of grand design was short-lived, as the cost savings of prefabricated stations became the norm of the industry. An additional advantage of this type of construction was the ability to relocate an entire structure if a location proved to be unprofitable. In large part, this remained the standard through the modern era.

Clean, white stations and matching uniforms were a key component in promoting full-service stations. This circa-1941 photograph is of the Kimo Shell on Route 66 in Kingman, Arizona. Kimo was an abbreviation of Ki for Kingman and mo for Mohave County.

Another aspect of gas station development came in the form of service. Attendants were often were in smart uniforms and were taught the finer points of pleasing the customer, such as checking the tire pressure, oil, spare tire, and radiator. But cleaning the windshield was the hingepin, for this service would make possible what the customer saw in the miles to come. This was the golden age of full-service stations.

With increased competition and rising costs, it soon became prohibitive to offer full service. The result has been the modern era of no service. With technological advancement, even this has been taken to a new level; some stations offer nothing but pay-at-the-pump service, with no attendant to be found.

It is with fondness that many remember the days of full service, the promise of clean restrooms, and the sound of the filling station's bell. But it's unknown as to how many people would pay for these services today, so the stations with class that treated customers like kings and queens remain as little more than memories.

Mini-Mart
A gas station's real product

They are as old as cars themselves. In the early days of the twentieth century, drugstores sold gasoline in gallon jugs. As the neighborhood drugstore became the gas station, the mini-mart was a ready-made business.

Some garages evolved into gas stations, and some roadside stores installed pumps out front. The profit on a gallon of gas has always been rather small, and the garage-style gas stations made more money selling wiper blades and fan belts than selling gas. Likewise, mini-marts made more selling maps and munchies for the road than selling gas.

They vary some, but the themes are the same: coffee for the sleepy driver, soda pop for the thirsty driver, cigs for the smoker, candy for the kids, maps for the stranger, batteries for the flashlight, a quart of oil for the car. In the Great Lakes area, a traveler far from home will stop for munchies and walk out with a little bag of different kinds of cheese and tiny sausages of heavenly Wisconsin quality—an exotic regional delight for someone from Arizona. Likewise, a traveler from Wisconsin can leave a mini-mart in the Southwest with a bottle of beer with a chili pepper floating in it.

The gas crunch in the early 1970s forced the closure of thousands of independent gas stations, and replacing a fan belt became more of a neighborhood garage repair than a roadside

Tee Pee Curios in Tucumcari, New Mexico, operated as a gift shop serving Route 66 after the highway was widened and left no room for gas pumps. The Tee Pee was never a garage, and its gift shop was originally a store, making it a surviving early mini-mart.

Eisler Brothers Old Riverton Store on Route 66 in Riverton, Kansas, represents the mini-mart in its original form. Leo and Lora Williams built the store in 1925 after a tornado destroyed a similar store next door. The store originally had gas pumps out front, and while selling gasoline was secondary to selling groceries, having a store fronting on a major highway that served the traveling public makes it one of the earliest surviving mini-marts in the United States. The store is frequented by those traveling Route 66 for pleasure, cementing its importance as a travelers' store.

repair at a gas station. Many gas stations became owned by the corporations supplying their gas, and their service bays became mini-marts. Some corporate television advertising touts the mini-mart while not mentioning the gasoline at all. The mini-mart will be with us for a long time—convenient but expensive.

251

Tanker Truck
Life blood of the highway

The explosion in the popularity of automobile manufacture and ownership between 1898 and 1905, in retrospect, is quite amazing. In addition, when one considers the near total lack of supportive infrastructure, as evidenced by the fact that gasoline was often delivered from refiners by horse-drawn tanker, this is even more phenomenal.

However, as with most aspects of the American automotive industry and related industries, the delivery of fuel also changed in the mere blink of an eye. The credit for the first motorized tanker truck has been given to Anglo-American, a subsidiary of Standard Oil, which began delivering fuel and oil-related products from railroad tankers to substations in 1905 without the use of a team of horses.

In the United States by 1910, the tanker truck was a common sight in most urban markets. However, in some of the more remote rural areas, the horse would still be doing the job well into the late 1920s. The tanks for both were initially built by the old-fashioned method of riveting, but by the end of World War I, acetylene and electric welding had proven to be a more efficient method of production. Another change during this period was the development of oval, rather than round, tanks to help subdue surging when the truck was on the road.

Standard Oil Company, the dominant force in the development of gasoline and oil-related services, spearheaded the use of tanker trucks in 1910. Oddly enough, in light of the numerous heavy-duty trucks available at the time, the company predominantly used Fords through 1915.

Oil companies developed a certain loyalty to truck brands during these formative years. The Texas Oil Company chose trucks built by Mack; the Kansas City Fuel Oil Company was partial to Federal. Texaco almost exclusively utilized REO, and the American Oil Company went for class by using Pierce-Arrow trucks.

By 1920, the tanker trucks had evolved into rolling billboards proclaiming the merits of the company and the products they produced. A decade later, styling began to play a key role in the selection of trucks, as oil companies vied for dominance. As a result, manufacturers responded with trucks that transcended the role of the workhorse.

To describe some of the trucks produced during the 1930s as futuristic would be a gross understatement. In late 1933, Diamond T introduced a streamlined tanker that featured integrated cab and tank unit in a complete rounded package. Even more revolutionary was its rear-mounted six-cylinder engine! White in 1936 introduced the 9000 series, which included a streamlined tanker with a V-12 engine. But Chrysler produced the crown jewel of streamlined Art Deco trucks.

The excitement generated by the introduction of the 1934 Chrysler Airflow car, or so *Chrysler Motors Magazine* of September 1937 said, served as the spark to introduce a line of Airflow trucks. The first Dodge Airflow tanker built for Texaco rolled from the Detroit factory in December 1934. By the end of January, an additional 29 had been built for Standard Oil of New Jersey.

The Airflow trucks had more than just revolutionary styling. The January 1936 issue of *Fleet Owner* described the advanced features of the truck in detail. Only six minutes were required to transfer the full load of 1,200 gallons (this conflicts with records from Gar Wood Industries and

the Heil Company, which manufactured the tank bodies and stated the capacity as 1,500 gallons). Pumps, meters, and hose reels were arranged so that products could be dispensed by gravity or pump. Hose connections allowed the product to be moved from the compartments separately or in tandem, and safety equipment included emergency valves and filters to ensure pure fuel.

Today, only four of these trendsetting trucks are known to exist. One has been fully restored and currently resides in the Henry Ford Museum in Dearborn, Michigan.

From the end of World War II until today, tanker trucks have been selected in large part as a means to present oil companies in a progressive, positive light. But like so many aspects of our auto culture that were once viewed with excitement, the tanker truck is now simply taken for granted.

By the 1930s the gasoline tanker truck had become an important part of an oil company's image. In addition to the delivery of fuel, it served as a rolling promotion.

6

The
Open
Road

Today many lament that the adventure of the open road has been relegated to pockets, much like the herds of bison have to parks. But how many people would really want the adventure that was the open road a few short decades ago, when they can now cruise along the interstate in air-conditioned comfort?

On Sunday, July 6, 1919, the *Washington Evening Star* offered a route map to Atlantic City, New Jersey, via Wilmington, Delaware. The paper also posted a listing of equipment that should be taken on such a journey.

This listing of "necessary equipment" included a set of ignition brushes; a tow rope; a fire extinguisher; a set of tire chains, chain tool, and extra links; a sweater and rain gear; a folding canvas; a pail, rags, fuses, and extra bulbs; a points file; an oil can; a small box of assorted nuts, screws, washers, and cotter pins; a small spool of copper wire; a voltmeter; a jack and handle, as well as blocks of wood for the jack base; a three-in-one valve tool; a tire-pressure gauge; and a wrench for the points. This listing hints at the adventure of the open road in that time.

In The Grapes of Wrath by John Steinbeck, set during the Great Depression, the Joad family seeks out a set of bearing caps in a wrecking yard and makes repairs along the road. The adventure of the open road had changed little since the Evening Star's article in 1919. By the 1950s, travels along the highways and byways of America had become much more civilized, and some routes, such as Route 66, had became legends in their own time.

Alcan Highway
The last frontier

Discussion of ways to join the United States with the Territory of Alaska via an overland route began before there even was a Lower 48. Nevertheless, in 1930, when President Herbert Hoover commissioned a feasibility study, the talk turned to serious action. This action was in turn followed by another 12 years of talk.

With the onset of World War II, concern for the vulnerability of Alaska pushed the idea to center stage. Added incentive came in June 1942 when the Japanese attacked the Aleutian Islands and continued territorial expansion throughout the Pacific. The end result was an engineering marvel equivalent to the construction of the Panama Canal: the 1,522-mile Alcan (Alaska–Canada) Highway. Crossing unmapped wilderness, forests, swamps, and rivers from Dawson Creek, British Columbia, to Fairbanks, Alaska, the highway connected a line of airfields known as the Northwest Staging Route.

Construction officially began on March 8, 1942. By June, more than 10,000 troops were on the job, including 3,695 African-American members of the 93rd, 95th, and 97th Regiments and the 388th Battalion (Separate) of the Corps of Engineers, collectively known as the Army's Black Corps of Engineers.

The incredible hardships endured during construction made its completion after 8 months and 12 days, on October 25, 1942, even more amazing. During this period, the men often worked 7-day workweeks, and fought thick clouds of mosquitoes and black flies. Poor-to-nonexistent communications between headquarters and field parties, a near-chronic lack of equipment and supplies, quarters that often consisted of little more than tents, and winter temperatures that hovered at minus-40 degrees Fahrenheit for weeks on end compounded the problems.

Today, even though is the Alcan is an all-weather road, it still presents the opportunity to experience automobile travel as it was several decades ago. Chuckholes, poor-to-nonexistent shoulders, and frost heaves still challenge the mechanical integrity of vehicles. Flying rocks and gravel, wildlife that ranges from 1,500-pound moose to grizzly bears, dust, mud, and clouds of mosquitoes also provide a hint of the same sense of adventure those Army Corps workers must have felt more than 60 years ago.

PROVED ON THE ALCAN HIGHWAY

Fifteen years after its completion, the Alcan Highway was still formidable enough for manufacturers, such as Chevrolet in 1957, to use it for the testing and promotion of the durability of their trucks.

Right: *This rare postcard shows the Alcan Highway under construction druing World War II.*

Breathalyser
The public got MADD

In the mid-1950s, Missouri State Highway Patrolman Tom Pasley saw a big-rig stopped in the middle of Route 66 near the little city of Rolla. Pasley asked the truck driver why he was blocking traffic, and the trucker said his truck had just stopped moving, but he didn't know why. The big-rig's trailer was a flatbed loaded with two huge blocks of granite, and when Pasley shined his flashlight under the trailer, he saw the back end of a 1955 Buick buried completely under the trailer. A car stopped, and a young man came running up screaming that his friends were in the car. A carload of soldiers had partied the night away in Saint Louis and were heading back to their base when the driver decided to drive with no lights on. One soldier begged the driver to stop and let him out, which the driver did. The carload of drunken soldiers then careened off into the distance, where they rear-ended the big-rig at extremely high speed. The big Buick was nothing compared to the many tons of granite, and the truck driver never felt the impact and couldn't understand why his truck suddenly ground to a stop.

Nearly 25 years later, Cindi Lamb's baby daughter was paralyzed when a repeat-offense drunk driver slammed into her car at 120 miles per hour. Shortly after, a man who had just been released from jail for drunk driving killed Candace Lightner's 13-year-old daughter while driving drunk. Lamb and Lightner formed Mothers Against Drunk Drivers in 1980, and a new era in traffic enforcement began.

Everyone wants drunk drivers off the road, but like any other crime, policemen must have probable cause to stop a driver. Sufficient evidence is also required for an arrest and conviction. A car weaving down the road and a staggering driver may be evidence of drunk driving, but the driver could also innocently have the flu and a high fever. The police officer must prove guilt, and that is where the breathalyzer comes into play.

An officer who suspects that a driver is drunk puts the suspect though a field sobriety test—walking a straight line, tilting back the head and touching the nose, reciting the alphabet—but still, a person with the flu could fail these tests. Breathalyzers started out as elaborate machines at police stations where the suspect breathed into a tube, and the machine measured the alcohol found in the invisible mist of moisture that leaves the lungs with every exhalation.

Ultimately, a blood test is the most accurate way to measure blood-alcohol levels, but it is necessary to have sufficient evidence before blood can be drawn. The breathalyzer gathers that evidence.

In the 1990s, police officers were armed with an even more effective device to aid their quest for probable cause. The PAS device—the passive alcohol sensor—fits in a shirt pocket, and this mini-breathalyzer is the officer's most effective tool early in the arrest process. The weaving car is pulled over, the driver staggers a little, the officer tells the driver to breathe into the little box, the officer gets a pretty accurate measure of blood alcohol, and the driver wakes up behind bars with a headache and a date with a judge.

Not all drivers are cooperative, though. "Some people will not want to blow into it," says Sergeant Ross Tarangle of the San Bernardino County Sheriff's Department in California. "Some people will try to beat it by putting their tongue on the end of the mouthpiece or manipulating it in other ways. Typically, they'll say they can't blow hard enough. Some people will try to play games because they think they can make it not give a reading. There are those who have been arrested multiple times for DUI, and they can be very uncooperative because they've been through the system and they know the process."

MADD claims that 55 percent of traffic fatalities were alcohol-related in 1980. By 2000, the number had fallen to an encouraging, but still tragic, 38 percent. Breathalyzers have played their part in helping the police make more probable-cause arrests and get more convictions.

Many people don't intend to drive drunk. They have a little too much wine at an afternoon party, they get into a hot car, their blood vessels dilate, and they're suddenly a lot drunker than they were when they first got into the car. Many people may thank the police and their PAS devices for saving them from a terrible mistake. Perhaps the PAS devices will quietly play their part in making New Year's Eve and the Fourth of July a little safer for the car-loving public.

San Bernardino County, California, Sheriff's Deputy Rich Daniel demonstrates the Passive Alcohol Sensor device on Department of Public Information Officer Roxanne Walker. The PAS device gives the officer in the field strong proof of probable cause to arrest a suspected drunk driver and helps greatly in the evidence-gathering process toward a conviction.

Automated Highway
1939 World's Fair, Next Exit

A fire truck comes bounding out of a fire station driveway with lights blazing and sirens screaming. There's a house burning down and no time to waste. The fire truck is emitting a radio wave, and as it approaches an intersection, a sensor on a traffic-signal mast picks up the frequency. Much like a garage-door opener, the sensor changes the light to green. The Opticon system lets emergency vehicles travel less hindered through heavy traffic.

The system is also a possible prediction of the day when cars equipped with computer chips will drive themselves on roads equipped with sensors that keep cars moving the same speed, the same distance apart, free of human error, and on pre-programmed paths. The day may come when traveling on a major highway is more like riding a train on tracks than actually driving.

The Automated Highway System, or Intelligent Transportation System, is closer to becoming a reality than neo-Luddites want to think and further away than techno-optimists like to imagine. The first permanently installed three-color traffic signal in America was introduced in 1919 in Detroit, Michigan, at the corner of Woodward and Michigan Avenues. In 1926, Chicago installed a system of traffic signals in its famous Loop area. The traffic signals were centrally controlled from a bank of timers in the basement of city hall. These were the beginnings of the AHS, but other than improved traffic volume–sensing equipment and computer controls, traffic signals have not changed much since the 1950s. However, the twenty-first century has dawned with GPS in moderately priced cars and car radios receiving broadcasts from satellites. The stage may be set for the fully automatic AHS.

Today's predictions for an Automated Highway System are probably as fantastic as the hyper-tech predictions of the 1939 World's Fair. This GPS navigational system may more accurately predict the extent of the AHS in actual use.

Engineers are sifting through several lines of thought. The Independent Vehicle Concept equips individual cars with computers and sensors, and lets them drive themselves on existing low-tech roadways. The Infrastructure-Supported and Infrastructure-Assisted Concepts combine the intelligence of the smart car with intelligent roadways, which guide the car along. The Cooperative Concept lets smart cars communicate with each other through wireless signals, which, in effect, would say, "Excuse me, may I merge?" and "Why, yes, you may." If nothing else, the Cooperative Concept would eliminate the need for wireless communication through middle fingers.

The 1939 World's Fair notoriously predicted a hyper-tech future in which fully automated robotic kitchens did all the cooking and washing up, leaving the glamorous housewife the leisure time to get a Claudette Colbert permanent. What the future actually held was a kitchen in which a heatless oven cooks with radio waves and has a little computer chip controlling its timer and output. Chances are, the AHS's future will parallel the World's Fair robotic kitchen, and it'll be a regular highway with high-tech help along the way rather than the fully automatic paradise predicted in the films *Metropolis* and *Things to Come*.

U.S. 99 and U.S. 101

Fraternal Twins—same parents, but they don't look alike

The San Gabriel, Sierra Madre, and Tehachapi mountain ranges all converge northwest of Los Angeles, and they form a wall so steep, broad, and impenetrable that by 1912 there was a political movement that very nearly split California into two states. An 18-foot-wide strip of concrete winding through the mountains from Los Angeles to the foot of the Grapevine Grade in the San Joaquin Valley kept the Golden State whole.

The 48-mile-long road teeters on the tops of ridgelines, had enough curves to make 219 complete circles, and had a 15-mile-per-hour speed limit for over 30 miles. The Ridge Route opened in 1915 and was completely paved by 1919. The route saved a state, but even by the standards of the 1920s, the tortured curves and steep grades made the road dangerous

Between Los Angeles and the San Joaquin Valley, the intersection of the San Gabriel, Sierra Madre, and Tehachapi Mountains is so rugged that California was very nearly split into two states in 1912. An 18-foot-wide strip of pavement kept the Golden State whole. The Ridge Route partly teetered atop a ridge line that was straight down on both sides, and it partly crawled through narrow canyons. The Ridge Route cut the path that was bypassed and converted to U.S. 99.

Right: *Serra who set up California's famous Catholic missions. The road connecting them was El Camino Real, and it set the path of U.S. 101 in the twentieth century. The original El Camino Real passes the Mission San Juan Bautista on the California Central Coast. The climactic scenes of Alfred Hitchcock's 1957 classic* Vertigo *were filmed in the courtyard up the hill at the left where James Stewart drove Kim Novak to her demise in a 1956 DeSoto.*

and obsolete. By 1932, the steam shovels were revving up, and U.S. 99 opened as the Ridge Route-Alternate in 1934, occupying canyons on the original road's west side for the most of the way.

Gaspar de Portolá was a Spanish explorer who took quite a walk up the California coast and immediate inland valleys in 1769. The same path linked the famous 21 California missions under the leadership of Father Junipero Serra in the following few years, and the road was named El Camino Real.

The San Andreas Earthquake Fault played its part in California history by forming the long, narrow valleys the wagon roads and highways would follow. Winding through the hills along this route, old alignments of U.S. 101 mark the path closer to the route of the original Camino Real. Like many highways in the eastern United States, the older versions of 101 followed the paths of the eighteenth-century roads they replaced.

The two roads, 99 and 101, connected the Mexican border with California, Oregon, and Washington, with U.S. 99 going all the way to the Canadian border. U.S. 101 hugged the coast, and U.S. 99 connected the valleys and traversed the mountain ranges well inland. The roads were twins, but they were very different, and they only shared common pavement in two places: Los Angeles and the city limits of Olympia, Washington.

For classic car buffs, the two roads still follow their original paths. Although 99 lost its U.S. highway status in the late 1960s, 101 remains a U.S. highway. Both routes retain much of their 1930s–1950s flair. In places, the original two-lane concrete winds through hills next to the freeway. In other places, the original two-lane from the 1920s, the expressway from the 1950s, and the modern interstate flow along with each other and give drivers the choice to take any of them, at least for a short distance. Guidebooks to the original paths of both highways guide the enthusiast along the way and point out the locations of gas stations, inns, and diners of the past.

Since 1917

After the Ridge Route parted the mountains to allow traffic to fall into the San Joaquin Valley, the Golden State Highway became a busy place. After the scary, miserable, day-long drive over the Ridge Route from Los Angeles, travelers were ready to stop, and Sweitzer's Tavern opened in 1917.

Beryl Mitchell's father had brought his family to California in 1930 as real-life Grapes of Wrath Great Depression refugees.

"We had a farm in southeast Illinois. We had an old Hudson, and we came to California to make a better life," Beryl Mitchell remembers. "We had a public sale and had enough money for a farm out here. We took Route 66 and stayed at camps where we cooked our meals. It took about two weeks to get here."

Sweitzer's Tavern was a popular place in the 1930s. The Sweitzers were close friends with the Fleischmann family of Fleischmann's Yeast fame. Local lore has it that Clark Gable and Carol Lombard were good friends of the Fleischmann family, and as evidence, a photo hangs in the former Sweitzer's Tavern showing Clark Gable posing by a doorway in the Sweitzer residence. One of the stories is that Gable would climb the Sweitzers water tower and hunt game birds in the swampy field across the road.

By the mid-1930s, the Golden State Highway had become U.S. 99, and through the 1930s and 1940s, Beryl Mitchell's family worked their farm up the highway from Sweitzer's. Beryl and her husband rented Sweitzer's in the 1950s and bought it in the 1960s, and Beryl's Café still has a sign on the front touring the location as Sweitzer's Corner.

"I bought this place because I thought they were going to build a housing development across the highway from us. I paid $20,000 for it. But, they never built the houses. We used to have lots of truck drivers. We had some wild little waitresses here, and the truck drivers liked them. The truck drivers called this the "Hay Hauler's Haven." On holidays and weekends, cars were just bumper-to-bumper on 99. Moving the highway didn't really hurt us, but later, they put up a sign [saying there were no services at our exit]."

Beryl's Café is a well-liked local business with a loyal customer base of Bakersfield truck drivers, farmers, and laborers with many travelers still wandering in off the newer alignment of 99, which had become a state highway in 1964. The building's roof sags charmingly, and while many nostalgic travelers are trying to step into places that take them back to the '50s, Beryl's takes the traveler back to the teens and '20s when the Golden State Highway was still a dirt road.

Beryl was born in 1911 but has entered the twenty-first century still working her café. Beryl is a tiny woman but not at all frail, and she smiles broadly at all her customers as she pours their coffee, while her daughter Doreen runs the grill and does the majority of the waiting on tables. Beryl has experienced the car culture's sad side, having lost three husbands to traffic accidents, but she still works every day and likes to tell stories about U.S. 99. "I think working all the time has kept me healthy."

U.S. 99 approaching Bakersfield, California. U.S. 99 was upgraded to four-lane expressway standards in the 1950s, and this old alignment still has long stretches of the islands and dimpled curbs that scream of the U.S. Highway system in the 1950s. U.S. 99 came out the north side of Bakersfield looking very much like this, but most of it has been destroyed by the modern California State Highway 99 freeway. Many of the driving scenes in Psycho were filmed on 99 just north of Bakersfield.

U.S. 99 and U.S. 101 left the Mexican border quite a distance from each other: 99 well inland in the harsh, low desert of Imperial County, and 101 right near the coast in San Diego. U.S. 99 headed north past the date farms of the Salton Sea and joined U.S. 60 near Palm Springs; the ghosts of 1920s concrete alignments still lay in the shifting sands.

U.S. 101 hugged the coast from San Diego, and was the path home or path never-to-return from for many thousands of World War II veterans who left Camp Pendleton for the Pacific Theater. There are long still-used neighborhood roads in southeastern Orange County made from the unmistakable concrete slabs banking through every curve.

U.S. 99 was co-signed with U.S. 60 and U.S. 70, which came in together from Arizona, and 99 traveled with them all the way to Los Angeles. There, 99 and 101 met briefly before they

Elaborate stonework along U.S. 99E near Oregon City. Dick Romm

The Pudding River Bridge and the Clackamas River Bridge are two of C. B. McCullough's masterpiece bridge designs on U.S. 99E between Salem and Portland, Oregon. The Clackamas River Bridge won the 1933 Most Beautiful Steel Bridge Award from the American Institute of Steel Construction. Dick Romm

The Siuslaw River Bridge on the central Oregon coast, built in 1936, could be the single most beautiful bridge on all of U.S. 101. It's the pride of the city of Florence.
Dick Romm

separated, as 99 headed for the Ridge Route and 101 returned to the coast, where its old alignments, cut off by erosion, still hang out over the crashing waves. Here, the two highways' true character becomes defined and different.

As it alternated between the coast and the first inland valley all the way to San Francisco, 101 was largely a path of tourism, giving families access to the beaches of Morro Bay, San Simeon, and Monterey. Farming on the Central Coast is of the luxuriant wine-grape variety, with the Salinas Valley being the only gritty farming along 101. John Steinbeck lived along 101 in the Salinas Valley, and two of his famous characters, George and Lenny, landed near the dusty little town of Soledad for their tragic end in *Of Mice and Men*.

U.S. 99, which sliced northward through hundreds of miles of the San Joaquin Valley, was all business: cotton, tomatoes, onions, garlic, alfalfa, and even petroleum. John Steinbeck wrote about U.S. 66 in *The Grapes of Wrath*, and for his famous family of Great Depression refugees, 66 was only a tool to get to 99, where their hope for a better future lay.

Above: *U.S. 101's bridge at Heceta Beach in central Oregon has been compared to the famous designs of the Roman aqueducts.*
Dick Romm

Left: *The only rival to Florence, Oregon's Siuslaw River Bridge is the Yaquina Bay Bridge at Newport. C. B. McCullough's bridges have arches that are much higher, longer, and more graceful than they need to be to function as load-bearing structures. They were meant to be beautiful.*
Dick Romm

U.S. 101 heads past San Luis Obispo, and a long piece of 1920s concrete winds its way up the terrible slope of the Cuesta Grade. Over in the Central Valley, U.S. 99 formed the main drags of Bakersfield, Fresno, and dozens of little towns. A long stretch of the 1950s-era 99 expressway glides along on the east side of the modern freeway south of Fresno, with the at-grade intersections and dimpled curbing only found along U.S. Highways.

In the 1950s, 101 wound past sophisticated jazz clubs and beatniks in coffee houses along the streets of San Francisco and headed for the majesty of the Golden Gate Bridge. Meanwhile, the working-class teenagers of Modesto were cruising 99; they were later immortalized in George Lucas' *American Graffiti*.

U.S. 101 stays on the coast nearly all the way to Olympia. North of the San Francisco Bay, 101 was known for a time as the Avenue of the Giants for taking tourists through the California Redwoods, the tallest trees in the world.

U.S. 99 split north of Sacramento. U.S. 99E linked the big towns, and U.S. 99W connected little towns and provided a bypass to get past the cities more easily. The routes rejoined in Red Bluff and took the driver past the oh-my-god sights that awaited in Northern California, including Mount Shasta.

As they neared the Oregon border, both highways 99 and 101 ran into trouble. The coastline became even less hospitable for 101. Inland, the Siskiyou Mountains loomed as another long, deep, high, steep barrier to 99, which negotiated the mountains with switchbacks and lovely 1920s arched bridges at Rock Point, Gold Hill, Myrtle Creek, and Winchester. U.S. 101 connected the lumber mills that dotted the coast and giant lumber barges moved that commodities up and down the coastline better than any highway or railroad could.

The business-versus-tourism theme followed 99 and 101 all the way through Oregon, whose natural wonders are rivaled by the creations of one of civil engineering's most imaginative minds. Some call C. B. McCullough *the* master bridge builder, and his designs are downright moving to those who appreciate old highways. McCullough's inland bridges have gentle concrete arches, tasteful ornamental railings, and lampposts that seem to have been placed for artistic qualities as well as safety. The giant coastal bridges McCullough designed for 101 are breathtakingly beautiful. Suspension bridges like the Golden Gate Bridge may win the beauty contests, but McCullough's bridges on the Oregon coast have a look—arches intermixed with ultra-square structures—and their intricate trestles and cantilevers show anyone looking exactly how the bridge works. The Siuslaw River Bridge at Florence and the Yaquina Bay Bridge at Newport are two of the most underrated bridges in the country, and 101 makes them even more special.

U.S. 99 crossed the Columbia River at Portland, and the original paths of 99 are still visible alongside Interstate 5 in Vancouver and Kelso, Washington. U.S. 101 ran out of road at Astoria, Oregon, and for 40 years, until the Astoria-Megler was built across the mouth of the Columbia River, it simply looked longingly at the Washington shore 4 miles away. Once again, 99 was the path of business, connecting Portland and the other cities of Oregon to the Washington capitol of Olympia and the city of Seattle beyond, while 101 waited for ferries to take cars across the river.

U.S. 101 hugs the shoreline of Washington's Willapa Bay and crosses some inland country before pulling into the once-bustling towns of Grays Harbor: Aberdeen and Hoquiam. Two steel bridges carry 101 though Hoquiam, and at the foot of the biggest one, there is a

small building with a booth on the second story that leans out over the highway. At one time, this was a radio station, and the disk jockey played records, gave weather reports, and waved to tourists from the windows of his glass booth. The gods of tourist travel watch over travelers on 101 as it circles Mount Olympus in a giant loop, and it eventually meets up with its long-lost twin, U.S. 99, in Olympia, where a sign reading "U.S. 101 END" once stood.

U.S. 99 lived on for a couple of hundred more miles, as it prowled the streets of Tacoma and Seattle, where its route can still be found and its flashy roadside architecture still survives. Bob's Java Jive coffee shop in Tacoma is shaped like a giant coffee pot, and the Twin Tee Pee Restaurant in Seattle is a neon gem. A giant set of cowboy boots looms in the distance, and the Hat 'n' Boots gas station comes into view with a giant cowboy hat to match the boots. U.S. 99 eventually stops at the Canadian border.

U.S. 99 and U.S. 101 were twins with very different personalities. Those with old cars can find much to love along these roads, with long stretches where there's nothing to remind the driver of the twenty-first century. From harsh deserts to green jungles with 65 inches of rainfall a year, from white beaches to rugged coastal cliffs or mountains abruptly rising from the Pacific shore, from dusty country folk to urban sophisticates, and from black night skies to neon glare, the two highways had them all—and still do.

U.S. 99 originally crossed the Cowlitz River at the town of Toledo on a steel truss bridge, but when the bridge was demolished and replaced with a safer concrete bridge in the early 1990s, the plaque dedicating the original bridge to the veterans of World War I was saved and moved to a monument nearby.
Craig Murphy

Dixie Highway
Adventure in the land of the confederacy

The Dixie Highway received its long-awaited designation on April 3, 1915, in Chattanooga, Tennessee. The official recognition of the highway was the culmination of a series of meetings initiated by Carl Graham Fisher, who had also been a driving force behind the creation of the Lincoln Highway and the establishment of the Indianapolis Speedway.

Initially the Dixie Highway was built to link the Upper Midwest with the sun and sand of Florida by tying together local roads and state-designated "highways." Fisher was also instrumental in the transformation of a large tract of Florida swampland into the cosmopolitan metropolis of Miami; the development of this route served more than his passion for improved roads.

By May, 1915, the northern portion of the route was expanded to two additional lines, one from Cleveland, Ohio, and one from Chicago, Illinois, that joined the main route at Cincinnati, Ohio. In 1916, Michigan joined the Dixie Highway Association, and the route was extended north to the Canadian border at Sault Ste. Marie, Michigan, via ferry between the upper and lower peninsulas.

In 1924, when the preliminary work began for the numbering and designation of the newly established U.S. Highway System, it was obvious that the Dixie Highway would not lend itself well to the proposed numeric designations. As a result, what was known as the Dixie Highway became Highways 25, 25W, 411, 19, 10, and 41 on November 11, 1926.

Still, the name persisted, and even as late as the 1950s much of the former route was still known or referred to as the Dixie Highway. The original good roads association for the area had given way to the U.S. 25 Dixie Highway Association, a co-op of businesses and communities along the route that had come together to promote tourism and travel.

In the days before the advent of the interstate highway, when getting there was at least half the fun, the Dixie Highway was touted as "North or South . . . Your Favorite Route to Florida or the Great Smokies."

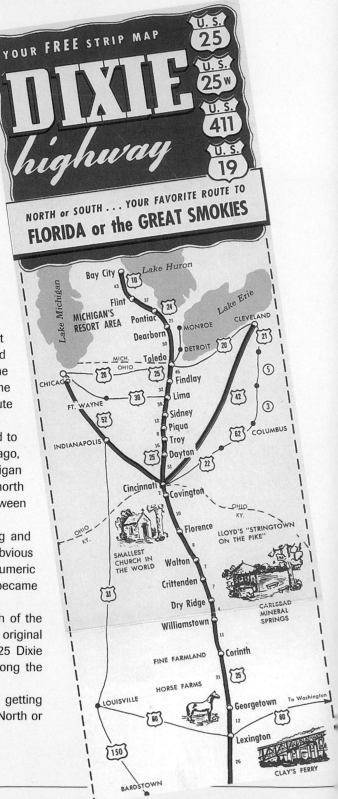

270

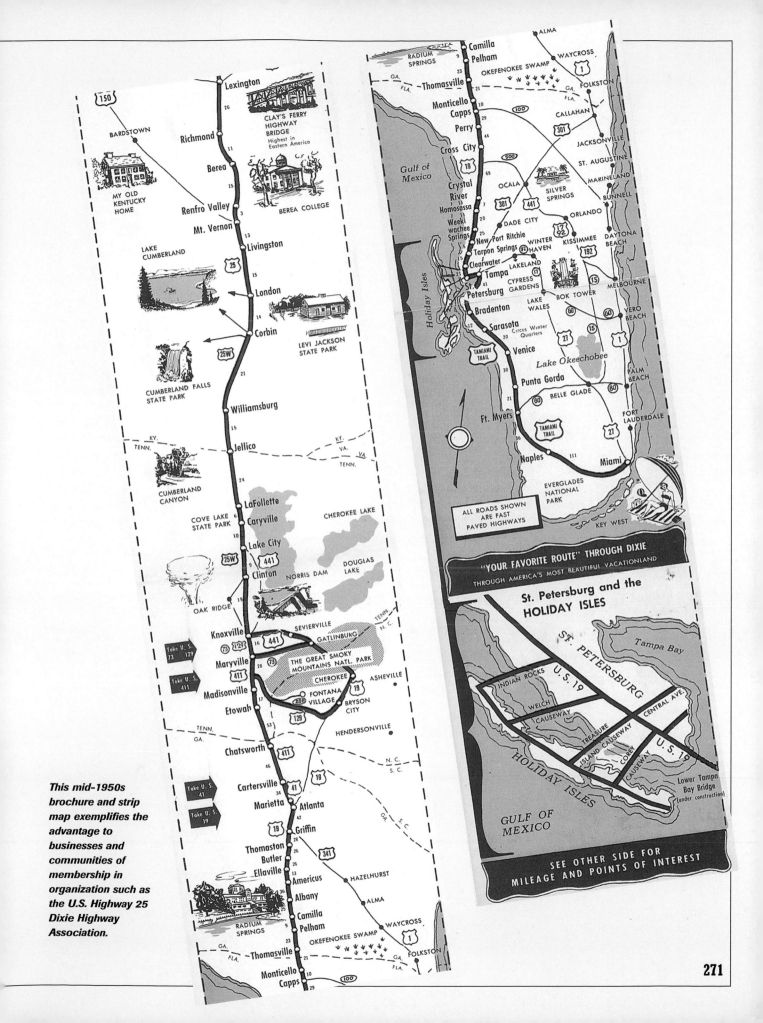

This mid-1950s brochure and strip map exemplifies the advantage to businesses and communities of membership in organization such as the U.S. Highway 25 Dixie Highway Association.

CLAY'S FERRY HIGHWAY BRIDGE
Highest in Eastern America

BEREA COLLEGE

MY OLD KENTUCKY HOME

LAKE CUMBERLAND

LEVI JACKSON STATE PARK

CUMBERLAND FALLS STATE PARK

CUMBERLAND CANYON

COVE LAKE STATE PARK

NORRIS DAM

DOUGLAS LAKE

THE GREAT SMOKY MOUNTAINS NATL. PARK

FONTANA VILLAGE

RADIUM SPRINGS

"YOUR FAVORITE ROUTE" THROUGH DIXIE
THROUGH AMERICA'S MOST BEAUTIFUL VACATIONLAND

ALL ROADS SHOWN ARE FAST PAVED HIGHWAYS

EVERGLADES NATIONAL PARK

St. Petersburg and the HOLIDAY ISLES

SEE OTHER SIDE FOR MILEAGE AND POINTS OF INTEREST

The Bridges
Connecting shore with shore

Rural bridges and roads at the dawn of the twentieth century were little improved from the days when Roman legions traversed the sands of North Africa and the moors of the British Isles. In some aspects, there had actually been digression. The turn of the century and an explosion in automotive ownership had resulted in little improvement.

Covered bridges were engineering marvels for their time, and today those that have survived into the modern era are highly treasured for their aesthetic value. However, during the infancy of the automobile, they were viewed as a detriment to the advancement of good roads at best and an outright danger at worst. The First Transcontinental Motor Train was a combination military exercise and promotional tour to drum up support for federal assistance in road development. The group encountered its first obstacle on the second day of its tour: a covered bridge with a roof that was too low for trucks to pass under.

Then, like a bursting dam, road construction and incredible feats of engineering swept across the land, forever changing it as well as the society it passed through. The Federal Highway Act was passed in 1921. The following year, the Lincoln Highway Association had what was considered an example of the perfect road constructed between Dyer and Schererville in Indiana. Among the many advanced features were a roadway that was 40 feet wide and had a surface of 10-inch-thick concrete reinforced with steel bars, a median divide, drainage, and lighting.

The Bronx River Parkway in New York, the first limited-access highway in America, opened in 1923. In 1929, Woodbridge, New Jersey, was home to the first cloverleaf interchange. By the end of the following year, the government had funded the construction of 10,000 miles of paved road in a 12-month period.

The covered bridge, though quaint and picturesque, came to be viewed as a hindrance once motor vehicles, especially trucks, began to dominate the roads of America.

In October 1927, ground was broken for a new six-lane bridge to span the Hudson River between upper Manhattan and Fort Lee, New Jersey. Incredibly, the 4,760-foot George Washington Bridge was finished in record time and opened to traffic on October 25, 1931. In 1946, an additional two lanes were opened on the upper level. When a lower level was opened on August 29, 1962, this made it the only 14-lane suspension bridge in the world. With traffic volume, according to 2003 traffic statistics, at 105,942,000, it is also the world's busiest. In 1981, the bridge was designated a National Historic Civil Engineering Landmark by the American Society of Civil Engineers.

On the West Coast, ground was broken for another engineering marvel, a bridge to span the Golden Gate, on January 5, 1933. This bridge was the longest span in the world at 1.7 miles, including the approaches, until the completion of the Verrazano Narrows Bridge in New York in 1964.

The logistics of the Golden Gate Bridge project were staggering. Shipped to the site by way of the Panama Canal were 83,000 tons of steel that was manufactured in New Jersey, Maryland, and Pennsylvania. The two main cables consisted of 27,572 strands of wire, and it took six months to spin them.

When the bridge was opened to automobile traffic on May 28, 1937, the toll was set at a half-dollar for one way, or one dollar for the round trip, with an

The George Washington Bridge, opened to traffic in October 1931, has become one of the busiest bridges in the world.

*Travel on U. S. Highway 34.
Shortest and Best Route thru Iowa,
Nebraska and Colorado*

World's Most Beautiful
FARES SLASHED!
MACKINAC BRIDGE

LINKING MICHIGAN'S UPPER AND LOWER PENINSULAS

Now you can drive across
MIGHTY MAC
for LESS than HALF!

World's Most Beautiful
MACKINAC BRIDGE

LINKING MICHIGAN'S UPPER AND LOWER PENINSULAS

MINNESOTA
LAKE SUPERIOR
ONTARIO
ST. IGNACE
OF MACKINAC
STRAITS
MACKINAW CITY
LAKE HURON
WISCONSIN
LAKE MICHIGAN
MICHIGAN
ILLINOIS
INDIANA | OHIO

STATE OF MICHIGAN
MACKINAC BRIDGE AUTHORITY

Hon. GEORGE ROMNEY, Governor

PRENTISS M. BROWN, Chairman
GEORGE A. OSBORN
BEN W. CALVIN
MURRAY D. VAN WAGONER
CHARLES T. FISHER !!I
WHEELER J. WITTE

ALLISON GREEN, Treasurer

LAWRENCE A. RUBIN, Executive Secretary
ORLANDO DOYLE, Chief Engineer

The Mackinac Bridge was financed through the sale of bonds to private investors. Total bond issue, including interest during construction was $99,800,000.00.

Litho in U.S.A.

Opened in 1957, the Mackinac Bridge is a modern engineering marvel that allowed traffic to flow between the upper and lower peninsulas of Michigan without the use of ferries.

additional nickel surcharge if there were more than three passengers in the vehicle. By 2002, the toll had risen to five dollars for southbound travelers, and there was no charge for northbound traffic.

The Golden Gate Bridge today holds the record for being the most photographed bridge in the world. However, it holds another less enviable record; it is unofficially the world's leading suicide location, with at least 1,200 people seen jumping or found in the water below since the bridge's opening.

These bridges and numerous others built during the same period are symbolic because they span more than just rivers or bays, they also bridge the era between the trail and the highway. With the May 7, 1954, groundbreaking for the Mackinac Bridge, proudly referred to as the "Big Mac" by the residents of Michigan, another chapter of bridging the gap was launched.

World's Most Beautiful Bridge

Designed by the late Dr. David B. Steinman

FARES:

CLASSIFICATION	RATE
Car (Incl. driver and passengers)	.$1.50
Car w/1 axle trailer or coach	2.50
Car w/2 axle trailer or coach	3.50
2 axle truck with 4 tires	1.50
2 axle truck with 6 tires	3.00
3 axle truck — single unit	3.50
Truck — comb. — 3 axles	4.50
Truck — comb. — 4 axles	5.00
Truck — comb. — 5 axles	5.50
Truck — comb. — more than 5 axles	6.50
Bus	3.50
Motorcycle	1.00

Subject to change without notice

BUS SERVICE—Passenger buses operated by the Mackinac Bridge Authority provide frequent service over the bridge between Mackinaw City and St. Ignace. One trip fare, 50¢; commuter books, 15 tickets for $5.50 good for three months, not transferable. Children under 12, with parents, free.

TRUCKS—COMMERCIAL VEHICLES — Load limits are the same as those in force on Michigan State Trunkline highways. Regarding vehicles over legal weight as defined in Act 300 P.A. 1949 as amended, the Mackinac Bridge Authority must be notified by means of a completed copy of the standard M.S.H.D. permit 48 hours prior to crossing. In regard to oversize vehicles (except house trailers) two hours notice by telephone is required. Scrip Books are available. Write, Comptroller, Mackinac Bridge Authority, P.O. Box 217, St. Ignace, Michigan 49781.

BICYCLE TRAFFIC on bridge is not permitted, but arrangements for transporting bicycles may be made with the bus drivers.

World's Longest Total Suspension

8,344 feet from cable anchorage to cable anchorage

There were more obstacles overcome and problems solved in designing and building the Mackinac Bridge than in any comparable project. Yet it is one of the safest and most beautiful spans ever built. ■ 33 marine foundations support the 4 mile long uninterrupted steel superstructure. All piers rest on bedrock. The two huge tower foundations are more than 200 feet below water — and all were built out on the water with boats, barges and ships handling the men, machinery and materials. ■ From 1884, when the people of Michigan first proposed bridging the Straits, until November 1, 1957, "Michigan first proposed bridging the that couldn't be built." On that eventful day Michigan's upper and lower peninsulas were permanently tied together and traffic began rolling smoothly over the historic Straits of Mackinac.

LENGTHS

Total Length of Bridge with Approaches (5 miles)	26,444 Ft.
Total Length Steel Superstructure	19,243 Ft.
Length — Suspension Bridge (Including Anchorages)	8,614 Ft.
Total Length — North Approach Spans	7,129 Ft.
Length — Main Span (Between Main Towers)	3,800 Ft.

HEIGHTS AND DEPTHS

Heights — Main Towers above Water	552 Ft.
Maximum Depth to Rock at Midspan	Unknown
Maximum Depth of Water at Midspan	295 Ft.
Maximum Depth of Tower Piers below Water	210 Ft.
Height of Roadway above Water at Midspan	199 Ft.
Underclearance at Midspan for Ships	155 Ft.
Maximum Depth of Water at Piers	142 Ft.
Maximum Depth of Piers Sunk through Overburden	105 Ft.

CABLES

Total Length of Wire in Main Cables	42,000 Miles
Maximum Tension in Each Cable	16,000 Tons
Number Wires in Each Cable	12,580
Weight of Cables	11,840 Tons
Diameter of Main Cables	24½ Inches
Diameter of Each Wire	0.196 Inches

Over the World's Greatest Inland Waterway

SPEED LIMITS—Maximum speed limit is 45 mph. Special speed limits will be posted, according to conditions

GENERAL REGULATIONS

- No U turns.
- No stopping on bridge.
- Posted speeds must be maintained.
- Pedestrian traffic prohibited.
- In the event of a flat tire or motor failure please remain in vehicle. Bridge Authority patrol cars constantly on duty will investigate, and assist. The Authority is prepared to service all breakdowns.

FREE PASSAGE — "No free use of such bridge shall be permitted, but all individuals or vehicles using such bridge shall pay the tolls and charges established for such use by the Authority. This provision, however, shall not apply to the operating personnel or vehicles of the Authority." Sec. 12 Act No. 214, Public Acts 1952.

DANGEROUS CARGO—Transportation of flammable liquids, liquid gases, or explosives will be governed by the rules and regulations established by the Fire Marshal Division of Michigan State Police, except that persons transporting explosives shall call the Fare Supervisor on duty at least 2 hours in advance of arrival on either side of the bridge. Phone 25, St. Ignace, Michigan.

TOURIST INFORMATION — Tourists may obtain information regarding Michigan's unexcelled vacation opportunities from the Michigan Tourist Council, Lansing; the Upper Michigan Tourist Association, Iron Mountain; the West Michigan Tourist & Resort Association, Grand Rapids; the East Michigan Tourist Association, Bay City; and the Southeastern Michigan Tourist & Publicity Association, 1404 Broderick Tower, Detroit.

CROSS OVER AND BACK ON MIGHTY MAC... WORLD'S MOST BEAUTIFUL BRIDGE

As early as 1883, ways of linking the upper and lower peninsulas of the Great Lakes State was the subject of lengthy discussion, proposals, and editorial discourse. It was 1923 before serious evaluation began. The project received an added sense of urgency in 1928, just five years after the State Highway Department initiated ferry service because of heavy traffic.

Circumstances, including the harsh economic conditions of the Great Depression and the diversion of resources toward the war effort during the period of 1940 to 1945, kept the project from progressing much further than the study stage. As a result, in 1947 the state legislature abolished the Mackinac Straits Bridge Authority. The next six years were marked by a flurry of citizens' committee organization, legislative action, and further evaluation, culminating in the building of the bridge.

Opened on November 1, 1957, at 5 miles in length, it was the longest suspension bridge in the world. With the opening of the "Big Mac," the era of the straits ferry that had served residents for a century ended.

The engineering involved in our greatest bridges must stand as one of the wonders of the modern age. In addition, for the traveler they serve as another milestone in the effort to overcome any obstacle that prohibits uninterrupted speed.

Ferries
Amphibious vehicles

In comparison to the engineering, construction, and technological accomplishments of the past century, the engineering and construction of the Great Pyramid pales in comparison. Even so, the most advanced technologies have their limitations; as a result, occasionally the only option available is to step back to tried-and-true methods such as the ferry.

On the Great Lakes, the ferry has long been an integral part of the transportation system. As transportation has evolved in the area, so have the ferries. Initially the focus was on cargo and passengers, but with the coming of the railroad a new chapter began.

The first car ferry, the *Ann Arbor*, was a wooden-hulled vessel that gave the Ann Arbor Railroad a decided edge in cross-lake cargo hauling. The Flint & Pere Marquette responded to the challenge with the launching of the first steel-hulled ferry in 1896. In addition to hauling loaded rail cars, the huge vessel proved to be an excellent icebreaker.

With the advent of World War I, cross-lake freight traffic as part of the nation's rail system boomed. As a result, in the summer of 1918, the United States Railroad Administration created the Lake Michigan Car Ferry Association. This allowed for operation of the 11 vessels of the Ann Arbor, Pere Marquette, and Grand Trunk railroads under the supervision of a single supervisory board. Return of the ships to their respective owners in 1920 began a new chapter in the history of car-ferry operation on the lakes.

An explosion in industrial activity on both sides of Lake Michigan during the following decade resulted in the commissioning of several new ferries. The Great Depression and the resultant decrease in commerce forced older ships from the lakes, setting the stage for the boom of World War II.

The modern era of lake traffic began in 1952 with two new additions to the Ludington, Michigan–based fleet, the SS *Spartan* and SS *Badger*. The high-water mark for Lake Michigan ferry service came in 1955 with the transport of 205,000 passengers and 204,460 freight cars.

In the years before the construction of the Mackinac Bridge, the Michigan State Ferries, founded in 1923, plied the waters of the Straits of Mackinac, providing the only direct automobile connection between the upper and lower peninsulas of Michigan.

ABOARD "THE STRAITS OF MACKINAC"
Michigan State Ferry

SET YOUR BRAKES

By 1975, the C & O Railroad was the last company to operate the ferries as part of its rail service. Citing the rising cost of ship maintenance and a litany of other expenses, the company ceased operations on the lake and sold the three remaining ferries in 1983.

The newly created Michigan–Wisconsin Transportation Company purchased the ferries, but revenue derived from passenger and auto transport proved to be inefficient in offsetting the cost of operation. On November 16, 1990, the SS *Badger* set sail on its final voyage.

The following summer, the ferry received a new lease on life, as new owners returned it to service between Ludington, Michigan, and Manitowoc, Wisconsin. In addition, in the summer of 2004 a new era of lake ferry service began with the launching of the state-of-the-art Lake Express, which offers high-speed service between Milwaukee, Wisconsin, and Muskegon, Michigan.

The ferries of the Great Lakes have a long and storied history. However, in the Pacific Northwest the ferry service is in large part merely a cog in the wheel of transportation.

Shortly after the turn of the nineteenth century, development on the islands of Puget Sound precipitated the need for regular ferry service. By 1929, the lucrative ferry service had been consolidated into two companies. Labor troubles as well as the economic conditions of the period narrowed this to but one company a decade later.

In 1951, the importance of reliable ferry service in the Sound prompted the state of Washington to buy the Puget Sound Navigation Company, which included all ferries and terminals except for those associated with the Seattle/Port Angeles/Victoria route. Initially the State Highway Commission and the Toll Bridge Authority operated the new ferry system jointly. The two agencies became part of the existing Washington State Department of Transportation in 1977.

The Washington State Ferry system is now the largest in the United States and serves 8 counties as well as the province of British Columbia in Canada. The state-operated system carried approximately 4 million passengers in the first year of operation. By 2000, passenger service had surpassed 25 million annually and vehicle transport had exceeded 10 million.

The most fascinating ferry service in operation today must be the Alaska Marine Highway System, as it provides a true link to the frontier heritage of the nation by being the only link between civilization and the wilderness. For many communities along the shores of Alaska and Canada, this ferry service is the only safe, reliable, and efficient means of transporting people, goods, and vehicles. The system has been providing year-round service since 1963. For those who wish to see the great state of Alaska without subjecting their vehicle to the rigors of the Alcan, it is the only viable alternative. During the past decade, this ferry system has transported an average of 400,000 passengers and 100,000 vehicles per year.

Ferries in the modern age seldom receive a great deal of thought unless you happen to live where they serve as an integral part of the transportation system. However, for the adventuresome, they provide a link to the past as well a break from the routine.

Operating between Ludington, Michigan, and Manitowoc, Wisconsin, the Badger *is the last steam-powered ferry to ply the Great Lakes. As a result, it provides a unique opportunity to experience travel from another era.*

The Las Vegas Strip
Glitter Gulch

The Las Vegas strip today is not the Las Vegas strip many envision. The strip today is Disneyland, neon, and the ultimate cruise, all rolled into one. The original strip was neon that crowded out the desert sky, glitter, and no illusion that this was anything more than a playground for adults.

Today the strip is roller coasters and casinos, towering spires, and volcanoes that erupt like clockwork. It is magic shows and monorails, fountains, and garish electric billboards. Its skyline is New York and Paris, with the Sphinx and Great Pyramid thrown in for good measure. In the past, the neon and glitter of the strip was a thin façade that hid a dusty desert oasis.

The strip today is known for billion-dollar resort/casinos such as the Mirage and the Bellagio. The old strip was the Frontier, Flamingo, Landmark, and Silver Slipper. The old strip can still be found, but it has a great deal of tarnish, while the current strip is a three-dimensional experience that floods the senses.

Attempts and suggestions to resurrect the old strip have run the gamut from converting the streets into canals for a neon recreation of Venice, to multi-million-dollar resorts built on the ruin of past glories. To date, these attempts have been of no avail, and the new strip reigns supreme—the King is dead; long live the King.

However, at its heart, the strip is what it has always been: a grand illusion. Fueling it is the grandest illusion of them all, which is the belief that riches are awaiting with one more roll of the dice or one more pull of the handle.

Even though gambling and other adult entertainment is still the lifeblood of Las Vegas, this aerial view of the new strip reflects the trend toward family entertainment.

Even under a cloudless blue desert sky, it's easy to see from this vintage post card why the original Las Vegas Strip was known as Glitter Gulch.

Highway Signs
Signs of the times

A confusing array of signage that ran the gamut from striped poles to hand-painted signs served as highway designation during the first years of the twentieth century. Good-roads associations and similar organizations attempted to rectify the problem through the creation of universal signage.

Automobile Blue Books of Chicago, Illinois, spearheaded this drive. In addition, they took the concept one step further. Their guidebooks included a listing of reputable businesses along each route. To designate these routes and businesses, white-lettered blue shields that resembled the Union shield used by the United States government were incorporated. Because of its wide recognition, the shield was selected to symbolize a U.S. highway designation on April 20, 1925, the same day the Joint Board on Interstate Highways decided that a numbering system was a preferable replacement for the name designation currently in use.

With the basic design agreed upon, the next order of business was to determine what would be placed in the center. The first proposal called for the top to be dominated by "U.S.A." with the route number below it. After heated debate, it was decided that the state name would be on top, followed by "U.S." and the route number.

Then there was the matter of color. The initial suggestions leaned toward yellow with black lettering, which many members felt was an advantageous combination, especially for winter visibility. The problem with this was that the combination had already been approved for signage warning of road hazards. In the end, it was agreed the signs would be white with black lettering and a black border.

In addition to this basic format, there were also official variants for specific purposes. At highway junctions, an *R* or *L* in smaller U.S. shields (the standard size was 18" x 18") designated the direction of turns. Another type of secondary sign was approved for city use; these signs were also smaller than the standard route markers (11" x 11") and featured "U.S." where the state designation would be, or "Business" and then "U.S."

Shortly before World War II, individual states began diversifying the concept. The first was Ohio in 1943, with a square sign that was embossed with the white U.S. shield. In 1950, Illinois began producing signs with the state name across the top and the removal of "U.S."

A 1953 court ruling stated that all U.S. highway signs must feature "U.S." as initially agreed upon. Other changes initiated included changing stop signs from yellow with black lettering to red with white lettering, and the allowance of states to adapt colors other than white with black lettering for U.S. highway signs placed with funds other than federally collected gasoline tax monies. The latter resulted in a short-lived but colorful chapter of highway signage. In 1956, Florida began color-coding its routes: orange for U.S. 41, yellow for U.S. 301, and so forth. Kansas experimented with green on the newly assigned U.S. 56. Arizona tried allocating different colors for directional signs, as a brief experiment to aid in clarifying directions. Today only the states of California and Virginia still use cutout U.S. shields to signify U.S. highways, as opposed to the now-standard black square with white shield, and the colored signs have been relegated to historic memorabilia.

While much has changed along the highways of America in the past 80 years, the U.S. highway shield has endured. As a result, it may be the most recognized of all highway signs. With the addition of the number 66, this recognition becomes global.

The Glidden Tour and the Great American Race

Where the past and present meet

In the infancy of the American auto industry, promoting the automobile as a viable means of transportation was the job of anyone who hoped to see them become more than a novelty. More often than not, wealthy industrialists who truly enjoyed their vehicles and the adventure of the open road were spearheading the movement.

Charles Glidden was just such a man. The wealthy New England industrialist dedicated his life and fortune to promoting automotive transportation. This was an outgrowth of his many adventures on the road, including countless tours through New York.

The Glidden Tours challenged motorists and vehicles in an effort to promote the need for improved roads as well as provide adventure for owners. The durability of vehicles like this 1908 Oldsmobile was sorely tested on these runs.

The Great American Race revived the spirit of the early Glidden Tours and for more than 20 years has provided the opportunity for owner as well as spectator to relive those exciting times.

THE GREAT AMERICAN RACE

Sponsored by

INTERSTATE BATTERIES

From ANAHEIM to INDY - MAY 21 thru 28, 1983

Grand Prize – $100,000.00

GREATRACE, Ltd. Dallas, Texas

In 1905, the American Automobile Association honored the numerous automobile manufacturers for their assistance in sponsoring cross-country reliability tours. Glidden saw tremendous opportunity for the manufacturers to sponsor a trophy for the winner of each event. As a result, they became known as the Glidden Trophy Tours.

Held annually between 1905 and 1913, the tours were highly competitive and provided a great deal of publicity as well as real-world experience for manufacturers. Many companies were eager to enter vehicles and sponsor teams.

The promotion of road improvement was another benefit of establishing the tour and other similar events. Since the deplorable condition of roads was a national issue, the route for the Glidden Tour was different every year.

The novelty of the automobile, combined with thrilling tales of adventure, was more than headline-grabbing news. For the manufacturer, publicity directly translated to sales.

Many of the earliest races and endurance runs were truly astounding in their scope. One epic was the New York-to-Paris race in 1908, which included fighting blizzards in the Hudson River Valley and deep mud in Ohio, encounters with wolves in Wyoming, and trekking through deserts in Mongolia and the wilds of Siberia.

The annual Glidden Tour came to end in 1913. However, with the post-war interest in vintage autos and rise of the collector car hobby, it was revived in 1946. The adventure of battling fractious mechanical contrivances as well as the elements and other competitors has now come full circle. In 1982, The Great Race burst onto the automotive scene, further stirring the spirit of the Glidden Tour in enthusiasts. As a timed endurance rally/race for street-legal vintage cars that are more than 46 years of age, The Great Race is without equal in the modern age. After all, what other opportunity will the owner of a 1916 Hudson have to race against the clock as well as other competitors through the heartland of America?

Interstate Highways
Coast to coast without a stoplight

It has been said that the interstate highway makes it possible to drive from coast to coast and never see anything. With all fairness, it might also be said that the interstate highway has made it possible to drive coast to coast without the fear of a head-on collision, narrow bridges, steep grades with no shoulder, or drivers cutting their pass too short as a result of oncoming traffic.

Tracing the origins of the interstate concept is fascinating. There are German engineering drawings for a limited-access highway that includes merging patterns with clover leafs dated 1912, and the adventures of a young, junior-grade military officer named Eisenhower fighting the mud on a 1919 cross-country convoy listed as the First Transcontinental Motor Train. Two decades later, this same officer had the opportunity to examine firsthand the wonders of the German autobahn and meditate on such a highway's role in national defense.

The success of the New Jersey and Pennsylvania Turnpikes related to safety and speed served as a precedent when the time came to take the concept to a national level. Mirroring this was the increased carnage caused by a dramatic rise in usage, as well as speed on highways such as Route 66.

While much has been written about the effect the interstate highway has had on mom-and-pop businesses,

communities, and American society as a whole, few
travelers today want to truly relive the imagined glory days of the two-lane
highway. In all honesty, this is the best of times, for we can take advantage of all the
interstate has to offer *and* have the luxury of enjoying the non-generic past in small doses.

The next time you find yourself believing the hype about Route 66, take the time for some
white-knuckle driving on a heavily traveled two-lane highway. To truly complete the time-travel
experience, consider traveling a lonely road at night not knowing if the station ahead closed at
sunset, whether the diner in the next town serves anything other than beans, or the hotel
looming on the horizon has seen the addition of modern improvement since 1946.

License Plates

In more aspects than one, the introduction of the automobile came about in a manner akin to having the can opener invented before the can. There was no infrastructure to support it and no laws to regulate it, or even a consensus as to what it was and how to define it.

The updated version of the Illinois Automobile Law put into effect in July 1909 stated that, "Whenever the term motor Vehicle is used in this Act, it shall be construed to include automobiles, Locomobiles, and all other vehicles propelled otherwise than by muscular power, except motor bicycles, traction engines, and road rollers, the cars of electric and steam railways. . . ."

Into this maelstrom of confusion came an even more serious problem: finding a way to regulate the number of vehicles that were exponentially increasing on the streets and to identify vehicles involved in illegal activity or that were stolen. Enter the license plate and vehicle registration.

The earliest license plates for motorized vehicles date to France in 1893. In the United States, the first license plates were required in New York beginning in 1901. These "plates" were either leather pads or flat metal plates with attached letters that were the owner's initials.

A few years later, Massachusetts became the first state to issue what was later considered a modern-type license plate. Among collectors these are known, respectively, as pre-state and state-issued plates. In Illinois, according to the 1909 statutes, a license plate consisted of, "a seal of aluminum or other suitable metal which shall be circular in form and not to exceed 2 inches in diameter, having stamped thereon the words, 'Registered Motor Vehicle No. . . .'"

In 1906, West Virginia and Pennsylvania became the first states to issue dated registrations and plates. Maryland joined suit in 1910, and other states soon followed.

Since that time, plates have become more standardized in size. But design, color, and even the metal used have varied wildly, as evidenced by the copper commemorative plates issued by Arizona during the 1930s and the colorful Michigan bicentennial plates issued in 1976.

Today, license plate collecting is a hobby that many thousands throughout the world enjoy. It provides a tangible link to the past and serves as a time capsule of sorts. What are the most sought-after American plates? In a recent article on license plate collecting, the 1921 Alaska plate topped the list as the rarest. The 1912 Mississippi plate ran a close second, unless the rumor that a 1911 porcelain plate from Mississippi really exists; then it would be a whole new ball game.

By 1929, the license plate had evolved into its standardized modern form. But in years to come numerous commemorative and special-edition plates would become highly sought after by collectors.

Lincoln Highway
Route 66 for an earlier generation

Today the romanticized view of the recent past is encapsulated in two lanes of asphalt designated 66. For the middle-aged generation during the 1940s and 1950s, it was the Lincoln Highway.

On July 1, 1913, a group of automobile enthusiasts, industrialists, and public officials came together and formed the Lincoln Highway Association. The purpose for founding the organization was, "to procure the establishment of a continuous improved highway from the Atlantic to the Pacific, to open lawful traffic of all description without toll charges." The proposed route ran from Times Square in New York City to San Francisco, California.

This ambitious goal was never fully realized until the introduction of the Federal Highway Act and the subsequent infusion of capital. However, with this intervention the era of named highways ended. Numbered routes became their replacement, and the Lincoln Highway became U.S. 1 along the eastern seaboard, U.S. 30 across the Upper Midwest and across the plains, U.S. 530 into Utah, U.S. 40 to Nevada, and U.S. 50 to the coast.

Even though it was designated a highway, was relatively well marked, and was the subject of extensive annually revised guides, the Lincoln Highway that future president Eisenhower experienced in 1919 as part of the First Transcontinental Motor Train was deplorable. It has been said that these experiences played a major role in his orchestration of the Interstate Highway System a quarter-century later.

However, the president who was most fundamental in the development of a modern highway system was Woodrow Wilson. Ames Brown wrote in the September 1916 issue of *Northwestern Motorist* an article entitled, "President Wilson the Motorist." In the piece he noted, "No more ardent motorist ever occupied the White House than President Wilson. . . . Mr. Wilson probably has spent an average of two hours a day in an automobile since he became President." His love for automobile travel provided him with intimate knowledge of the need for improved roads. This knowledge led to his membership in the Lincoln Highway Association and his signature on the Federal Aid Road Act of 1916.

Lincoln Highway, Lyons and Fulton Bridge over Mississippi River
Official Gateway to Iowa and Illinois.

This vintage post card of the Lyons and Fulton Bridge attests to the rapid advancement of road conditions immediately following World War I with the notation, "Official crossing of Lincoln Highway . . . over paved roads."

Fold-out brochures and post-card booklets were popular souvenirs of a trip on the Lincoln Highway. This set dates from circa 1920.

With the replacement of named highways in 1926, the Lincoln Highway and the crucial role it had played in the development of a modern highway system began to fade from the national conscience. The association ceased activity at the end of 1927, with its final contribution being to mark the route as a memorial to Abraham Lincoln. This was done by the Boy Scouts of America in 1928, with the placement of thousands of small concrete markers adorned with a small bust of President Lincoln.

However, as with Route 66, the Lincoln Highway has become the focus of a new generation interested in the history of the American highway and its culture. To aid in this endeavor and ensure preservation of what remains, the Lincoln Highway Association was reactivated in 1992.

LINCOLN HIGHWAY BETWEEN IRWIN AND EAST PITTSBURGH.

ON LINCOLN HIGHWAY, BETWEEN FORT LOUDEN AND McCONNELLSBURG.

ROLLER COASTER ON LINCOLN HIGHWAY BETWEEN IRWIN AND GREENSBURG.

RA SUMMIT, SHOWING McCONNELLSBURG, HAGERSTOWN PIKE AND LINCOLN HIGHWAY.

AG ROCK, WASHINGTON PARK ON LINCOLN HIGHWAY ON LIGONIER MTS.

Meter Maid

The Enforcer

Technically, they're parking enforcement officers, but. . . .

"We're called meter maids. That's what we're called, and if you don't like it, don't apply for the job," says Holly Wilson, who really likes her job.

Drivers make faces as they drop hard-earned coins into the little timers. The motorists reasonably assume that parking meters collect money to maintain the streets, but really, parking meters are traffic-control devices that keep cars moving. A shop owner feels it in the wallet if the same cars camp out in front of his store all day long, keeping away new customers.

Downtown Sayre, Pennsylvania, has a triple-problem with parking. Sayre's once-booming railroad industry has been replaced by a huge hospital as its largest employer, and hospitals are busy places. Sayre is also land-locked—clamped between two big rivers on the east and west sides, which come together at the south end—and capped by the New York state line on the north side. On top of this, downtown Sayre is old-fashioned parking-wise, with cars diagonally parked where the parking meters stand guard.

"Years ago, when these old towns were laid out, people never had a clue how many cars there would be, and they did not permit for the growth of the automobile," Holly Wilson says. "So, they had to come up with something to control parking-related traffic jams."

Parking meters were the answer, and for the first couple of decades, policemen in most cities checked parking. With time, most city governments decided chasing burglars was a better use of a policeman's time. Then cities hired civilian enforcement officers, usually women, and they quickly became known—most of the time affectionately—as meter maids. Sayre installed parking meters in 1943 and hired its first parking enforcement officer in 1964, three years before the Beatles' "Lovely Rita" made meter maids cool. Sayre's first meter maid served for 37 years before Holly Wilson took over the long-held post in 2001.

Many cities provided the meter maids with three-wheeled motorcycles or Cushman motor-carts, but Sayre is small enough for Holly to walk a beat. She always varies her route to remain unpredictable for potential parking-space time thieves. Sayre police officers joke with her that she should get a camouflage uniform and hide in the trees. Holly's comfortable with the job and tries to give people a chance before putting tickets on violators' cars, but she's out there for all to see, and she had to get used to it.

"At first, I felt like I was *out there*, with everybody looking at me. I was a little intimidated. I had a lot of people yelling at me and throwing tickets on the ground. I didn't like that, but I'm the kind of person who likes to make them laugh, and for the most part, that gets me through it. People have just gotten used to me. I try to work with the shop owners because I don't want to drive their customers away."

Holly's heard all the excuses. "I was only in there two seconds," they tell Holly, who had seen the meter running for a half-hour, but Holly puts the ticket on the car, and hopefully the three dollar fine later appears in the lock-box on the nearby post.

"I get a lot of notes in the box from people telling me their children were sick, or they'll never shop in Sayre again. People bend coins and use pieces of paper to jam the meters—anything to park free. Then, there are the people who drive around the streets until they find a parking meter with time still left on it, and for most of them, it's just the principle of the thing. Sometimes, if they don't pay, they'll say, 'All I had was a quarter, and I didn't want to put it all in there because I'll only be a minute.' I say, 'Think of it as your good deed for the day. Think how happy the next guy will be!'"

Sometimes, it's the machinery that causes the problems: "One day, a girl's gas tank was leaking badly in front of the pharmacy, and it was right where the pharmacy girls come out and smoke their cigarettes. Another time, a tractor-trailer came around the corner and knocked over a post with two parking meters on it, and these two kids picked it up and started running with it. Those things are heavy, and it was in the snow. I don't think they would have gotten far with it, and I don't think they could have busted into the meters either. They had underage drinking charges brought against them, too!"

Parking enforcement is an all-weather job, and the only time Holly is not on the beat is when it's raining too hard for

Officer Richard Bowman of the Sayre, Pennsylvania, police force points out a parking violation fine collection box, circa 1955. Cities assigned police officers to enforce parking regulations, but with time, police departments decided chasing burglars would be a better use of a policeman's time. So they hired civilian parking enforcement officers—usually women—who became known as meter maids.

The fearsome presence of Sayre parking enforcement officer Holly Wilson deters would-be violators from overstaying their parking time. Sayre police officers joke that Holly should wear camouflage and hide in the trees.

her to open her ticket book. On any other weekday, she's out there listening to retired Italian men tell stories from the old days, making friends with the local kids, and keeping the traffic moving.

"We have a large elderly population here, and I've helped them in and out of their cars, and I helped an old lady move into an apartment one time. Some days, I get frustrated with the litter, and I grab a garbage bag and start picking it up because I can't stand it."

It's not a job for everyone, but Holly likes cars, likes people, and likes to walk. "You only live once, so you might as well have a good time at it."

Parking Meters
"Small town. Not much to do in the evening . . ."

The first thing you see is a pair of hands working a pipe-cutting tool. Around and around, the tool etches a deeper groove. Lucas Jackson is drunk and cutting the heads off parking meters in the middle of the night—suicidally decapitating unseen authority figures, knowing fully the crime will land him in the hands of that authority. Being in the military during World War II had already taught him that in order to fight against authority, he first had to get close to it. Paul Newman played Lucas Jackson in *Cool Hand Luke*, where the parking meters represented rules, authority, and permission-giving devices. He hated them.

Tacy Collini decides she can cook in the house trailer while it's being towed down the road. While many people are rightfully uncomfortable with the sadistic nature of slapstick, Lucille Ball's tumbling, tossing, flour-and-egg-splattering scene in *The Long, Long Trailer* appeals to viewers because they all have been guilty of looks-good-on-paper thinking and wound up covered with flour and eggs of some kind. The funny scene is followed by something chilling: The long, long trailer is parked at the curb, taking up several spaces, and Desi Arnaz, as Nicky Collini, is walking along putting coins in parking meter after parking meter, with vehicular and marital troubles that are no longer funny showing in his face.

Parking meters did not come from the bustling boulevards of Manhattan, the mechanized industrialism of Detroit, or the parking-starved streets of San Francisco. Parking meters were a Midwestern invention, and sprang from the sidewalks of a city known more for cattle drives than automobile drives. In 1935, downtown Oklahoma City had old-fashioned storefronts with office spaces on the upper floors, and in the days before urban sprawl, parking lots did not exist in great numbers. Office workers from the second floors or from around the corners took up all the parking spaces in front of retail stores.

Carl Magee was a newspaperman who had settled in Oklahoma City in 1927 and founded the *Oklahoma News*. He followed the parking space controversy with interest. The Oklahoma City Chamber of Commerce appointed Magee to its Traffic Committee, and Magee had an idea. He came up with a crude timed parking meter, and he got Oklahoma State University engineering students involved in a contest to see who could perfect the parking meter under the leadership of Professor H. G. Thuesen and OSU engineering graduate Gerald Hale. The leaders announced a winner, and the result was nicknamed "Black Maria." Oklahoma City installed 175 of them as a test operation in critical areas during July of 1935.

The idea worked. The parking meters ensured that there was a turnover of cars at the curbs. Because their primary purpose was to keep traffic moving, the cost to park was only a nickel, but the nickels added up and generated revenue to maintain the streets. The fine for a violation was a whopping $20 at a time when $50 would buy a nice used car.

Magee's invention was a hit, and he formed a group of investors to cement a deal with a Tulsa, Oklahoma, timing-device manufacturer and founded the Dual Parking Meter Company. Its first product was called the Magee-Hale Park-O-Meter. Other companies followed. The best yo-yo a kid could buy in the 1970s was the Duncan Butterfly, but how many would guess the Duncan who made the yo-yo was the same Duncan who made Duncan parking meters? Donald Duncan had already been successful in the yo-yo business when he purchased Miller Meter in the late 1930s.

Not a tonic offering temporary relief, but a sure permanent cure against inoperative meters due to cold weather.

Quality Duncan meters are specifically engineered to operate dependably regard-less of inclement weather conditions. To insure continuous operation of your city's metered parking control program twelve months of every year . . . Add Duncan dependability today.

WRITE TODAY
DUNCAN PARKING METER
DIVISION OF NAUTEC CORPORATION
835 NO. WOOD ST. • CHICAGO 22, ILL.
For more data, circle No. 407 on reply card
March 1964 • THE AMERICAN CITY

The idea spread to many other cities. The earliest parking meters were manually wound, and a city employee would walk a foot-beat winding the meters, which were then tripped into action by the patron parking his car. Later, parking meters became self-winding, and the driver would wind the meter himself without realizing it as he turned the clock to the desired allotment of time.

Parking meters have entered the twenty-first century in an electronic form with digital readouts, like everything else. Some of them have sensors that clear the time when a car drives away, and some of the most sophisticated can photograph a car after its time expires.

Americans who think of themselves as free must ask a hard-faced little machine for permission to park at a curb their taxes have already paid for, or else face grim consequences from a cop on a tricycle. It's doubtful that the parking meter will live in the treasured-memory corner of the car enthusiast's mind, where the drive-in theater speakers play the dialogue from *Cool Hand Luke*.

Motorcycle Cop
The long, maneuverable arm of the law

Motorcycle police officers seem motivated by freedom. It's not the overly romanticized freedom of the open road—the *Easy Rider* version of escaping constraints. Rather, it's the uninhibited ability to get to the victim or the perpetrator that keeps coming up in conversations with motor officers.

Most often, these officers work traffic details, and a motorcycle is the best way to get to the speeder or the drunk before he kills someone, or the best way to get to the traffic accident while the police cars and ambulances are stuck in traffic.

"You could call me a native Los Angelino, but at the same time, I hated LA with a purple passion as far as living in it is concerned," said Buzz Banks in Jon G. Robinson's book, *Route 66: Lives on the Road* (MBI Publishing, 2001). Banks' way out of the big city was to join the California Highway Patrol (CHP) in 1941 at age 27, a decision that also gave him the "certain extent of excitement and adventure" he was looking for and a home in Route 66's desert town of Victorville.

Motorcycles were often the first vehicles used by communities to motorize their police departments. This patrol officer is pulling over a 1909 Packard.

Excitement and adventure are certainly found in Banks' 1994 book, *Policing the Old Mojave Desert*. Banks had a need for freedom, and he chose to work on a motorcycle.

The United States entered World War II in December, 1941, shortly after Banks joined the CHP, and General George S. Patton was put to the task of training tank crews to fight the Germans in North Africa. Patrolman Banks escorted General Patton's tank divisions down U.S. 66 from Victorville to Amboy under some measure of secrecy. Patton took rather long, strange routes through the desert, and Banks escorted the tanks, keeping the tanks and the public from running into each other. His motorcycle gave him the maneuverability to work among the tanks and to quickly get to where he was needed.

"We had to be careful," Banks recalls. "We couldn't use the radios much. We had orders to operate with our headlights off, and we even had to shield our red taillight lenses. You could fly over the desert for years after the war and see tank tracks all over the place."

Tom Pasley of the Missouri State Highway Patrol (MSHP) is another member of Banks' generation, and he began working the outskirts of Saint Louis in 1939. He was eventually based in Rolla and joined the MSHP Safety Squadron. The squadron was a group of 13 motorcycle officers who worked special details all over Missouri, such as the state fair; dangerous stretches of highway that needed extra enforcement; and the role of "good cops" who helped people change tires on narrow two-lane highways. The maneuverability of their motorcycles made the Safety Squadron perfect for conducting manhunts, as Pasley found out one night in the 1940s on narrow rural farm roads and cow paths with killers lurking in the brush.

"We had worked a 12-hour day on the motorcycles, and we were coming in for the evening," Pasley remembers. "An officer by the name of Potts drove up on a car to check it, and the fellow leaned out the window and shot Potts with a shotgun. Only a few of the pellets hit him, so it didn't kill him. So, they called everybody in, including all the boys on motorcycles, and we had a manhunt all the way from Joplin to Baxter Springs [Kansas]. I was the only one who

In this photo of the Missouri State Highway Patrol Safety Squadron, circa 1940, Tom Pasley is in the front row at the right. In addition to 33 years of service to the MSHP, Pasley had been an art student, and he designed the Safety Squadron's gas-tank logo and the MSHP patrol-car logo that has been in use for nearly 60 years. Missouri State Highway Patrol collection

didn't get into a car, because we didn't have enough cars. I stayed out all night on the motorcycle. Potts and another trooper named Grammar were in a car, and they came down a country road, and there was a log across the road. Grammar got out to move the log, and he got shot in the back end with a shotgun. The [bad guys] were lying in a ditch because their car had broken down or something.

"Now, the manhunt was on foot, and I was out in Kansas on that little old motorcycle. It was a foggy morning with a lot of dew on the ground, and I saw a light coming across the field. Of course, it startled me, and I was hiding behind my motorcycle with my gun drawn. It turned out to be two old farmers. One of the [bad guys] had gone in and tried to rob a farmer of his car, and these farmers jumped him. They tied him up with barbed wire around his wrists! Later, when I was an instructor at the [police] school, I told all my recruits that if they ran out of handcuffs, they could just go get some barbed wire."

Times and styles change, but policing highways from a motorcycle has changed very little since Banks' and Pasley's era. In the decades since, the sometimes silly but always positive TV show *CHiPs* made motorcycle cops look cool in the eyes of a whole generation in the 1970s. Their choice to be motorcycle officers brings them the sense of excitement and adventure that Buzz Banks sought generations before, while at the same time living up to their choice to keep the traveling public safe on the roadways.

San Bernardino Country Sheriff's Deputy Ross Tarangle works as a motorcycle officer in the twenty-first century and echoes the sentiments of generations of motorcycle officers who came before him. "Personally, the thrill of riding a motorcycle and the excitement of police work creates a total package," Tarangle says. "It's the enjoyment of working out in the open and working outside. Having the added mobility of being on a motorcycle certainly allows you to work enforcement in more areas than someone who's working in a car. Ultimately, the goal of traffic enforcement is to reduce injury from traffic collisions. Because you have the advantage of being able to maneuver in places that cars can't get to, it probably allows you to be more effective in traffic enforcement. It's less physically inhibited, and you have greater visibility, but certainly, it is a lot more dangerous than being in a car, and you may not have time to react to that."

The excitement and sense of immediate effectiveness seem to outweigh the dangers for America's two-wheeled traffic-enforcement officers, and they don't seem to mind being called motorcycle cops.

The Lincoln Tunnel

Marvels of the modern era

In 1930, initial plans were announced for a twin-tube tunnel under the Hudson River between West 38th Street in Manhattan and Weehawken, New Jersey. The most significant accomplishments represented by the tunnel were not its initial completion in 1937, but in the engineering utilized in its construction. The engineering evolution has enabled it to grow with expanding traffic-control needs and the safeguards instituted in its construction.

A series of sealed air locks provided workers with a properly pressurized environment. Additional state-of-the-art safeguards resulted in the Lincoln becoming the first major tunnel to be constructed without a single fatality.

The first tube is today's center tube, and it was opened on December 22, 1937, at a completion cost of $75 million. Traffic congestion resulted in the initiation of a second tunnel, but war-related delays prevented its opening until 1945. It was decided in 1951 that a third tunnel was needed; this was completed in 1957 at a cost of $85 million. In contrast, the Port Authority is currently engaged in an improvement project that includes the reconstruction of the toll plaza with an estimated cost of $50 million.

According to Port Authority figures, the Lincoln tunnel complex carries approximately 120,000 vehicles per day. This makes the Lincoln Tunnel one of the busiest in the world.

This 1940s post card is of the Lincoln Tunnel entrance from the New Jersey side of the Hudson River.

New Jersey Turnpike
The finest highway in the world

"In 1949, we determined to build in New Jersey the finest highway in the world, linking the interstate crossings of the Hudson River with the interstate crossings of the Delaware River, for the convenience of the citizens of New Jersey and our sister states. The project was called the New Jersey Turnpike. Our Turnpike Authority has substantially completed the project with incredible speed." So read the introduction to an understated proclamation made by New Jersey Governor Alfred E. Driscoll in a *New York Times* interview.

One of the innovative features of the turnpike would become an industry standard with the introduction of the Interstate Highway System: Particular emphasis was given to signage along the turnpike. As the roadway's design allowed for higher speeds, the first sign announcing an interchange was posted two miles before the exit, announcing the route name, number, and the town to which the interchange gave access. This was repeated one mile after the first sign, and again at the interchange.

This souvenir booklet features numerous views of the New Jersey Turnpike, a revolution in highway design that would serve as a case study for the development of the Interstate Highway System.

PLACE STAMP HERE

Typical Toll Plaza New Jersey Turnpike

TICHNOR QUALITY VIEWS, BOSTON, REG. U. S. PAT. OFF.

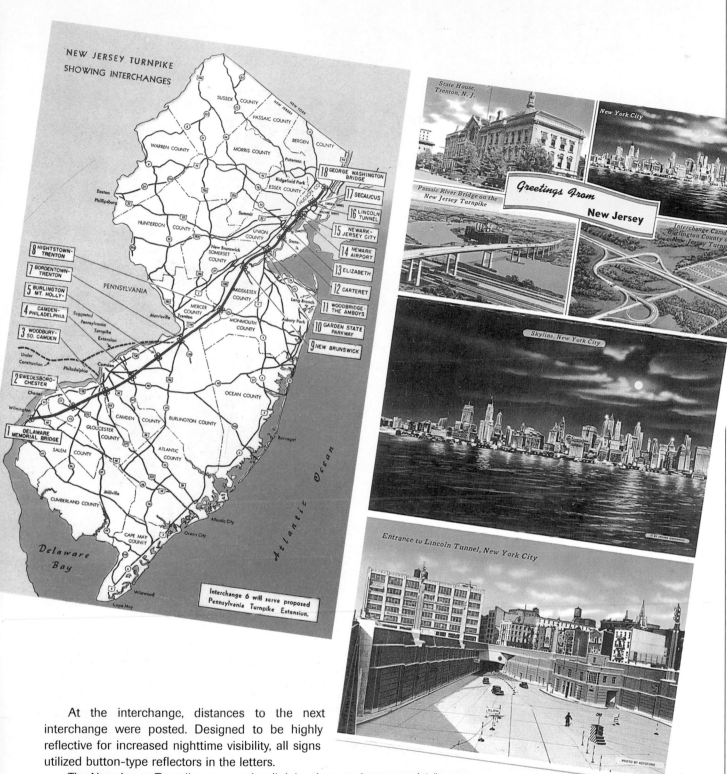

NEW JERSEY TURNPIKE
SHOWING INTERCHANGES

Interchange 6 will serve proposed Pennsylvania Turnpike Extension.

18 GEORGE WASHINGTON BRIDGE
17 SECAUCUS
16 LINCOLN TUNNEL
15 NEWARK– JERSEY CITY
14 NEWARK AIRPORT
13 ELIZABETH
12 CARTERET
11 WOODBRIDGE– THE AMBOYS
10 GARDEN STATE PARKWAY
9 NEW BRUNSWICK
8 HIGHTSTOWN– TRENTON
7 BORDENTOWN– TRENTON
5 BURLINGTON– MT. HOLLY
4 CAMDEN– PHILADELPHIA
3 WOODBURY– SO. CAMDEN
2 SWEDESBORO– CHESTER
1 DELAWARE MEMORIAL BRIDGE

State House, Trenton, N. J.

New York City

Passaic River Bridge on the New Jersey Turnpike

Greetings From New Jersey

Interchange Camden & Burlington County on the New Jersey Turnpike

Skyline, New York City

Entrance to Lincoln Tunnel, New York City

PHOTO BY KEYSTONE

At the interchange, distances to the next interchange were posted. Designed to be highly reflective for increased nighttime visibility, all signs utilized button-type reflectors in the letters.

The New Jersey Turnpike was another link in what was known as the "eastern turnpike complex," which was a forerunner to the modern Interstate Highway System. The Pennsylvania Turnpike, completed in 1940, was the first link. The Maine Turnpike followed in 1947, the New Hampshire Turnpike in 1950, Ohio by 1955, New York as well as Indiana in 1956, Massachusetts by 1957, Connecticut and Illinois by 1958, and Delaware and Maryland in 1963. Much of the interlinked turnpike system was absorbed into the interstate system by the close of the 1960s.

Road Striping

It's a fine line between life and death

It's late at night, and he's been driving since this morning. He slows his big 1950 Buick to a stop sign, flips on his turn signal, looks both ways, and makes his left turn onto the highway. He's driving along on the right side of the road watching the dotted white line go by on his left.

There's one little problem. He's far from home and in unfamiliar territory, and he doesn't know that this highway has just been widened. He did not turn onto a two-lane road. He turned onto one half of a new four-lane road, but he doesn't know it until two sets of headlights come straight at him side-by-side over the next rise. A yellow line on one side of the road would have told him he was on the wrong side, but it would be quite a while before the entire highway system arrived at that conclusion.

U.S. highways were widened all over the country in the 1950s, and the circumstance of confusing, unsafe lane markings is easy to imagine when, at that time, all pavement markings were white. It's especially embarrassing to consider this when the first paved highway to have a stripe up the middle to divide opposing traffic was paved around the year 1600 near Mexico City. According to a report by Professor H. Gene Hawkins, Ph.D., of Texas A&M University, the ancient Mexican highway was paved with stone and divided with a line of lighter colored stones up the middle. Hawkins goes on to say that other pavement markings were extremely rare on city streets and wagon roads before the era of automobiles, other than some painted lines on bridge decking.

As the automobiles came into favor, they cried out for better traffic-control devices. Some sources claim the earliest known pavement markings for automobiles were stop lines used in Portsmouth, Virginia, in 1907. New York City appears to have been the first to install painted crosswalks in 1911, and Providence, Rhode Island, and Minneapolis, Minnesota, quickly followed.

Automobiles could cross county lines and state borders as quickly as a locomotive could, but the automobiles didn't have a professional conductor watching the signs ahead to warn the engineer of circumstances. Average folks drove cars, and they drove them in unfamiliar territory. They needed traffic signs and pavement markings, and the signs and markings needed to be the same from place to place.

The American Association of State Highway Officials published the first national manual on traffic markers in 1927: *Manual and Specifications for the Manufacture, Display, and Erection of U.S. Road Markers and Signs*. The manual completely ignored pavement markings because, in 1927, there wasn't much pavement to mark.

The AASHO merged with the National Conference on Street and Highway Safety, and the new joint committee published the 1935 edition of the *Manual on Uniform Traffic Control Devices* (*MUTCD*), which allowed for pavement markings of any color. Much of the time, roads only had markings in danger areas. It may surprise the modern driving enthusiast to learn that many pavement markings were done in black, which seems like a lard-headed idea until one learns that many highways were paved in white concrete, and black markings provided better contrast than white paint—at least, until it rained.

Yellow had been allowed in pavement markings, but the 1948 edition of the *MUTCD* emphasized the need for it. Higher speeds, multi-lane roads, and more cross-country driving made changes necessary for safety's sake. Most broken center lines would be white, but double center lines on multi-lane roads and no-passing zones on two-lane roads would be yellow. This was because the public had become used to yellow as a symbol of warning, because it was the color of lights on traffic signals and "Stop Ahead" signs. Oddly enough, the biggest debate while the 1948 edition of the manual was being

Floods hit the deserts of Southern California hard in 1969 and 1978, but which flood destroyed this mile-long stretch of road and caused it to be bypassed by a new alignment? The 1971 Manual on Uniform Traffic Control Devices *dictated that broken center lines be yellow, so this road, with its white line, was most likely destroyed in the 1969 flood.*

compiled was whether highways should have solid edge lines.

Nostalgists who haunt Route 66 and other bypassed highways enjoy identifying U.S. highways by the dimples that appear on center-island curbing. The dimples were designed to catch a car's headlights at night and make the island more visible. However, better ideas were in the works, and the 1954 *MUTCD* issued directives for the use of reflective paint.

Through the 1950s and 1960s, the Interstate Highway System crept across the country, bringing with it a whole set of new rules. Yet, the two-lane highways didn't change much until 1971, when the new edition of the *MUTCD* dictated that all center lines be reflective yellow. People who grew up in the 1970s may recall seeing the outline of the old white line sticking out from under the new yellow line.

Those "roadies" who tromp through the weeds seeking out old alignments of highways are modern archeologists with a love of cars and roads, and they conduct their searches and identifications as seriously as those who unearth tombs. Along with width and pavement materials, the ghosts of pavement striping help them identify the likely period a piece of road was paved.

Here and there, a white line will reappear as newer yellow lines deteriorate or as a new layer of paving flakes away. Many people would not notice, but there are those enthusiasts of car culture who notice it, and it takes them back to their father's Nash and puts Elvis back on the radio.

Route 66
The highway of dreams

To say the reason for the international fascination with the stretch of asphalt called Route 66 is one of the great mysteries of our time would be a gross understatement. In the years before the interstate highway rendered the final verdict that it was obsolete, everyone who had driven it already knew that. From the Midwest to the coast of California, it was not the most direct route nor was it the most scenic. The highway received its numerical designation in 1926, but was not fully paved until 1937. Until 1954, there was a section in western Arizona more than 30 miles long that was too mountainous for large trucks and most buses. Why has the "Double-6" come to be viewed as the quintessential American highway?

From its inception, there has been something unique about this road. In 1933, it was promoted as the most direct and scenic route to the Los Angeles Olympics, while at the same time it was being promoted to the victims of the Dust Bowl and hard times of the Great Depression as the route to the promised land.

During World War II the western leg was, in large part, little more than a corridor through the arsenal of democracy. In the years before it was fully bypassed, it was the road of dreams and the family vacation, as well as the title for a popular television show. Promotion gave Route 66 the edge, and a romanticized view of what once was has kept it alive.

The modern roots of the U.S. highway designated number *66* began in 1916 with the passage of the Federal Aid Road Act, which provided states with the revenue needed to improve or expand existing roads within their borders. Stage two in the creation of Route 66 came in 1921 with the Federal Highway Act, which required each state to place a minimum of seven percent of its highways into the federal system.

The wave of nostalgia that has swept Route 66 to international recognition has served to revitalize communities bypassed by the interstate highway.

In towns such as Kingman, Arizona, it is easy to see why Route 66 was known as the Main Street of America.

For those who know where to look, there are vestiges of Route 66 that would have been familiar to the Joads as they headed for California. This portion of the pre-1939 alignment is to be found at the east end of the Sacramento Valley in northern Arizona.

In rapid succession, the two remaining stages came together. In 1924, a commission was formed to assign numeric designations to the federal highway system. On November 11, 1926, the work was finalized and improved, and an American legend was born.

Almost from its inception, Route 66 was larger than life. John Steinbeck immortalized it as the route of refugees in his classic work *The Grapes of Wrath*. A generation later, times had changed, and Nat King Cole encouraged those "motoring west" to "get their kicks on Route 66."

Today the tradition continues as adventurers from throughout the world take Mr. Cole's advice and help make Route 66 one of the most famous roads in America. Surprisingly, the popularity of the old highway shows no signs of slowing down.

From Santa Monica, California, to Chicago, Illinois, old roadside businesses are being resurrected or re-created. Merchandise adorned with the Route 66 shield runs the gamut from shot glasses and toilet paper to post cards and root beer in what is now a multi-million-dollar-per-year industry. Many communities along the route have capitalized on its popularity by hosting events that, for just a weekend, allow a small glimpse into a time when Route 66 was the Main Street of America.

Maybe that's the reason for the popularity of this legendary highway: it's still an avenue for escape, if ever so briefly, from the ordinary, just as it has been for more than three-quarters of a century.

Traffic Signal

We put the "Stop" and "Go" in stop-and-go driving!

"Red light! Green light!"

The words are shrieked from playgrounds and have been a staple childhood game for generations of Americans. Babies who are too young to talk know from watching through the windshield that red means stop and green means go.

Well before the advent of the automobile, there were reckless driving laws, and a person who ran a horse or a wagon through a busy urban American street could expect a date with a judge. Photographs and motion pictures from the first decade of the twentieth century show city streets jammed with horses, wagons, bicycles, and trolleys on tracks. The results were frustrating, messy, and deadly when automobiles were added to the mix. Policemen stood in the intersections directing traffic with their whistles and white gloves, and with time, they got technological help. Some cities gave a policeman a red stop light which he stood next to in the intersection and operated with a switch. The New York City Police Department had experimented with manually operated semaphores—arms with "Stop" and "Go" signs that rose and fell from a box—but the situation called for far better technology. The NYPD built a traffic tower at the intersection of 42nd Street and Fifth Avenue in 1916, and a policeman stood in the tower 16 feet above the street and operated the red, yellow, and green lights manually.

Many cities realized that a traffic cop was a waste of a perfectly good policeman who could be out chasing criminals. The City of Detroit, Michigan, put police inspector William L. Potts in charge of solving the problem, and Potts oversaw the installation of what is reputed to be the first permanently installed, automatic, three-color traffic signal in the United States. The signal tamed the intersection of Michigan Avenue and the famous Woodward Avenue.

Traffic signals spread rapidly across the country in the 1920s. Some hung from ornate masts decorated with wrought iron. Some had both lights and semaphore arms with a bell that would ding upon the "Go" signal. Signal design became more consistent through evolution, but the 1935 edition of the *Manual on Uniform Traffic Control Devices* standardized the colors and some design elements. There were even allowances made for left-turn arrows, but they were usually only found in big cities, and most rural areas wouldn't see left-turn arrows consistently until the 1970s.

Timers controlled the signals, and the timers became more sophisticated through experimentation and research as traffic patterns were studied. Timers changed the signal intervals depending on the traffic volume the research found. The City of Chicago centralized a vast array of signal timers in the basement of city hall in 1926, beginning with a signal on 49th Street in the Loop area.

Traffic signals that sense traffic and signal accordingly are called "actuated signals," and the first examples were operated by sound. A signal stayed green on the street with the most traffic, and a driver on the smaller street could honk his car's horn to trip the signal for his turn. The signals were marked with signs that read "Honk for Green."

In the 1940s, outside sun visors were extremely popular automotive accessories that kept cars cooler and reduced glare, but they made traffic signals hard to see. The most popular aftermarket sun visor was the Fulton Sun Shield, and it could be bought with another accessory called the Fulton Traffic Viewer, a round glass prism that looked something like a magnifying glass that mounted to the dashboard. The Traffic Viewer brought the traffic signals into the driver's view, even if the signal was way too high over the intersection for the driver to see it without hanging his head out the window.

By the 1950s, traffic signals with brains were phasing in. Reportedly, Houston, Texas, had some intersections where the signals were actuated through pressure plates in the street that sensed a car's weight. These devices, no doubt, frustrated motorcyclists.

The most common traffic signal sensors in the late twentieth century and beyond are "inductive loop" actuators. The observant driver is used to seeing a sealed-over circle or rectangle in the street pavement at intersections, where a slit has been cut, wires laid in, and the slit sealed over. There is a wire coil looped through this circle with an electric current

flowing through it that sets up a magnetic field. When a car stops over it, the massive amount of iron in the car interferes with that magnetic field. The computer in the signal control system makes note of the car and trips the signal when either the one car has sat there a long time or more cars have pulled up behind the first one and been counted by the inductive loops farther back.

It's rush hour, the streets are full, and traffic is backed up at all the intersections. How does a police car, fire truck, or ambulance get through heavy traffic in an emergency? Many cities have installed the Opticon system, which works something like a garage-door opener. When an emergency vehicle turns on its lights or siren, the vehicle puts out a radio wave, which is picked up by a little sensor on the traffic signal mast. Then, the traffic signal and left-turn arrow are turned green for the emergency vehicle, keeping it on its way.

Signals are still different enough from each other to be interesting, and a state's unique traffic-signal design can be one of the little discoveries a car enthusiast can enjoy on a long trip. In most parts of the United States, traffic signals are mounted on masts, painted black or dark green, and have a shield around them to block the sun and make the lights more visible. In parts of the East and South, traffic signals for the whole intersection are housed in one big unit that hangs over the middle of the intersection on cables, and some of the units are painted a bright yellow. Texas and New Mexico mount their traffic signals with the lights arranged horizontally, and Texas lore has it that this design was arrived at after a hurricane beat up the traffic signals near the Gulf Coast. Times and methods may have evolved, but as long as vehicles roll on rubber tires, the three cheerful colors will be among the comforting constants in an ever-changing world.

This 1941 ad for the General Electric Novalux traffic signal touted the unit's virtues to city engineers everywhere. The unit offered 16 color intervals to choose from to control an intersection's unique patterns. Optional equipment included yellow flasher circuits for low-use intersections and emergency flashers for fire lanes.

U.S. 1

The road to paradise is a bridge over troubled waters

Arguably, it could be said that it is the oldest road in the U.S. highway system, since it is designated number 1. But this would be the proverbial splitting of the hair, since each of the original highway designations was approved on the same day: November 11, 1926.

As with most of the original U.S. highways, 1 linked many existing trails and roads into one coherent route. In the Northeast, this often meant the motorist was literally following in the footsteps of the nation's founders through Boston, past Bunker Hill, into Providence, and on to Philadelphia.

Common sense would dictate this to be a coastal highway. However, it has been said that common sense has no place in government. Highway 1, which should be a coastal highway, exemplifies this axiom with a decidedly inland turn at Washington, D.C. At this juncture, the road becomes a trip through the Old Dominion and the heart of the Confederacy. The names of the communities through which it passes ring with the sounds of battle from a time when a nation was torn asunder: Fredricksburg, Richmond, and Petersburg.

The front of this simple, colorful post card portrays the northern and southern terminuses of U.S. Highway 1, but on the reverse side 15 major East Coast cities through which it passes are listed.

As the highway continues south, it maintains its inland track. Then, at Waycross, Georgia, it begins a wide swing to the Atlantic coast. Running the length of the Sunshine State, Florida, it hugs the beach, making it a drive through paradise for those who may have come south to escape the cold and snow of the north.

Highway 1 initially had as its northern terminus Fort Kent, Maine, on the Canadian border, and Miami, Florida, the southern. In 1938, the highway was extended to what was then the southernmost community in the United States, Key West, in an astounding marvel of modern engineering labeled the Overseas Highway. This is where the highway truly becomes a one-of-a-kind driving adventure.

The idea of connecting the chain of keys to the mainland dates to the late nineteenth century. By 1917, the idea had grown to a full-fledged effort as evidenced by an approved bond measure, in the amount of $100,000 in Monroe County to link Key Largo, Big Pine Key, and Stock Island.

Initially it was the prospect of getting pineapples to market faster that gave incentive to the project. By 1921, it was limes and an even bigger cash cow: a boom in real estate development as well as speculation.

GREETINGS FROM
U.S. ROUTE No. 1 MAINE to FLORIDA
FORT KENT, MAINE ...... KEY WEST, FLORIDA

U.S. 12

The trail becomes a highway

U.S. 12, from Detroit, Michigan, to Aberdeen, Washington, is a near-perfect time capsule of highway development in America, with a history that spans more than 200 years.

In Michigan, a large portion of the highway follows two key Native American trails, including the Great Sauk Trail. With the coming of European and American settlement, the trail played a key role in the development of southern Michigan, and many vestiges from that time, such as the historic Walker Tavern, attest to its importance.

The infant automobile industry quickly centered in southern Michigan, most notably Detroit, Jackson, and Kalamazoo. As a result, the trail took on new importance and experienced further development.

Much of the early system of highway designation can be quite confusing, and what would become U.S. 12 was no exception. The highway received official designation on November 11, 1926. The first official routing used the Detroit-Lincoln-Denver Highway, between Detroit and Kalamazoo. In Indiana, it incorporated the route of the Dunes Highway. This was a deviation from the original plans released one year before. In the original concept the highway was to run from Detroit to Saginaw, north along the shore of Lake Michigan to Ludington and then, by ferry, to Manitowoc, Wisconsin. The official routing, utilizing the southern route, turned north through Chicago and in Wisconsin followed what had been the Black and Yellow Trail. In Eau Claire, Wisconsin, it picked up the Yellowstone Trail, a prominent early automobile road that ran from Boston to Seattle.

Today, as with many early highways and trails, U.S. 12 has been fragmented. Still, in southern Michigan much of its alignment is a veritable time capsule from when the Model A Ford was the talk of the town. Along some portions, especially in the summer when the towering trees cast dappled shadows on the blacktop, one can almost come to expect Chief Pontiac and his warriors to emerge from the woods that press in from both sides.

By 1945, the postmarked date for this post card, the route of U.S. 12 had been an important traffic corridor for more than 120 years.

This post card from circa 1930 accentuates the many modern and advanced features belying the importance of U.S. 12 as a major transportation route.

Woodward Avenue

Cruising a historic path from Ted's to the Totem Pole

Detroit's Woodward Avenue is a broad multi-lane boulevard. It has three histories: the eighteenth-century story of settlement, nineteenth- and early-twentieth-century stories of industrialization and automotive genius, and the 1940s-to-1960s story of cruise nights, hot rods, drag races, and drive-in restaurants.

The French settled Detroit in 1701, and the founder's name, Antoine de la Mothe, Sieur de Cadillac, would be famous for other things 200 years later. The Detroit River connects Lake Saint Clair to Lake Erie, and the narrow river made for a good place to cross into what would later be Ontario, Canada. The little fur-trading post grew to be a small city and surrendered to British rule in 1760. The Saginaw Trail connected Detroit to Saginaw Bay farther north, traversing the Thumb of Michigan. Detroit was a U.S. city when it burned to the ground in 1805, and President Thomas Jefferson sent a trustworthy judge, Augustus Woodward, to Detroit to rebuild it.

The judge must have had an artistic streak because, in the heart of Detroit, his new road system radiating outward from Grand Circus Park's curving border resembled, in plan, a necklace, by which name it became affectionately known. Woodward Avenue sliced through the middle of the Necklace and followed the Saginaw Trail, pointing the way toward the cities of Pontiac, Flint, and Saginaw.

Henry Ford lived one block off Woodward Avenue, and he set up his first Model T assembly-line plant on Piquette Avenue. General Motors' headquarters is at the foot of Woodward downtown, and Chrysler's headquarters is farther out in the suburb of Highland Park.

Detroit's east-west streets are numbered at one-mile intervals counting northward, and Eight Mile Road marks the City of Detroit's northern border. Within Detroit, the culture of early history and industrial history rule, and historians claim the first mile of paved concrete highway in America was Woodward Avenue between Six and Seven Mile Roads. They further claim that the first automatic three-color traffic signal was at Woodward and Michigan Avenues.

After World War II, the fondly remembered postwar American culture swept up Woodward Avenue, and two drive-in restaurants marked each end of Woodward's cruising scene. The Totem Pole Drive-in marked the southern turn-around near Ten Mile Road, and the northern turn-around was a drive-in called Ted's at Square Lake Road, which was also technically Nineteen Mile Road. In between were over nine miles of six-lane boulevard, alive with flashy cars, early rock music, french fries, and massive egos.

"Something you had to remember about Woodward is that no matter who you were, you had the fastest car, or you had a buddy who could beat the fastest car," John Jendza says about Woodward Avenue bragging rights. Jendza was born in 1946, which was just in time to put him in the thick of early 1960s cruising culture. With his moniker Top Hat John, Jendza is a past

WOODWARD AVENUE BY NIGHT. DETROIT, MICH.

chapter president of the Society of Automotive Historians and an enthusiastic Woodward Avenue storyteller with especially fond memories of a particular Woodward establishment.

"Ted's Drive-in Restaurant was the capitol of cruising culture on Woodward, along with Maverick's and the Totem Pole," Jendza tells. "Ted's had a great menu and the biggest and best hamburger you could get. The Ted's Five-by-Five hamburger was five inches high by five inches wide, and it was gourmet, first class, and huge! They had the largest and best onion rings you could buy. Folks would come out just to talk cars, and they could put 200 cars in the parking lot realistically. It was fun just to be there and maybe go out to look for a race. You could go there on Friday or Saturday night, and it was not unusual to see the big drag cars from the 1960s: Color Me Gone, The Ram Chargers, and Royal Pontiac's drag cars. Royal Pontiac (11 blocks off Woodward Avenue in Royal Oak) was *the* dealer to get a hot Pontiac from. Royal Pontiac was the place to get your Pontiac super-tuned. They called it the Royal Bobcat Package."

Woodward Avenue physically lent itself to the kind of cruising that was popular at the time. "It was a long road, and it was three lanes north and south," Jendza explains. "It was a safe road, and it was controlled by lights that were a minimum of one mile apart. It wasn't a commercial road. There were lots of residential neighborhoods, but you didn't have houses right on Woodward. The majority of the drive-ins were outside the city limits of Detroit, and you could get into a race anywhere. You could be at the corner of Ten Mile Road and Woodward, and if two guys met at that signal and wanted to race, they went at it."

The gas crunch, low-horsepower cars, and the changing youth culture of the 1970s ended cruising as it was known in the 1950s and 1960s. However, after a 20-year cruising drought, various business, municipal, and tourism entities initiated the Woodward Dream Cruise in 1994. It has grown to be possibly the biggest car show in the world. Although it may be overly and inaccurately nostalgic for the hot rod culture, it's still of Woodward Avenue, and under the pavement, it's connected to Sieur de Cadillac, Thomas Jefferson, Augustus Woodward, Henry Ford, Walter Chrysler, Elvis Presley, and Chuck Berry. As John Jendza says, "It was *Woodward!*"

Woodward Avenue had a classy appearance within the Detroit city limits in the 1920s. The cruising culture would blossom behind the photographer's vantage point in the 1950s and '60s.

RADAR/LIDAR

Caught in the Beam

If it moves, men will race it—horses, dogs, chariots, ships, boats, locomotives, automobiles, motorcycles, and airplanes. It's a safe bet people ran foot races before their language was developed enough to say, "Let's race!"

The quest for speed will never stop, but unfortunately, some people take it to the public streets without the judgment to see what's wrong with traveling 20 miles per hour faster than the surrounding traffic. Some people are in a hurry, and some are just low-self-esteem cases who only feel good about themselves when they're passing someone on the highway. The police are there with radio waves and lights from the Lidar system to help them.

The Duryea brothers of Springfield, Massachusetts, invented the American auto industry in 1896 when they built about a dozen "motor wagons" specifically to be sold to the public. Within a year, a Duryea automobile gave the United States its first recorded traffic accident when the driver hit a woman on a bicycle in New York City. The bicyclist had a broken leg, and the driver of the car went to jail. The need for traffic enforcement was clear. Reckless driving laws already existed prohibiting riding a horse or driving a wagon through a town in a dangerous manner, but speeding in a car was a new and intolerable homicidal activity.

Radar (radio detection and ranging) helped the Allies win World War II. It told the Allies from what direction and at what speed the Axis planes and ships were approaching.

When a train rolls by fast ringing its bell, the listener will hear the bell drop in pitch after the train goes by. Most people have heard this phenomenon called the Doppler effect. Radar speed detection works the same way, and radar technology came to the policeman's aid in the early 1950s. Early radar speed enforcement was awkward because the radar unit had to be plugged into a power source, and the policeman had to leave the radar unit or send out a second police car when a speeder tripped the equipment.

Gene Tinnin of the Missouri State Highway Patrol started using radar speed-enforcement equipment in the late 1950s on U.S. 66, near the small city of Lebanon. By that time, the equipment was powered only by the patrol car's 12-volt electrical system, but it still took more than one patrol car to perform the speed enforcement operation—a radar car and chase car. "The radar head sat outside the car on a tripod, and it looked something like a camera," Tinnin recalls. "The meter was in the car, and another patrol car down the road would actually chase down the speeder. The trooper in the car with the meter would radio down to the chase car, 'We have a black Ford coming in at 75,' and the second car would pull over the speeder. Sometimes, in heavy traffic areas where speeders had been a problem, we would have two or three chase cars waiting for the message from the car with the radar unit."

Radar speed-detection equipment, like everything else, became transistorized in the 1960s, and patrolmen became a lot more agile. There were problems, though. Radar guns spread the signal over a wide area, and on a multi-lane highway, the officer had to make careful and difficult observations to know precisely which of the many cars on the road was actually tripping the radar. Drivers hell-bent for speed also purchased radar detectors of their own to try to outfox police radar units. Laws against consumer radar detectors were considered,

because law-enforcement people thought of radar detectors as devices designed to aid a person in committing a crime.

The debate over radar detectors ended in the 1990s as police departments moved away from radar and into lidar: light detection and ranging. The principle is the same, but these devices use a tightly focused beam of light instead of a scattered radio signal. Thus, the lidar unit locks in a car's speed accurately in about one-third of a second, so the speeder cannot hit his brakes quickly and fool the lidar. The lidar unit has a sight, and the policeman knows exactly which car he's reading, leaving speeders without much of a defense. Nevertheless, there are still legal arguments over lidar. Some believe the policeman's range of vision is so limited by the sight on the lidar unit that he can't tell if the driver was trying to pass a slow-moving vehicle or speeding up to avoid an accident, as does happen. Also, with radar's continuous-speed display, a policeman can watch traffic and see if a speeding car is only speeding for a few seconds to pass another car or avoid an accident and, then, slowing back down to a legal speed. Lidar, on the other hand, takes such a quick sample of a car's speed that it does not allow the policeman to make a judgment about why the car was speeding.

Ultimately, both devices are useful in speed enforcement, and lidar units are also placed on tripods and used to take all sorts of quick measurements after an accident, to make a graph, which maps out how the accident happened. Accident-scene measurements that once took hours now take minutes with lidar doing the legwork.

Ninety percent of a policeman's job is just being seen. When a policeman is seen in a car or on a motorcycle with a hand-held speed detection unit, traffic just tends to control itself. The speeders behave themselves, and the good drivers feel safer.

Rich Daniel of the San Bernardino Sheriff's Department watches for speeders with lidar (light detection and ranging).

Tollbooth
Car culture in Cather Country

The Tri-State Tollway and the East-West Tollway hum day and night through Chicago. The Turner Turnpike and the Will Rogers Turnpike slice through the eastern Oklahoma farmland. The Garden State Parkway navigates the Jersey Shore from end to end, and the historic New Jersey Turnpike connects Philadelphia and New York City. Out west, the Golden Gate Bridge is suspended in space and time as an Art Deco masterpiece.

All of them are toll roads with bustling tollbooths where operators shout quick thank-yous through the carbon monoxide over the never-ending traffic whir. Here, change clangs in automated toll-taking machines, which beep and open gates or hit the sirens and red lights when a car passes through without paying.

Tollbooths have a long history in the United States. From pre-colonial times, landowners charged travelers to cross their land or use bridges they had built. An elegant little tollbooth from earlier times still stands on U.S. 40 outside Uniontown, Pennsylvania. The John Brown Toll Road negotiated the treacherous Cajon Pass in California and was a constant battle to maintain until the automotive era, when Route 66 eventually paved the path.

There are still remnants of old-fashioned toll roads dotted around the country, and one of the best is the Plattsmouth Bridge across the Missouri River. A little, old-fashioned tollbooth still remains with a smiling operator who probably belongs more to the nineteenth century than to the twenty-first. In 1928, a group of private investors put up the cash to build the Plattsmouth Bridge, the United States Congress approved the bill to allow a bridge across a navigable waterway, President Coolidge signed the bill into law, and the engineers went to work. As the bridge appeared, U.S. Highway 34 was inching its concrete slabs across western Iowa toward the Plattsmouth Bridge.

In the infancy of the automobile, there were countless scenes where the past and future seemed to overlap. Imagine the scene in this vintage photo post card with a horse and carriage as well as with a horseless carriage.

Herkimer, N.Y., Old Turnpike Toll Gate.

The Plattsmouth Bridge has entered the twenty-first century as the perfect playground for antique cars. While looking through a flat windshield at the back of a headlight mounted on the side of the radiator on a 1930s car, or looking through the split windshield and under the sun visor of a 1940s car, the driver can get the undistracted feeling of exactly what it was like to encounter a U.S. highway, a no-nonsense steel-truss bridge, and a tollbooth in the prewar world. The classic car glides west across Mills County, Iowa, and the Plattsmouth Bridge rises out of the trees with a giant Burlington-Northern railroad bridge on its north side. The bridge is narrow, and it's a steep climb through the steel to Cass County, Nebraska, where the land is much higher. It's a sudden, tight left curve at the end of the bridge that angles the car to a stop in front of the little toll house, where Lou Study leans out and says hello. It's an experience right out of 1930, 1940, or 1950, with nothing to tell the driver that many decades have passed.

Lou Study (pronounced STOO-dee) is a Plattsmouth native with a traditional Midwestern accent and style of dress—the type of man who's worked this tollbooth from the beginning. Study was born in the mid-1930s and is a native to the bridge as well as Cass County.

"I remember hiding in the trunk of my dad's car to save the toll when I was a kid," Study recalls. "They used to charge a nickel for everybody in the car but the driver, and my dad used to hide me in the trunk to save the toll. After we went across, Dad would say, 'All right, boy, come on out!' Money was a little hard to come by in the 1940s. There was a time when all seven of us kids hid in the trunk of the car, and Dad told us to keep quiet. That way, he saved 35 cents every time he crossed the bridge with us kids."

Tollbooth operators in big cities are surrounded by authority, but isolated, small-town operators are the authority. Study offers this example: "The tollbooth workers have saved a lot of kids from abduction across this bridge—mostly parents trying to steal the children from each other. I just had a little girl come running up here yelling, 'Help, help! My daddy's trying to steal me, and I don't want to go!' I told her to wait in my vehicle until I could get the law out here. I've had to call the law on some kids who were diving off the railroad bridge into the river."

Speaking of the law, Cass County Sheriff Bill Brueggemann says the Plattsmouth Bridge and tollbooth have played roles in police drama, as when kidnappers tried to cross the state line and the pursuit sended at the bridge. "They took off on foot and ran down into the woods," Sheriff Brueggemann says, "and we first heard about it when word got to us that there were Iowa officers in our county shooting guns. The tool booth operator was actually the one who called 911 and told us what was going on. Most of the pursuits that come across that bridge wind up meeting that dirt embankment at the sharp curve by the tollbooth."

Other than novice truck drivers sliding into the embankment by the tollbooth on icy winter days, life is pretty peaceful for these nineteenth-century tollbooth operators on the Plattsmouth Bridge. "This is my home away from home!" Lou Study says to a customer. "I love it out here. I get to look at all the pretty girls and flirt with them and get away with it because I'm an old man. I've done steel work, ranch work, and construction work, so this job is gravy for me!"

Pennsylvania Turnpike

The concept that all-weather roads were imperative for the development of remote rural areas predated the advent of the automobile by at least 100 years. In 1791, the legislature for the Commonwealth of Pennsylvania approved a transportation plan. The first fruits a year later were the creation of the Philadelphia and Lancaster Turnpike Company for the construction of a 62-mile road, which was log surfaced.

Even though the road was replaced with a canal shortly after 1800, the idea was not entirely forgotten. In the early 1880s, the old roadbed received new attention as William Vanderbilt and Andrew Carnegie sought a route for a railroad that was run between Harrisburg and Pittsburgh. The Allegheny Mountains, however, proved to be a formidable obstacle. In 1885, with over one-half of the roadbed for the railroad and seven tunnels nearly complete, the endeavor went broke.

By 1910, as the automobile became more prominent, serious discussion and study were given to converting the abandoned railway into a highway. By 1934, the idea had gained enough momentum that a state-funded study was approved. The concept and merits of limited-access highways had already been at the forefront, with the construction of the Henry Hudson Parkway, the Arroyo Seco Parkway in Los Angeles, the Bronx River Parkway, and the Merritt Parkway.

In 1937, with the full support of President Roosevelt, the governor of Pennsylvania signed a bill creating the

This early souvenir post-card booklet highlights the scenic as well as man-made wonders and attractions found along the Pennsylvania Turnpike.

THE PENNSYLVANIA TURNPIKE

The Pennsylvania Turnpike meets one of the country's greatest needs—safe and rapid motor transportation through the Appalachian Mountains.

Furthermore actual savings in money is possible for all who use it. And money savings naturally appeal to owners and operators of motor cars. This is primarily significant in the operation and maintenance of trucks.

While there are some monetary savings in the operation of passenger cars, the principal reason why such motorists will use the Turnpike is because of the added convenience, safety and comfort as well as saving in time. The Turnpike eliminates 90 per cent of all causes of accidents—no head-on collisions, no sideswiping, no grade crossings or intersections, no striking of pedestrians or stationary objects along the right-of-way. Hazards of snow, ice and fog now found on roads over the mountain at nearly all seasons of the year are materially lessened. The Turnpike is above established flood levels, thus assuring through travel in event of disastrous floods.

Tourists from far and near use the Turnpike to see the magnificent mountain views and enjoy 160 miles of happy motoring.

Here are a few of the Turnpike advantages over other highways:

1. Safe operation at higher speeds in all kinds of weather.
2. Reduced fuel cost.
3. Reduced tire cost. (Because of lower grades and reduced braking effort.)
4. Reduced maintenance cost. (Because of lower grades and easy super-elevated curves, with resultant lessening of strain on transmission, brakes and engine.)
5. Utilization of lower powered trucks for the same pay load and of increased pay load for present size of unit.
6. Saving of time ranging from two to six hours per trip between Harrisburg and Pittsburgh.
7. Reduction of accidents with corresponding saving in insurance rates.
8. Ease of passing trucks and other slow moving vehicles provided for by extra 12-foot lane.

SERVING THE PUBLIC

Throughout the entire length of the Turnpike gasoline service stations and restaurants are located on both sides of the roadway at staggered points. The stations provided by the Standard Oil Company of Pennsylvania are unique and de luxe service stations. They are built along early Pennsylvania architectural lines. The stations are one-story buildings and two miles east of the Bedford Interchange, features an elaborate two-story building which provides many modern innovations. Nestled in the beautiful hills of Bedford County, this de luxe service station offers relaxation, comfort and the finest cuisine service, whether meals are served in the colonial dining room or on tables appropriately decorating the flagstone terrace. The scenery surpasses many of America's famous mountain resorts.

West-bound motorist will park their cars on the north side of the Turnpike and use the pedestrian tunnel to reach the main dining room in the south building. This tunnel entrance is in the lobby of the north building. No vehicles are permitted to cross the parkway dividing strip.

Special accommodations are available for truck drivers at this point. A dormitory will provide sleeping facilities for 38 drivers. Smoking lounge and recreation are included for their comfort.

The management of all restaurants is under the direction of the well-known caterer—Howard Johnson.

While the Standard Oil Company of Pennsylvania received the service station concessions on the Pennsylvania Turnpike by reason of its being the highest competitive bidder for these rights, yet the rates to be charged for gasoline, oil and food on the Turnpike can not exceed those prevailing on the free highway system.

The service station facilities on the highway are as modern as the Turnpike itself.

GENUINE CURTEICH-CHICAGO   C. T. ART-COLORTONE   CREATION (REG. U.S. PAT. OFF.)

D-6768

Pennsylvania Turnpike Commission. The economic conditions of the time, and skepticism of venture capitalists as to the potential profitability of a super toll road, resulted in the project being financed by a loan for nearly $41 million, with an additional $29 million in grants from the New Deal Reconstruction Finance Corporation.

A detailed scale model of the new superhighway was the hit of the General Motors Highways and Horizons Futurama exhibit at the 1939 New York World's Fair. The real thing was even more astounding, especially considering the brief scheduled time for completion, which was the case with numerous engineering marvels constructed during the 1930s. In this instance, it was 20 months!

Six of the seven unfinished railway tunnels were completed and widened. Also built were 9 interchanges with 10 service plazas, more than 300 bridges, and 11 tollbooths. Near Everett, 1.1 million cubic yards of rock were removed to create the largest open road cut in the world. When possible, the turnpike was laid out with southern exposure in mind to aid in snow removal.

The 160-mile project, from Middlesex to Irwin, was an engineering marvel that incorporated many revolutionary features and established engineering precedents that would later be used on the Interstate Highway System. Straight sections were designed for 100-mile-per-hour speeds. Curves were banked to accommodate speeds of 70 miles per

Moonlight on Pennsylvania Turnpike

hour. Maximum grades were set at 3 percent in a time when highway grades as steep as 9 percent were common.

On October 1, 1940, the Turnpike officially opened. Initially plans called for usage by 1.3 million vehicles annually. Soon it became apparent that this prediction was far short of the mark, as 10,000 vehicles per day were often recorded. As a result, the construction bonds were retired early, and other states began to plan for turnpikes of their own.

The Pennsylvania Turnpike is a true milestone in the evolution of the American highway. As an integral part of the Interstate Highway System, with continual improvements, its role is still important.

Acknowledgments

The Authors would like to thank all the people who went to great lengths to find photographs, provide information, and took the time to tell their stories. Like all cultures, the car culture is made of people, and this book would not have been possible without these people.

US 99 and US 101: Beryl Mitchell, Beryl's Cafe, Bakersfield, California; Richard Engeman, Oregon Historical Society, Portland, Oregon; Jeff Smith, Columbia River Maritime Museum, Astoria, Oregon; David Freece, Cowlitz County Historical Society, Kelso, Washington; John Larson, Polson Museum, Hoquiam, Washington. Craig Murphy, Lacy, Washington.
Toll Booth: Greg Schneider, Lou Study, Plattsmouth Bridge Company, Plattsmouth, Nebraska; Sheriff Bill Brueggemann, Cass County Sheriff's Department, Plattsmouth, Nebraska.
McDonald's: Julie Pottebaum, McDonald's, Oak Park, Illinois.
Yellow School Bus: Ken McCoy, Gary Russell, Antelope Valley Transportation Agency, Lancaster, California.
AMC Pacer: Virginia Johnson, Hesperia, California.
Parking Meters: Rodger Harris, Oklahoma Historical Society, Oklahoma City.
Odometer: Bill Slaughter, Church of Jesus Christ of Latter-day Saints, Salt Lake City, Utah; Chuck Zimmerman, Hesperia, California.
Dash Board, AM Radio: Chuck Zimmerman.
Volkswagen Beetle: Howard and Doretta Kegel, Apple Valley, California; Darryl Evey, Desert Autohaus, Victorville, California.
Motorcycle Cop, Radar/Lidar, Breathalyzer: Roxanne Walker, Sergeant Ross Tarangle, Deputy Rich Daniel, San Bernardino County Sheriff's Department/Hesperia Police, Hesperia, California; Cheryl Cobb, Missouri State Highway Patrol, Jefferson City, Missouri; Gene Tinnin, retired, Missouri State Highway Patrol; Tom Pasley, retired, Missouri State Highway Patrol; Buzz Banks, retired, California Highway Patrol.
Automatic Transmissions: Chris Engelman, Apple Valley, California.
Air-Conditioning: Dave Duricy, Hamilton, Ohio.
Earl Scheib: Beth Axelrod, Earl Scheib Inc., Sherman Oaks, California.
Air Bags, Crash Test Dummies: Frank Richardson, Jerry Kratzke, Matt Ivory, John Williams, Matt Hubbard, Karco Engineering, Adelanto, California.
Movie Manor Motor Inn: George Kelloff Sr., Monte Vista, Colorado.
Chrysler Airflow: Julie Butkus, Kimbery Ray, Daimler-Chrysler, Auburn Hills, Michigan.
Indian Motorcycles: Dave Wright, Stellican LTD; Bob Stark and Rick Silvercloud, Starklite, Riverside, California.
Traffic Signals, Pavement Markings: H. Gene Hawkins PhD, Mary Cearly, Texas A&M University, College Station, Texas.
Auto Mechanic: Mike Shattuck, Shattuck's Automotive, Hesperia, California; Allen Davenport, Ranken Technical College, St. Louis, Missouri.
Woodward Avenue: "Top Hat John" Jendza, Mount Clemens, Michigan; Jim Conway, Detroit Historical Museum, Detroit, Michigan; Deborah Schutt, Schutt and Company, Detroit, Michigan.
Graceland: Kelly Hill, Todd Morgan, Susan Sherwood, Elvis Presley Enterprises, Memphis, Tennessee.
Car Hops: Celina Abernathy, Sonic, Oklahoma City, Oklahoma.

Meter Maids: Chief Kevin Guinane, Holly Wilson, Sayre Police Department, Sayre, Pennsylvania; Jim Nobles, Sayre Historical Society, Sayre, Pennsylvania.
Tires, Windshield Wipers: Rudy Hester, Hesperia, California.
Cadillac Ranch: Jeff Meyer, Chicago, Illinois; Cadillac Ranch, copyright 1974, Ant Farm, Chip Lord, Hudson Marquez, Doug Michels.
Mini-Marts: Scott Nelson, Old Riverton Store, Riverton, Kansas.
Promotional Giveaways: Delbert Trew, Devil's Rope Museum, McLean, Texas.
The Club: Karen Winner-Hale, Winner International.
Concept Cars: Joe Bortz, Debra Powless, Bortz Auto Collection, Highland Park, Illinois; Julie Butkus, Kimbery Ray, Daimler-Chrysler, Auburn Hills, Michigan.
American Grafitti, Steven Weiss, Mel's Drive-In; Edward Orr, PrinTop, Hollywood, California.

Great appreciation to all those who conducted **photography** for Jon Robinson: Dick Romm, Craig Murphy, Marc Mirabile, Jason Egbert, Jeff Meyer.

Jon Robinson offers special thanks to: All the engineers and factory people who built the **1950 DeSoto** that carried him the 5,000 miles it took to write this book. **Scott and Susan Nassif and the whole crew of NAPA Auto Parts,** Hesperia, California. The makers of **coffee** and fine **scotch whiskeys** everywhere.

Bibliography

American Road, Pete Davies, Henry Holt & Company, LLC, 2002.

Born To Be Wild, Paul Garson, Simon & Schuster, 2003.

The History of the Standard Oil Company, Volumes 1 & 2, Ida Tarbell, MacMillan Company, 1904.

The Illustrated Encyclopedia of the World's Automobiles, David Burgess Wise, Chartwell Books, Inc., 1979.

Standard Catalog of Independents, Ron Kowalke, Krause Publications, 1999.

Americans on the Road: From Autocamp to Motel, 1910 – 1945, Warren Belasco, The MIT Press, 1979.

Early Cars, Michael Sedgwick, Octopus Books Limited, 1972.

BMW Isetta: Und Ihre Konkurrenten, Eine von Walter Zeichner, Schrader Automobil-Bucher, 1986.

Case, Carleton – Ford Smiles – Shrewsbury Publishing Company, 1917.

Georgano, G.N. – A History of Sports Cars – Bonanza Books, 1970.

Hopper, Gordon – Model A Ford Restoration Handbook – Polyprints, 1966.

Witzel, Michael Karl – The American Gas Station – Barnes & Nobles, Inc., 1992.

Robinson, Jon – Route 66: Lives on the Road – MBI Publishing Company, 2001.

Patton, Phil – American Heritage, Volume 47/Number 7, 1996.

Burness, Tad – American Truck & Bus Spotter's Guide 1920-1985 – Motorbooks International, 1985.

Clymer, Floyd – Treasury of Early American Automobiles – Bonanza Books, 1953.

Kimes, Beverly Rae and Clark, Jr., Henry Austin – Standard Catalog of American Cars 1805-1942, Second Edition – Krause Publications, 1986.

Dyke, A.L. – Diseases of a Gasoline Automobile and How to Cure Them – A.L. Supply Company, 1903.

Chappell, Pat – Standard Catalog of Chevrolet: 1912-1990 - Krause Publications, 1990.

Yost, Stanley and Bassett, Kathryn - Taxi! A Look At Checkers Past – Misc. Enterprises, 1990.

Bromley, Michael – The Motor Bandits: Cars, Crimes and Philosophy-SAH Journal: Issue 212- September/October 2004.

Mattar, George – 1958 Pacer Panache, Hemmings Classic Car, January 2005.

Motor Car Values Blue Book – Kelly Kar Company, October 1926.

Meridith, Alex – 1965Ford Falcon vs. Mustang – Special Interest Autos, #110, April 1989.

Brownell, Tom and Bunn, Don – The Heavyweight Book of American Light Trucks 1939-1966 – Motorbooks International, 1988.

Parker, Lowell –Cactus derby, part one to three, Arizona Republic, December 8, 1975.

Los Angeles/Phoenix Route Map, Harry Locke-Publisher, 1914.

Touring Topics – October 1913, November 1913, December 1910, August 1910, November 1911, July 1911, October 1914, November 1914.

Abbott, Lyle – Barney Oldfield Earns New Title "Master Driver" – Arizona Republican, November 12, 1914.

Brown, Arch – The Most Magnificent Auburn of All, Special Interest Autos #109, February 1989.

Work, Josiah – 1933 Ford V8 vs. Terraplane Eight, Special Interest Autos #109, February 1989.

Keefe, Don – 1956 Olds Golden Rocket, Hemmings Classic Car, December 2004.

Reader Digest, America From the Road - 1982.

Hinckley, James – Checker Cab Company: Photo History, Iconografix, 2003.

Clymer, Floyd – Floyd Clymer's Historical Motor Scrapbook, Polyprints, 1954.

Juneau, Bud – 1928 Martin: Plainly Aerodynamic, Special Interest Autos #165, May/June 1998.

Hinckley, James – Corvair With A Lived In Look, Special Interest Autos #151, January/February 1996.

Katz, John – 1965 Mustang GT 2+2, Special Interest Autos #164, March/April 1998.

Brown, Arch – Chevy's First V8, Classic Auto Restorer, December 1993.

Martin, Mark – Running Hot: Great Race '93, Classic Auto Restorer, December 1993.

Ingle, Paul – End of the road, Illinois Times, September 25, 2003.

Hays, Kristen – Drive-thru strippers latest in convenience, The Associated Press, September 17, 2000.

Lavender, Dave – Library puts in drive-thru window, The Herald Dispatch, December 14, 2003.

Oldham, Joe – Cars Magazine, May 1974.

Robinson, Jon – Classic Chevrolet Dealerships, MBI Publishing, 2003.

Our Glorious Century, Readers Digest, 1994.

Keefe, Don – 1955 Biscayne, Hemmings Classic Car, October, 2004.

Patton, Phil – Designer of the American Dream, American Heritage, November, 1996.

Index